Parker, Suzi.
1000 best bartender's
recipes /
2005.
33305209658875
ca   02/21/06

000
BEST

BARTENDER'S
RECIPES

D0452244

SUZI PARKER

SOURCEBOOKS, INC.®
NAPERVILLE, ILLINOIS

Copyright © 2005 by Suzi Parker
Cover and internal design © 2005 by Sourcebooks, Inc.
Sourcebooks and the colophon are registered trademarks of
Sourcebooks, Inc.

All rights reserved. No part of this book may be reproduced in
any form or by any electronic or mechanical means including
information storage and retrieval systems—except in the case of
brief quotations embodied in critical articles or reviews—without permission in writing from its publisher, Sourcebooks, Inc.

This publication is designed to provide accurate and authorita-
tive information in regard to the subject matter covered. It is
sold with the understanding that the publisher is not engaged
in rendering legal, accounting, or other professional service. If
legal advice or other expert assistance is required, the services
of a competent professional person should be sought.—*From a
Declaration of Principles Jointly Adopted by a Committee of the American Bar Association and a Committee of Publishers and Associations*

All brand names and product names used in this book are trademarks, registered trademarks, or trade names of their respective
holders. Sourcebooks, Inc., is not associated with any product or
vendor in this book.

Some recipes contained herein may call for raw or undercooked
eggs. Please consult with your physician prior to consumption.

The Author and Sourcebooks, Inc. shall have neither liability
nor responsibility to any person or entity with respect to any
loss, damage, or injury caused or alleged to be caused directly
or indirectly by the information in this book.

Published by Sourcebooks, Inc.
P.O. Box 4410, Naperville, Illinois 60567-4410
(630) 961-3900
FAX: (630) 961-2168
www.sourcebooks.com

Library of Congress Cataloging-in-Publication Data

Parker, Suzi.
  1000 best bartender's recipes / Suzi Parker.
    p. cm.
  ISBN 1-4022-0547-3 (alk. paper)
  1. Bartending. 2. Cocktails. I. Title: One thousand best bartender's recipes. II. Title.

TX951.P35 2005
641.8'74--dc22

                                        2005016586

Printed and bound in the United States of America.
LB 10 9 8 7 6 5 4 3 2

To Estelle and Billy Parker who advised me to mix the drinks instead of drink them and my partner-in-crime Glen Hooks, always calm as Gandhi in my wild universe.

TABLE OF CONTENTS

ACKNOWLEDGMENTS

It may seem strange to thank your parents first and foremost in a cocktail book, but I have to thank mine—Billy and Estelle Parker. Because I was an only child, I always got to tag along with my dad and mom on business trips around the country. These often occurred in swanky restaurants in the heyday of disco—the 1970s. While the food was delicious, the business conversations were dull for a kid. The flashing lights and glittery bottles of the adjoining bars, on the other hand, fascinated me, and I fell in love with bars and mixing at an early age. Later in life, when I realized I needed a trade to fall back on in case journalism failed, my dad sent me to bartending school. So thanks, Mom and Dad.

I'd also like to thank the numerous friends and colleagues who sent me ideas for drinks for this collection. In no particular order: Lucy Tallon, cocktail goddess extraordinaire of London and Africa; Stephanie Owen, vintage cocktail archivist; Stephanie Caruthers, creator of the most unique cocktail thus far in the twenty-first century; Alex Heard, long-time editor who knows a good Southern cocktail; and Wanda Stone and Kathy Williams, keepers of the cookbooks.

A special thanks to the person who keeps me on track for all projects, my agent, Erin Reel—Los Angeles superbabe and visionary who listens carefully and makes wise decisions about the future and direction of my work.

Most of all to Wonder twin Glen Hooks who went beyond the call of duty to help with this book. As always, he offered unwavering support, silly laughter (especially when I was drowning in thousands of cocktail recipes at an ungodly hour of the night), keen insight, sage advice, and the desperately needed push (with plenty of Starbucks coffee) to make sure this book was born.

INTRODUCTION—
Set-ups

No argument: cocktails are sexy and sophisticated. They sparkle with mysterious possibilities. Imagine a night in a neon-lit club. A handsome man spots a gorgeous woman. He sends a drink over. She wonders: who is this good-looking man who just bought me a Cosmopolitan? He wonders: if I buy her two, will she go back to my place? After three, will she still be standing?

Endless seduction lingers in a cocktail glass regardless of season or setting. The beauty of a cold clear martini, a glass of perfect red sangria, or a sparkling vintage concoction transformed into a twenty-first century incarnation is liquid anticipation. For some, the thrill is in the warmth that comes with downing one of these potables. For others, it's all in the shake, stir, or blend.

When I was four, I toddled into a bar adjoined to a restaurant owned by my parents' friend. Instantly, I was hooked, not by the darkness of the joint or the local television celebs who frequented the place, but by the jewels behind the bar. The bottles of amber and emerald, sapphire and ruby hypnotized me. I had never seen anything more beautiful.

The fascination continued through my teens. Whenever I dined out, a Shirley Temple was a must. My dad preferred scotch and water; my mother straight water. Curiosity about how liquor tasted was never my game; the life of a barfly was hardly appealing. No, I wanted to mix. Let me behind the bar and I'd whip up a concoction to rival any.

Eventually bartending school beckoned as a wacky adventure I longed to have, and I mixed to my heart's content. Mixology is certainly a handy trade to have at parties to win friends and influence people. And practice does, indeed, make perfect.

It's impossible to learn all the drinks in the world. Literally thousands exist and more are created every day along with new liqueurs—some even appear to glow in the dark. Certainly, in the early part of the twentieth century, a mixer would have better luck learning all the cocktails than he or she would today. Mixologists often named cocktails after the hotel or bar that birthed them or for the patron who desired them. Cocktails such as the Daiquiri and the Mojito became famous in other countries and found their way to popularity in the United States. In today's fast-paced world of starlets and playboys jetting around the globe, the international cocktail is no longer so easy to define.

But a good drink is. Whether it's a Bloody Mary before noon, a non-alcoholic Safe Sex on the Beach after a sweaty workout, or a Garza's nightcap at bedtime, a well-made drink can be exhilarating, like, well, sex. And, depending on the category, just as complicated. Take tropical drinks, which are built with various kinds of rum and juices to get that island feel. But the classic drinks, the ones that have stayed through the decades from Sinatra to Sting, often only have two ingredients, but they are no less for it.

In the end, drinking—like wardrobes and lovers—comes down to personal taste. You can wear the most popular fashions, but that isn't nearly as much fun as finding your own style or yes, your own cocktail. That's where this book comes in. Use it to try something new and unexpected. Maybe, after a healthy amount of sampling, you'll find that you really do like the same kind of martinis your friends, or even your dear old dad, like. Or you may simply be happy to stick with the frozen daiquiri you loved in college. With a little courage and experimentation, though, you might just find your drink of choice is something else entirely.

So explore the liquor store. Buy something exotic. Begin mixing. Expect a whole new world of adventure to open up. And remember this toast: may your enemies be lethargic and your lovers energetic.

Publisher's Note: This book and the recipes contained herein are intended for those of a legal drinking age. Please drink responsibly and ensure you and your guests have a designated driver when consuming alcoholic beverages.

BARTENDING 101

Just like in a kitchen, a functional bar requires certain basic items: liquors, liqueurs, wine and beer, mixers, garnishes, booster ingredients, barware, and glassware.

THE LIQUORS
Bourbon
Brandy
Canadian whiskey
Dry gin
Rum
Scotch whiskey
Tequila
Vodka

THE LIQUEURS
Triple sec
Crème de menthe
Crème de cacao
Kahlúa (or a coffee liqueur)
Amaretto

Drambuie
Benedictine
Cointreau

WINE AND BEER
Dry vermouth
Sweet vermouth
White wine
Red wine
White zinfandel
Champagne (optional)
Beer—one six-pack regular, one six-pack light

MIXERS
Bloody Mary mix (store-bought or homemade)
Club soda
Cola
Cranberry juice cocktail
Cream (heavy and light)
Cream of coconut
Ginger ale
Grapefruit juice
Grenadine
Lemon juice
Lime juice (Most popular: Rose's. Not to be used as a
     substitute for fresh lime juice.)
Orange juice
Orgeat
Piña Colada mix
Pineapple juice
Seltzer
7-Up
Sour mix
Tomato juice
Tonic water
Water

GARNISHES AND THEIR FRIENDS
Cherries (maraschino, of course)
Cinnamon sticks

Lemons
Limes
Nutmeg
Olives
Pickled pearl onions
Oranges

The Friends: picks, straws, and swizzle sticks

BOOSTER INGREDIENTS
Celery salt
Ice (The three C's: cubes, cracked, crushed)
Salt
Sugar (Don't forget saucers for salt and sugar for
    frosting the rims of glasses.)
Tabasco
Worcestershire sauce

ESSENTIAL EQUIPMENT
Bar glass
Bar spoon
Bottle opener
Champagne bucket
Corkscrew
Cocktail napkins
Covered cocktail shaker
Cutting board
Electric blender
Knife—paring or bar
Lemon/lime squeezer
Martini pitcher
Shot glasses
Measuring cup
Measuring spoons
Mixing pitcher
Muddler
Seltzer bottle
Speed pourers (optional, but handy)
Strainer
Towels

GLOSSARY

MIXOLOGY

Build: When ingredients are poured into the glass in which the cocktail will be served. The ingredients are floated on top of each other. Sometimes a swizzle stick is used, allowing the ingredients to be mixed.

Float: The final ingredient of a drink is added by pouring on top, over the back of a mixing spoon.

Puree: A smooth mixture usually obtained by blending and then passing through the sieve.

Muddle: When ingredients are crushed with a pestle in a muddler in order to extract the most flavor from fruit or mint garnishes.

Shake: Firmly grabbing cocktail shaker and aggressively shaking it about a dozen times to fully mix the ingredients. Shaken drinks will be cloudier but more thoroughly mixed and colder.

Stir: Pour ingredients into a shaker or mixing glass full of ice and stir with a long twist-stemmed bar-spoon at least six times in 360 degree complete rotations. Strain the drink into a cocktail glass and leave the "used" ice in the mixing glass.

INGREDIENTS

Absinthe: Now illegal in the United States, a redis-tilled alcohol with an anise taste that contains wormwood; absinthe substitutes will suffice in place of the real deal. (See Pastis.)

Aquavit: A Scandinavian caraway-infused spirit.

Adovokaat: An eggnog liqueur popular in Holland.

Amaretto: An almond-flavored liqueur made from apricot pits.

Anisette: A licorice-flavored liqueur made from anise seeds.

Apple brandy: An apple liqueur, also known as Cal-vados or applejack.

Apricot liqueur: A cordial made from apricot pits.

Banana liqueur: A banana liqueur also known as crème de banana.

Benedictine: A soft herbal liqueur that has been pro-duced commercially since the 1860s by the Bene-dictine monks in France.

Bitters: Angostura bitters—A brand of bitter aromatic tonic used to flavor aperitifs and longer drinks. It was invented around 1825, in Venezuela, by a French doctor to fight illnesses among Bolivar's troops.

Orange bitters: A bitter liquor made from the dried peel of unripe, sour, or bitter oranges, steeped in gin or alcohol.

Peychaud bitters: The brand name of a bitters produced in the southern United States.

Blackberry liqueur: A cordial made from blackberries.

Bourbon: A brown liqueur made from at least 51 percent corn mash with wheat or rye grains and aged for at least two years in white oak casts.

Brandy: A liquor distilled from wine or fermented fruit. Introduced to Northern Europe by Dutch Brandy products traders in the sixteenth century, the name brandy comes from the Dutch word brandewijn, meaning "burnt wine."

Burgundy: The unblended wines (both white and red, but mainly red) of Burgundy, France. Used in punch or in heated winter drinks.

Campari: A bright red type of orange bitters named after its Italian producer.

Chambord: A French liqueur made from small black raspberries.

Chambraise: A French liqueur made from wild strawberries.

Chartreuse (green or yellow): Green Chartreuse is the only green liqueur in the world with a completely natural color. It also comes in yellow. Only three men in the world, brothers of the Chartreuse order cloistered monks in France, know the names of the 130 plants and how to blend, distill, and age them to produce this liqueur.

Coffee liqueur: A coffee-flavored liqueur. The most popular is Mexican-produced Kahlúa.

Cointreau: An orange-flavored liqueur made from the skins of curacao oranges. The generic term is Curacao. If redistilled clear, it is triple sec.

Cognac: A fine brandy from the Cognac region of western France. All cognac is brandy but not all brandy is cognac. It is rated the best brandy in the world, smooth with a heady scent.

Cranberry liqueur: Cranberry-flavored cordial.

Crème de cacao: A chocolate-flavored liqueur that comes in light and dark varieties.

Crème de cassis: A black currant-flavored liqueur that is notable in the Kir Royale.

Cream of coconut: A coconut syrup used in tropical drinks especially Piña Coladas.

Crème de menthe: A mint-flavored liqueur that comes in white or green varieties.

Crème de noyaux: An almond-flavored liqueur also known as crème de almond.

Crème de violette: A violet-flavored liqueur made with the oil of violets and vanilla.

Curacao: A delicate orange-flavored liqueur that comes in orange and blue.

Drambuie: A honeyed and herbal liqueur with a scotch malt whiskey base made on the Isle of Skye in Scotland.

Dubonnet: A vermouth from the south of France that comes in sweet (red) or less-sweet (blonde).

Fernet Branca: A bitters made of herbs, with a strong medicinal flavor that is produced in France and Italy.

Fino sherry: A very dry type of sherry.

Framboise: A raspberry-flavored liqueur that is often replaced with the more common Chambord.

Frangelico: A hazelnut-flavored liqueur produced in Italy.

Gin: An alcoholic drink distilled from malted grain and flavored with juniper berries. Invented by a Dutch chemist in the seventeenth century as a remedy, it was brought to England and developed there as a favorite liquor for the working class.

Dutch Genever gin: A type of gin of very superior quality mainly produced in the Netherlands. Its production is very similar to that of malt whisky, with juniper and flavoring added to the final product.

Gordon's gin: A famous brand of gin made in England.

Galliano: A golden Italian liqueur with an anise, licorice, and vanilla flavor.

Grand Marnier: An orange-flavored French liqueur with a brandy base.

Grappa: The name of an Italian brandy made from the stalks of grapes.

Grenadine: A pomegranate-flavored syrup with pomegranate used as flavoring and sauce.

Irish cream liqueur: A liqueur made with Irish whiskey blended with fresh cream, spirits, and a little chocolate. The most popular is Bailey's Irish Cream.

Kirsch: A white brandy distilled from cherries and usually aged in a paraffin lined cask to prevent it from taking on the color of the wood. Also known as cherry schnapps.

Licor 43: A sweet, bright yellow citrus and vanilla-flavored Spanish liqueur made from a combination of forty-three ingredients, including citrus and fruit juices, herbs, spices, and vanilla.

Lillet: A sweet French aperitif wine containing quinine and spices in two varieties: sweet (red) and less-sweet (blonde).

Madeira: A specific Portuguese sweet fortified wine.

Malibu: A coconut rum liqueur.

Mandarine Napoleon: A Belgian liqueur made with rare mandarines whose skins are soaked in a Cognac base.

Maraschino: A cherry-flavored clear liqueur.

Marsala: A fortified Sicilian wine (dry or sweet).

Ojen: An anise-flavored Spanish liqueur popular in New Orleans.

Orange flower water: A non-alcoholic diluted orange flower extract in water used as a mixer.

Orgeat: A non-alcoholic syrup made with almonds, orange flower water, and sometimes barley water used as a mixer.

Ouzo: An anise-flavored Greek aperitif spirit made from pressed grapes, herbs, and berries including aniseed, licorice, mint, wintergreen, fennel, and hazelnut.

Parfait Amour: A light purple curacao flavored with rose petals, vanilla, and almonds and made in France.

Pastis: An anise-flavored absinthe substitute that does not include wormwood, not to be confused with anisette. Brands include Absente, Herbsaint, Pernod, and Ricard.

Pisco: A Peruvian or Chilean unaged brandy.

Punsch: A rum-based liqueur with a spicy sweet flavor.

Rose's lime juice: A famous brand name for concentrated lime juice.

Rum: A liquor made from fermented and distilled molasses. Light rums are usually produced in Puerto Rico, Barbados, and Cuba and do not age for very long. Dark rums come mostly from Jamaica, Martinique, and Haiti and can mature from three to twelve years. The color of rum is due to the aging process.

Sabre: An orange liqueur with a hint of chocolate produced in Israel.

Sake: Japanese wines made from rice, spring or mountain water, yeast, and a fungus known as Koji mold.

Sambuca: A popular Italian licorice-flavored liqueur with an infusion of elderberry. Sambuca is similar to anisette but with a higher alcohol content. Black sambuca is similar but opaque black in color.

Sangria: A beverage originating from Spain made with red wine, sugar, and fruits, and garnished with fresh fruits and berries.

Scotch: A term used to designate whisky made in Scotland.

Schnapps: Another name for spirit, usually implying quite a strong alcohol content.

Sloe gin: A berry-plum liqueur made from sloe berries steeped in gin.

Sour Mix: A mixture of lemon juice and sugar syrup. Also called sweet and sour mix or bar mix.

Southern Comfort: A blend of bourbon, orange, and peach liqueur.

Strega: A delicate, mild, and colorless herbal Italian liqueur.

Tequila: A spirit that is only produced in two regions of Mexico and that is made with a minimum of 51 percent distilled blue agave sap.

Tia Maria: A coffee-flavored, rum-based Jamaican liqueur.

Tonic: A tall drink made with ice, spirits, and tonic water.

Triple sec: An orange-flavored clear liqueur similar to Cointreau. Known in nineteenth century as "white curacao."

Vermouth: French or French-style dry fortified wine and herb aperitif. The two most common types are: sweet red and Italian, and dry white and French.

Vodka: A clear alcoholic spirit made from grain that originated in Russia.

Whiskey: Blended whiskey—Whiskey produced from a combination of whiskeys and/or neutral spirits containing at least 20 percent straight whiskey.

Canadian whiskey: A whiskey mainly made of rye, usually lighter-bodied than American whiskeys. It usually matures in oak casks for five years, but can be bottled at two years.

Irish whiskey: A whiskey made from malted cereals, barley, water, and yeast. It is passed through the still three times (creating a high alcohol level), blended, and aged minimum five years in used Sherry casks.

Jack Daniels: A sour mash whiskey made in Tennessee.

Jim Beam Bourbon whiskey: The name of a sour mash bourbon made in Kentucky.

Rye whiskey: A whiskey made from a mash that contains a minimum of 51 percent rye, and is aged in new oak barrels.

Tennessee whiskey: A smoky sweet type of whisky that is produced like Bourbon, but is mellowed before being stocked in barrels. It is considered by law as a separate category of whiskey.

Yukon Jack: A Canadian-whiskey-based liqueur with citrus and herb flavors.

TYPES OF DRINKS

Aperitif: An alcoholic drink taken before a meal or any of several wines and bitters.

Collins: A tall drink made typically with gin or vodka, sour mix, and club soda.

Cooler: A drink made with ginger ale, club soda, and a fresh spiral or twist of citrus fruit rind, served in a collins or highball glass.

Cordial: Sweetened spirits. The same as liqueurs.

Fix: A sour drink that usually includes pineapple juice and crushed ice.

Fizz: Very similar to a Collins but made with sour mix, sugar, and club soda; often includes an egg.

Flip: A chilled, creamy drink made of eggs, sugar, and a wine or spirit.

Frappe: A partially frozen, often fruity drink, that is usually a mixture of ingredients served over a mound of crushed ice.

Highball: Any spirit served with ice and club soda in a medium to tall glass (often a highball glass).

Julep: A traditionally Southern spirited drink made with fresh mint muddled with sugar, bourbon, and plenty of crushed ice. It's served in an iced silver or pewter mug.

Lowball: A short drink made of spirits served with ice, water, or soda in a small glass.

Mist: Liquor served over a glass filled with crushed ice, often a way of serving liqueur as an after dinner drink.

Nightcap: A spirited drink taken at bedtime.

Pousse Café: A drink made by floating one ingredient on top of another.

Punch: A party-size beverage consisting of fruit, fruit juices, flavorings and sweeteners, soft drinks, and a wine or liquor base.

Rickey: A drink made with a liquor, usually gin, a half lime, and club soda. It is sometimes sweetened, and often served with ice in a rickey glass.

Shooter: A straight shot of whiskey or other kind of spirit taken neat. Also the name for drinks made using various liquors served in a shooter glass without ice.

Sour: A short drink consisting of liquor, lemon/lime juice, and sugar.

Toddy: A sweetened drink of liquor, hot water, and spices.

Virgin: A non-alcoholic drink.

GLASSWARE

Beer mug: A glass with an handle that holds 12 to 16 ounces that is typically used to serve beer, but may be used for frozen margaritas and Bloody Marys.

Brandy snifter: A round balloon on a short stem with a lot of room for swirling that can hold 3, 6, or 12 ounces depending on the size that is used for straight brandy.

Champagne flute: A long slender glass with a stem that replaced the champagne saucer in the 1970s because of its ability to hold effervescent champagne bubbles longer. A similar design is the champagne tulip.

Champagne saucer: The classic round champagne container with either a solid or hollow stem. Legend says it takes its shape from Marie Antoinette's breast.

Cocktail: The classic V-shaped glass associated with cocktail culture holds 4 1/2 ounces and is extremely similar to the famous martini glass.

Collins: A tall 12-ounce glass named for an 1880s London waiter that is associated with the family of Collins drinks and is also used for a variety of tall drinks.

Delmonico: A 5-ounce glass used for drinks containing sparkling water like fizzes. Typically known as a breakfast juice glass.

Double rocks: A 12-14 ounce old-fashioned glass used typically for drinks with heavy liquors.

Highball: An 8-12 ounce glass similar to a collins glass used for most standard mixed drinks.

Hurricane: A 22-ounce glass in the shape of a hurricane lamp. It was created to serve the classic Hurricane at Pat O'Brien's in New Orleans but is now used for other tropical or frozen drinks as well.

Martini: A V-shaped glass that is similar to the cocktail glass design but only holds 4 ounces.

Old-fashioned: A small squat glass with a thick base also known as a rocks glass or a lowball that is used for 6-ounce drinks "on the rocks" (with ice). It is also used for straight liquor if shot glasses aren't available.

Parfait: A specialty glass anywhere from 4 to 7 ounces that is used for drinks that contain liqueurs, ice cream, and fruit.

Pilsner: A tall glass that holds around 14 ounces and is typically used for beer but is also occasionally used for various mixed drinks.

Pony: A small liqueur glass that traditionally holds 2 ounces.

Pousse café: A narrow, tall 1-ounce liqueur glass used to layer "floated" drinks with the heaviest liqueur on the bottom and the lowest density liqueur floating on top.

Sherry: A 2-ounce stemmed glass used for sherry but in the nineteenth century it was commonly used as a wine glass.

Shot: A small and compact glass with a standard size of 1 ounce, which is also called a jigger that can be used to measure ingredients, hold one liquor, or serve mixed shooters. A long shot holds 2 ounces.

Sour: A classic 4-ounce small stemmed glass, narrow at the stem and tapering out to a wider lip used for drinks like whiskey sours. These days, sours are served in Delmonico glasses but are more classic in this original glass.

Wine (Red): Commonly called a balloon wine glass, this stemmed glass holds about 12 ounces and is used for red wine cocktails and sangria.

White: An 8-ounce oblong, slightly tapered wine glass used for white wine.

Zombie: A narrow, sleek tall glass, frosted or clear, that is used for the Zombie and other tropical drinks.

1

BREAKFAST AND BRUNCH COCKTAILS—
The All-Night Party Crowd's Eye-Openers

Leather-clad rock-and-rollers, the sequined jet set, even seer-sucker wearing Southerners who still fancy plantation lifestyle bask in sleeping late and discovering a cocktail awaiting them at brunch. For sleepy-eyed morning haters, a nip or two—just so the boss can't smell— in the juice offers the jazzy jolt needed to embrace stark sunlight. Weekend pajama-happy rebels play naughty by downing a fizzy cocktail before noon on a lazy Sunday morning while diving into the newspaper. Then consider pool parties in the Hamptons or country club bridal brunches where a cocktail is just what the bartender ordered. Whether spicy or fizzy, breakfast cocktails jump-start the day with a boisterous bang.

1. BLOODY MARY

Say Bloody Mary three times before bedtime. When you wake up in the morning, be sure to have one.

1 1/2 ounces vodka (or peppered vodka for spice)
3 ounces tomato juice
1/2 ounce lemon juice
Dash or two Tabasco sauce
Dash or two Worcestershire sauce
Pinch of celery salt
Pinch of pepper
Dab of horseradish

1. Chill a cocktail shaker.
2. Add vodka, tomato juice, lemon juice, Tabasco sauce, and Worcestershire sauce.
3. Add salt, pepper, and horseradish to taste.
4. Pour into a chilled collins glass or beer mug.
5. Garnish with a lime slice or a celery stalk. Also preferred as garnishes: pickled green beans, okra pods, and garlic stuffed olives.

(See page 52 for original Bloody Mary mix.)

2. PEACH FUZZ

Soft and downy, the perfect serum for getting the dish on your brother's bride.

3 ripened peaches
6 ounces pink lemonade
6 ounces vodka
Ice cubes to fill blender

1. Put peaches, pink lemonade, vodka, and ice in a blender.
2. Blend until iced is crushed.
3. Place in freezer for four hours.
4. Scoop into highball glasses.
(Serves 6)

3. VODKA MINT

Caution: An oft-used tool for sweet-faced motherly interrogators.

6 ounces frozen limeade
6 ounces vodka
17 mint leaves

1. Combine limeade, vodka, and mint leaves with enough ice to fill blender.
2. Blend at highest speed until slushy. Pour into cocktail glasses.
4. Top with thin slices of lime and mint leaves.
(Serves 4)

4. BLOODY BULL

For the morning after. Solves problems from last night's out-of-control bachelorette party.

10 1/2 ounces consommé
24 ounces tomato juice
3 tablespoons lemon juice
2 tablespoons Worcestershire sauce
1 teaspoon celery salt
1 teaspoon garlic salt
2 teaspoons salt
9 ounces vodka

1. Mix all ingredients in a pitcher.
2. Serve in highball glasses with ice.
(Serves 6)

5. MILK PUNCH

A truly old-school beverage—served at weddings and brunches through the decades.

8 ounces cold milk
1/2 ounce bourbon
3/4 ounce crème de cacao

1. Fill cocktail shaker with ice.
2. Add milk, bourbon, and crème de cacao.
3. Shake.
4. Pour into a goblet.

6. COFFEE FLIP

Wow. This makes the cobwebs run screaming.

1 ounce cognac
1 ounce tawny port
1 small egg
1 teaspoon sugar

1. Fill cocktail shaker with ice.
2. Add cognac, port, egg, and sugar.
3. Shake.
4. Strain into a chilled delmonico glass.
5. Dust with nutmeg.

7. BRANDIED FLIP

Tastes so good you'll do cartwheels and somersaults until four.

1 ounce brandy
1 ounce apricot flavored brandy
1 small egg
1 teaspoon sugar

1. Fill cocktail shaker with ice.
2. Add brandies, egg, and sugar.
3. Shake.
4. Strain into a chilled delmonico glass.
5. Dust with nutmeg.

8. MADEIRA MINT FLIP

Another Madeira, my dear-a?

1 1/2 ounces Madeira
1 ounce chocolate mint liqueur
1 small egg
1 teaspoon sugar

1. Fill cocktail shaker with ice.
2. Add Madeira, liqueur, egg, and sugar.
3. Shake.
4. Strain into a chilled delmonico glass.
5. Dust with nutmeg.

9. POLYNESIAN PICK ME UP

*No, this does not involve carting a virgin off to the volcano.
Your fate is much more pleasant.*

4 ounces pineapple juice
1 1/2 ounces vodka
1/2 teaspoon curry powder
1/2 teaspoon lemon juice
1 tablespoon cream
2 dashes Tabasco sauce
4 ounces crushed ice

1. Pour all ingredients into a blender.
2. Blend for 10 seconds on high speed.
3. Pour into a chilled old-fashioned glass.
4. Dust with cayenne pepper.

10. CITRONELLA COOLER

For a guaranteed mosquito-free brunch.

1 ounce citrus vodka
Dash of lime juice
2 ounces chilled lemonade
1 ounce chilled cranberry juice

1. Build vodka, lime juice, lemonade, and cranberry
   juice in a collins glass.
2. Top with a squeeze of fresh lime.

11. MAY BLOSSOM FIZZ

*As sweetly intoxicating as springtime flowers. Your guests
just may frolic around the May Pole.*

1 teaspoon grenadine
1/2 ounce lemon juice
1 ounce club soda
2 ounces Punsch

1. Fill cocktail shaker with ice.
2. Add grenadine, lemon juice, club soda, and Punsch.
3. Shake.
4. Strain into an old-fashioned glass.
5. Top with soda.

12. SANGRIA

Perfect setting: pitcher for two, Melrose Avenue, a night of endless possibilities.

1/5 dry red wine
1 ripe peach
6 slices lemon
1/2 ounce cognac
1 ounce triple sec
1 ounce maraschino liqueur
1 tablespoon sugar
1 whole orange
6 ounces chilled club soda

1. Pour wine into a glass pitcher.
2. Add peeled and sliced peach and lemon slices.
3. Add cognac, triple sec, maraschino liqueur, and sugar.
4. Stir to dissolve sugar.
5. Carefully place the orange in the pitcher. (See below.)
6. Let mixture marinate at room temperature for at least 1 hour.
7. Add soda and 1 tray of ice cubes to pitcher.
8. Stir.
9. Pour into wine goblets.
(Serves 6)

(For orange: cut orange peel into one long strip, beginning at stem end and continuing until spiral reaches bottom of fruit. Make sure to expose the fruit while cutting. Leave peel attached to orange bottom to suspend fruit in pitcher.)

13. MEXICAN WEDDING BREAKFAST COCKTAIL

Goes well with huevos rancheros and a blushing bridal afterglow.

1 1/2 ounces sherry
1 egg
1 teaspoon powdered sugar
Drop of Tabasco sauce or dash of cayenne pepper

1. Fill cocktail shaker with sherry, egg, powdered sugar, and Tabasco sauce or cayenne pepper.
2. Shake.
3. Strain into a cocktail glass.

14. PEACH MIMOSA

A sweet twist on the classic brunch favorite.

1 ounce peach schnapps
Orange juice
Champagne

1. Pour peach schnapps into a champagne flute.
2. Add enough orange juice to fill half of the glass.
3. Top with champagne.

15. PEACH BELLINI

A favorite of the most discerning June brides.

1 peeled and pitted peach
Champagne

1. Puree peach and place in a champagne flute.
2. Add champagne.

16. TWIST OF A SCREWDRIVER

Everybody wants a turn.

3 1/2 cups orange juice
4 ounces vodka
2 teaspoons lemon juice
2 teaspoons triple sec

1. Combine all ingredients in a pitcher.
2. Stir.
3. Chill in refrigerator.
4. Pour into highball glasses with ice.
5. Garnish with orange slices.
(Serves 4)

17. PERFECT PEACH JULEP

Even more Southern than the mint julep—if that's possible.

1 medium fresh chilled peach
2 ounces bourbon
Crushed ice
Mint sprigs

1. Peel, pit, and slice peach.
2. Puree the peach in a blender.
3. Add sugar and process.
4. Stir in bourbon.
5. Pour over crushed ice in silver julep cup.
6. Garnish with mint springs.

18. BAY BREEZE

A nice compliment to lazy mornings on the Outer Banks.

1 ounce vodka
Splash of pineapple juice
Splash of cranberry juice

1. Pour vodka into a highball glass with ice.
2. Splash with juices.

19. SEA BREEZE

Drink while watching America's Cup. Wish for a sailboat of your own.

1 1/2 ounces gin
3/4 ounce apricot flavored brandy
1/4 ounce grenadine
1 ounce lemon juice
Club soda
Mint sprigs

1. Build gin, brandy, grenadine, and lemon juice in a highball glass.
2. Add ice.
3. Fill with club soda.
4. Add mint sprigs.

20. CAPE COD

Conjures up morning memories from Martha's Vineyard. Even if you've never visited.

1 1/2 ounces vodka
1/2 ounce lime juice
1 ounce cranberry juice
1/2 teaspoon sugar

1. Fill cocktail shaker with ice.
2. Add vodka, juices, and sugar.
3. Shake.
4. Strain into cocktail glass.

21. BLOODY MARIA

Ay Caramba! Tequila in the morning!

1 1/2 ounces tequila
2 dashes Worcestershire sauce
Sprinkle of salt
Sprinkle of pepper
Sprinkle of celery salt
Tomato juice

1. Build tequila and Worcestershire sauce in a double old-fashioned glass.
2. Sprinkle salt, pepper, and celery salt.
3. Fill with tomato juice and ice.

22. AZALEA COCKTAIL

Sip while swinging on a plantation veranda amidst a colorful burst of bloom.

3/4 ounce lime juice
3/4 ounce pineapple juice
2 1/4 ounces gin
4 dashes grenadine

1. Fill cocktail shaker with ice.
2. Add juices, gin, and grenadine.
3. Shake.
4. Strain into a cocktail glass.

(This drink can be made frothier by adding 1 1/2 ounces heavy whipping cream. If adding heavy whipping cream, use a goblet as glassware.)

23. RAMOS GIN FIZZ

Fun fact: Whenever legendary Louisiana governor Huey P. Long traveled to New York City, he took his own New Orleans bartender so he could have this drink made right.

1 1/2 ounces gin
2 tablespoons cream
1/2 ounce lemon juice
1 egg white
1 tablespoon powdered sugar
3 to 4 drops of orange flower water
1/2 ounce lime juice
1/4 ounce club soda

1. Fill cocktail shaker with ice.
2. Add gin, cream, lemon juice, egg white, powdered sugar, orange flower water, and lime juice.
3. Shake.
4. Strain into a goblet.
5. Top with chilled club soda.

24. CLAMDIGGER

Put on your short pants and grab the shovel and pail!

1 1/2 ounces vodka
3 ounces clam juice
3 ounces tomato juice
Dash of Tabasco sauce
Dash of Worcestershire sauce
Salt and pepper to taste

1. Fill a highball glass with ice.
2. Pour in all ingredients.
3. Stir.
4. Garnish with a lime slice.

25. SUMMER RAIN

As refreshing as a surprise downpour in August.

3 ounces cranberry liqueur
Apple juice
Lime wedge

1. Pour cranberry liqueur into a highball glass half-filled with ice.
2. Top with apple juice.
3. Add a squeeze of lime.
4. Stir.
5. Garnish with a lime slice.

26. SUNRISE MIMOSA

A reward for getting up earlier than the other guests.

1 tablespoon apricot nectar
1 tablespoon orange juice
2 ounces champagne

1. Pour apricot nectar and orange juice into a champagne flute.
2. Slowly add champagne.
3. Garnish with an orange slice or two raspberries.

27. CHAMPAGNE LEMON GRANITA

Sinfully slushy and utterly satisfying. No way to go wrong with this tangy one.

4 scoops lemon sorbet
2 ounces citrus vodka
2 ounces champagne

1. Put lemon sorbet into a blender.
2. Blend on low speed, slowly adding vodka.
3. Add champagne.
4. Pour into chilled highball glasses.
5. Garnish with fresh mint.

28. RED ROOSTER

Cock-a-doodle doo! Wake up and face the day.

1 1/4 ounces 151-proof rum
1/2 ounce crème de noyaux
6 ounces guava juice
Splash of grenadine

Build in a collins glass with ice.

29. RUSSIAN BRUNCH

Try this one with a side of borscht. Or not.

8 ounces vodka
12 ounces orange juice
8 ounces champagne

1. Pour vodka and orange juice into a blender with ice.
2. Pour into a large pitcher.
3. Add champagne.
4. Stir.
5. Pour into goblets.
(*Serves 4*)

30. COUNTRY CLUB COOLER

No membership dues required. Drink up! It's an open tab.

1/2 teaspoon grenadine
2 ounces club soda
2 ounces dry vermouth
Ginger ale

1. Pour grenadine and club soda into a highball glass.
2. Stir.
3. Fill glass with cracked ice.
4. Add dry vermouth.
5. Fill with ginger ale.
6. Garnish with lemon and orange peel spirals.

31. PINEAPPLE COOLER

Tiiiiiny bubbles...in the wiiiine...

2 ounces pineapple juice
1/2 teaspoon powdered sugar
2 ounces club soda
2 ounces dry white wine
Ginger ale

1. Pour pineapple juice, powdered sugar, and club soda in a highball glass.
2. Stir.
3. Fill glass with cracked ice.
4. Add white wine.
5. Fill with ginger ale.
6. Garnish with lemon and orange peel spirals or pineapple chunks.

32. PASSION FRUIT COOLER

Everybody needs a little passion. Passion fruit cooler, that is.

1 ounce orange juice
1/2 ounce lemon juice
1/2 ounce gin
1 1/2 ounces light rum
3 ounces passion fruit nectar

1. Fill cocktail shaker with ice.
2. Add juices, gin, rum, and passion fruit nectar.
3. Shake.
4. Strain into a highball glass with ice.

33. BRUNCH PUNCH

If Mike and Carol served this, it would be called Brady Bunch Brunch Punch.

3 quarts chilled tomato juice
1 liter light or dark rum
2 1/2 teaspoons Worcestershire sauce
5 ounces lemon or lime juice
Salt and pepper to taste

1. Combine all ingredients into a large pitcher.
2. Stir.
3. Pour into a punch bowl with a block of ice.
4. Garnish with thinly sliced lemons and limes.
(Serves 40)

34. APRICOT FIZZ

A sugary kick-start to chase away lingering drowsiness.

1 ounce lemon juice
3/4 ounce lime juice
1 teaspoon sugar
1 1/2 ounces apricot flavored brandy
Club soda

1. Build ingredients in a highball glass.
2. Fill with ice.
3. Top with club soda.

35. FRAISE FIZZ

Start the morning off right with a confectionery straw-berry and lemon combo.

1 1/2 ounces gin
1 ounce fraise liqueur
1/2 ounce fresh lemon juice
1 teaspoon sugar
Club soda

1. Fill cocktail shaker with ice.
2. Add gin, fraise liqueur, lemon juice, and sugar.
3. Shake.
4. Strain into a highball glass.
5. Fill with ice.
6. Top with soda.
7. Garnish with a lemon twist and a strawberry.

36. GRAND ROYALE FIZZ

Fit for a French king...or those still in their pajamas.

1/2 ounce orange juice
1 ounce lime juice
1 teaspoon sugar
2 ounces gin
1/4 ounce maraschino liqueur
1/2 ounce cream
Club soda

1. Fill cocktail shaker with ice.
2. Add orange juice, lime juice, sugar, gin, maraschino liqueur, and cream.
3. Shake.
4. Strain into a highball glass.
5. Fill with ice and club soda.

37. APRICOT CREAM SPRITZ

A great change of pace for the adventurous brunch crowd.

6 ounces milk
4 ounces apricot nectar
2 tablespoons apricot flavored brandy
Sparkling wine

1. Fill chilled cocktail shaker with milk, apricot nectar, and apricot flavored brandy.
2. Stir until smooth.
3. Pour into 6 red wine glasses.
4. Add equal amounts of wine into each glass.
(Serves 6)

38. FROSTY SOUR

Pleasantly cold and invigorating, yet quickly warms your guests.

12-ounce can frozen lemonade concentrate
1 tablespoon frozen orange juice concentrate
6 ounces bourbon
12 ounces crushed ice

1. Put lemonade and orange juice concentrate, bourbon, and ice in a blender.
2. Blend until liquefied.
3. Strain into sour glasses.
4. Garnish with orange slices and cherries.

(Serves 8)

39. MANGO COOLER

Step 1. Get up. Step 2. Have these for brunch. Step 3. Race each other back to the bedroom. An aphrodisiac delight.

1 1/2 ounces vodka
1 1/2 ounces orange juice
1/2 ounce lemon juice
1/2 ounce Cointreau
3 ounces mango nectar

1. Build ingredients in a highball glass.
2. Fill glass with ice.
3. Garnish with a mango slice.

40. OJEN FRAPPE

Lean on Ojen, a sweet anise-flavored liqueur, to get the morning going.

1 ounce Ojen
1/3 ounce sugar syrup

1. Fill cocktail shaker with ice.
2. Add Ojen and sugar syrup.
3. Shake.
4. Pour into a highball glass.

41. OJEN COCKTAIL

A popular choice for New Orleans carnival revelers who need a pick-me-up to keep catching the beads.

2 1/2 ounces Ojen
2 dashes Peychaud bitters

1. Fill cocktail shaker with ice.
2. Add Ojen and bitters.
3. Stir.
4. Strain into cocktail glass.

42. ABSINTHE FRAPPE

Some say absinthe is the devil's tool. Lord, don't let it be so.

1/3 ounce sugar syrup
1 1/2 ounces Pernod

1. Pour sugar syrup and Pernod into a chilled high-ball glass with crushed ice.
2. Stir vigorously until frost appears on sides of glass.

43. AMBASSADOR'S MORNING LIFT

Even more effective than the embassy's elevator.

32 ounces prepared dairy eggnog
6 ounces cognac
3 ounces Jamaican rum
3 ounces crème de cacao

1. Pour all ingredients into a punch bowl.
2. Stir.
3. Dust each serving with nutmeg.
(Serves 10–12)

44. MORNING CALL COCKTAIL

Sip gently while reliving—or forgetting—the previous night's antics.

1 ounce pastis
3/4 ounce fresh lemon juice
3/4 ounce maraschino liqueur

1. Fill cocktail shaker with ice.
2. Add pastis, lemon juice, and maraschino liqueur.
3. Shake.
4. Strain into a cocktail glass.

45. PERNOD CLASSIQUE

The absinthe breakfast of champions.

1 ounce Pernod
5 ounces water
2 ice cubes

1. Pour the Pernod in a tall glass.
2. Add the water and ice cubes.
3. Stir.

46. ICED DANISH MARY

An alternative to the classic Bloody Mary. Guests will surely want to know the secret ingredient.

1 1/2 ounces aquavit
Bloody Mary mix (store-bought or freshly mixed; see below.)

1. Pour aquavit into a double old-fashioned glass with ice.
2. Add Bloody Mary mix.

47. BLOODY MARY MIX

You can buy something similar in a can, but why not be a domestic diva and make it from scratch?

2 46-ounce cans tomato juice or V-8 juice*
1 teaspoon coarsely-ground fresh black pepper
1 teaspoon celery salt
4 ounces lemon juice
1 5-ounce bottle Worcestershire sauce
Tabasco sauce to taste (for heat)
Salt to taste

1. Mix all ingredients thoroughly in a pitcher.
2. Refrigerate.

* If you like it hot, use spicy V-8.

48. MADRAS

The quintessential preppy potable. Biff and Muffy can't get enough of these.

1 1/2 ounces vodka
4 ounces cranberry juice
1 ounce orange juice

1. Pour vodka and juices into a highball glass with ice.
2. Garnish with a lime wedge.

49. BREAKFAST COCKTAIL

Sneak in a flask of this and even IHOP is bearable.

2 ounces gin
1/2 ounce grenadine
1 egg white

1. Fill cocktail shaker with ice.
2. Add gin, grenadine, and egg white.
3. Shake.
4. Strain into a chilled cocktail glass.

50. BREAKFAST EGGNOG

Most people don't drink eggnog other than at Christmas. But they should. An eye-opener for any day of winter.

1 egg
2 ounces brandy
1/2 ounce orange curacao
3 ounces milk

1. Fill cocktail shaker with ice.
2. Add egg, brandy, curacao, and milk.
3. Shake.
4. Strain into a tumbler or goblet.
5. Dust with nutmeg.

51. GOOD MORNING FIZZ

Prepares you to face even the most annoyingly perky Susie Sunshines.

1 ounce lemon juice
1 teaspoon sugar
2 ounces gin
1/2 ounce anisette
1 egg white

1. Fill cocktail shaker with ice.
2. Add lemon juice, sugar, gin, anisette, and egg white.
3. Shake.
4. Strain into a highball glass.
5. Fill with ice and soda.

52. ROSE IN JUNE FIZZ

The bride may choose a colorful bouquet of fresh-cut flow-ers. But what she really wants is one of these.

1 1/2 ounces gin
1 ounce framboise liqueur
1 1/2 ounces orange juice
1 ounce fresh lime juice

1. Fill cocktail shaker with ice.
2. Add gin, framboise liqueur, and juices.
3. Shake.
4. Strain into a highball glass.
5. Fill with ice and soda.

53. SHERRY FLIP

A drink that is perfect for winter brunches in mountain cabins when five feet of snow covers the ground. Blazing fire, optional.

1 egg
1 teaspoon sugar
1 1/2 ounces sherry
1/2 ounce cream (optional)
1/4 ounce light crème de cacao (optional)

1. Fill cocktail shaker with ice.
2. Add egg, sugar, sherry and optional ingredients, if desired.
3. Shake.
4. Strain into a cocktail glass.

54. BIRD OF PARADISE FIZZ

This bird of paradise will send you flying.

1 1/2 ounces gin
1/2 ounce lemon juice
1/2 ounce blackberry brandy
1/2 ounce sugar syrup
1 egg white
4 ounces club soda

1. Fill cocktail shaker with ice.
2. Add gin, lemon juice, blackberry brandy, sugar syrup, and egg white.
3. Shake.
4. Strain into highball glass.
5. Fill with club soda and ice.

55. SPARKLING STRAWBERRY MIMOSA

Don't dare serve these without a heaping helping of French toast topped with whipped honey butter.

2 ounces orange juice
2 ounces strawberries
1/2 ounce strawberry syrup
4 ounces champagne

1. Blend orange juice, strawberries, and strawberry syrup in a blender until smooth.
2. Pour into a cocktail glass.
3. Top with champagne.
4. Garnish with a strawberry and an orange slice.

56. BREAKFAST MARTINI

The high-roller's breakfast drink of choice before he heads back to the table.

1 1/2 ounces gin
3/4 ounce lemon juice
3/4 ounce Cointreau
1 teaspoon light marmalade

1. Fill cocktail shaker with ice.
2. Add gin, lemon juice, Cointreau, and light marmalade.
3. Shake.
4. Strain into a chilled martini glass.

57. CHAMPAGNE BLUES

I got the champagne blues...I got nothin' left to lose...I need some more booze.

1/5 blue curacao
8 ounces lemon juice
4/5 dry champagne
Peel of two lemons

1. Chill all ingredients.
2. Pour curacao and lemon juice into a punch bowl (with no ice).
3. Stir.
4. Add champagne.
5. Stir gently.
6. Float lemon peels in the bowl.
(Serves 25)

58. CHAMPAGNE PUNCH WITH KIRSCH

For wedding parties that strive for just a hint above ordinary.

4 fifths iced brut champagne
5 ounces iced Kirsch liqueur
5 ounces cream sherry
4 ounces iced lemon juice
16 ounces iced orange juice

1. Pour all ingredients into a chilled champagne bowl.
2. Stir.
(Serves 25)

59. CHAMPAGNE DU MARCO

Perfect for the decadent second marriage.

1 ounce vanilla ice cream
2 dashes maraschino liqueur
4 dashes orange curacao
2 dashes cognac
Champagne

1. Pour ingredients into chilled deep-saucer champagne glass.
2. Fill with champagne.
3. Garnish with fruits in season.

60. CHAMPAGNE FLIP

The mother-of-the-bride sips this while the bride is getting dressed. The mother of the groom downs two.

1 egg yolk
1/2 teaspoon sugar
3 ounces champagne
1/4 ounce brandy

1. Fill cocktail shaker with ice.
2. Add egg yolk, sugar, and champagne.
3. Shake.
4. Strain into a cocktail glass.
5. Float brandy on top.

61. SANGRIA ESPECIALE

When normal sangria just won't do.

2/5 red wine
1/5 champagne
4 ounces gin
4 ounces cognac
Sugar to taste
Juice of 2 oranges
Juice of 2 lemons

1. Pour ingredients into a punch bowl.
2. Stir.
3. Add ice.
4. Garnish with orange and lemon slices.
(Serves 12–15)

62. WHITE GRAPE, TANGERINE, AND SPARKLING WINE PUNCH

Guests expecting the same old champagne punch? No way. Zig and keep them guessing.

48 ounces unsweetened white grape juice
6 ounces frozen tangerine juice concentrate, thawed
8 ounces club soda
3 ounces brandy
2 ounces lemon juice
1/5 sweet sparkling wine
Thin slices of tangerine

1. Pour ingredients into a punch bowl over a block of ice.
2. Stir.
3. Cover punch bowl and refrigerate until cold.
4. Add sparkling wine prior to serving.
5. Float tangerine slices.

(Serves 15–20)

63. CHAMPAGNE SHERBET PUNCH

The punch that has launched a thousand nuptials.

24 ounces chilled pineapple juice
2 ounces lemon juice
1 quart pineapple sherbet
1/5 chilled champagne

1. Pour juices into a punch bowl.
2. Add sherbet just prior to serving.
3. Add champagne.
4. Stir.
(*Serves 20*)

64. CHAMPAGNE PUNCH

Welcome Baby New Year with this bubbly brew.

Juice of 12 lemons
Powdered sugar
8 ounces maraschino liqueur
8 ounces triple sec
16 ounces brandy
2/5 chilled champagne
16 ounces club soda
16 ounces strong tea, optional

1. Add enough powdered sugar to sweeten lemon juice in a small bowl.
2. Pour mixture in punch bowl over ice.
3. Stir.
4. Add maraschino liqueur, triple sec, brandy, champagne, club soda, and strong tea, if desired.
5. Stir.
6. Decorate with seasonal fruits.

(Serves 20–25)

65. BACCIO PUNCH

This happy-go-lucky concoction will make the gods bow to you.

16 ounces champagne
16 ounces grapefruit juice
16 ounces dry gin
4 ounces anisette
Sugar to taste
16 ounces mineral water

1. Pour ingredients into a punch bowl.
2. Stir well.
3. Surround bowl with ice cubes.
4. Decorate with fruit.
5. Serve in goblets.
6. Garnish with several grapes.
(Serves 8)

66. HOT GOLD

Now we know what kept the 49ers going during the Gold Rush.

6 ounces warmed orange juice
3 ounces amaretto

1. Pour orange juice into a large mug.
2. Add amaretto.
3. Stir with a cinnamon stick.

67. COFFEE COOLER

This one is not on the Starbucks menu. But it can be on yours.

1 1/2 ounces vodka
1 ounce cream
1 ounce coffee liqueur
1 teaspoon sugar
4 ounces cold black coffee
1 small scoop coffee ice cream

1. Fill cocktail shaker with ice.
2. Add vodka, cream, coffee liqueur, sugar, coffee, and coffee ice cream.
3. Shake.
4. Strain into a highball glass.

68. BULLDOG HIGHBALL

Arf! No need to save these for when you're putting on the dog.

1 1/4 ounces orange juice
2 ounces gin
Ginger ale

1. Build orange juice and gin in a highball glass with ice.
2. Fill with ginger ale.

69. GINGER FIZZ

You've got to think that the Gilligan's Island starlet was craving one of these after her first week on the island.

1 ounce lemon juice
1 teaspoon sugar
1 1/2 ounces gin
Ginger ale

1. Fill cocktail shaker with ice.
2. Add lemon juice, sugar, and gin.
3. Shake.
4. Strain into a highball glass with ice.
5. Fill with ginger ale.

70. MORNING FIZZ

For the rock babe who needs just a little morning glory help from the bottle.

2 ounces blended whiskey
1/2 egg white
1/2 ounce lemon juice
1 teaspoon sugar
1/2 teaspoon Pernod
Chilled club soda

1. Fill cocktail shaker with ice.
2. Add whiskey, egg white, lemon juice, sugar, and Pernod.
3. Shake.
4. Strain into a tall glass.
5. Add splash of soda
6. Fill glass with ice.
7. Stir.

71. ROBERT E. LEE COOLER

Generally speaking, one should never surrender one's hold on this drink. Feel free to rise again and mix another.

1/2 teaspoon sugar
2 ounces club soda
3/4 ounce lime juice
1/4 ounce pastis
1 1/2 ounces gin
Ginger ale

1. Dissolve sugar in club soda in a collins glass.
2. Add ice.
3. Build lime juice, pastis, and gin.
4. Fill with ginger ale.
5. Garnish with lemon and orange spirals.

72. ORANGE OASIS

No mirage here, thirsty traveler. Come on in, but leave the camel outside.

1 1/2 ounces gin
1/2 ounce cherry liqueur
4 ounces orange juice
Ginger ale

1. Build gin, cherry liqueur, and orange juice in a collins glass with ice.
2. Fill with ginger ale.
3. Garnish with an orange slice.

73. STRAWBERRY SPARKLE

A sprinkle of pink cheer for the most carefree of occasions.

1 cup sliced fresh strawberries
2 ounces frozen strawberry daiquiri fruit juice concentrate, thawed
6 ounces chilled champagne
4 ounces chilled lemon-flavored sparkling water

1. Put fresh strawberries into a blender.
2. Blend until smooth.
3. Pour strawberry puree into a glass pitcher.
4. Add juice concentrate.
5. Stir well.
6. Cover and refrigerate.
7. Prior to serving, stir in champagne and sparkling water.
8. Pour into chilled champagne flutes.
9. Garnish with fresh strawberries, if desired.

74. STRAWBERRY-CRANBERRY FROST

This is how Jack Frost lures you in so he can nip at your nose.

2 ounces vodka
4 ounces sliced frozen strawberries, in syrup, partially
  thawed
4 ounces cranberry juice cocktail
3 ounces ice

1. Pour vodka, frozen strawberries, cranberry juice, and ice in a blender.
2. Blend until smooth.
3. Pour into a large goblet.
4. Garnish with a whole strawberry and a mint sprig.

75. AFFAIR

Definitely to remember.

2 ounces strawberry schnapps
2 ounces cranberry juice
2 ounces orange juice
Club soda (optional)

1. Pour schnapps, cranberry juice, and orange juice in a highball glass with ice.
2. Stir.
3. Top with club soda, if desired.

76. FROZEN MINT JULEP

Sultry summer days call for one of these. Make that two.

2 ounces bourbon
1 ounce lemon juice
1 ounce sugar syrup
6 mint leaves
6 ounces crushed ice

1. Muddle bourbon, lemon juice, sugar syrup, and mint leaves in a glass.
2. Pour mixture and ice into a blender.
3. Blend at high speed for 15 or 20 seconds.
4. Pour into a chilled highball glass.
5. Garnish with a mint sprig.

77. LAKE BREEZE

While the kids are gathering wood for the campfire, sneak a few of these.

4 ounces cranberry juice
2 ounces pineapple juice
1 teaspoon coconut liqueur
Lemon-lime soda

1. Fill cocktail shaker with ice.
2. Add juices, liqueur, and soda.
3. Shake.
4. Strain into a collins glass with ice.
5. Fill with soda.

78. FANCY FIX

The much-needed dose for those who like it posh.

Juice of 1/2 lemon or lime
1 teaspoon powdered sugar
1 teaspoon water
2 1/2 ounces champagne

1. Squeeze juice of lemon or lime into a collins glass.
2. Add sugar and water.
3. Stir.
4. Fill glass with shaved ice.
5. Add champagne.
6. Stir well.
7. Garnish with a slice of lemon and a straw.

79. PIMM'S CUP

London Lucys love this classic British upper class libation.
Perfect for a day at Wimbledon, Ascot, or the Henley Royal
Regatta.

2 parts lemonade or ginger beer (Bartender's choice)
1 part Pimms No.1
Slice of vodka-soaked orange; cucumber; lemon;
   apple; a strawberry

1. Pour lemonade into a highball glass with ice. (Use
   a pitcher if making more than one drink.)
2. Add Pimm's Cup No. 1.
3. Drop in vodka soaked fruit.
4. Garnish with a mint sprig.

80. PISCO SOUR

A Chilean favorite that always tastes better in Santiago. But works fine in Santa Fe.

1 1/2 ounces pisco brandy
1/2 ounce lemon juice
1 teaspoon sugar
1/2 egg white
Dash of Angostura bitters

1. Fill cocktail shaker with ice.
2. Add pisco brandy, lemon juice, sugar, egg white, and bitters.
3. Shake.
4. Strain into a cocktail glass.

81. MANGO BATIDA

A South American cooler that refreshes the weariest globetrotter.

1 ounce orange juice
2 1/4 ounces mango juice
1 1/2 ounces cachaca

1. Pour juices and cachaca into a cocktail shaker.
2. Shake.
3. Pour into highball glass with crushed ice.
4. Stir.

82. BLUE FIX

The absolute antidote for the funks. Kiss those blues good-bye.

Juice of 1/2 lemon or lime
1 teaspoon powdered sugar
1 teaspoon water
2 1/2 ounces blue curacao

1. Squeeze juice of lemon or lime into a collins glass.
2. Add sugar and water.
3. Stir.
4. Fill glass with shaved ice.
5. Add blue curacao.
6. Stir well.
7. Garnish with a slice of lemon and a straw.

83. HAPPILY EVER AFTER

The wedding party essential for the toast that guests will remember forever after.

1 ounce peach schnapps
1 ounce cranberry juice
1 ounce ginger ale

1. Pour peach schnapps, cranberry juice, and ginger ale into old-fashioned glass with ice.
2. Stir.

84. ALOHA BUBBLY

Fun Fact: Aloha means love, luck, and happiness. Say Aloha Nui to those you really love. That means lots of aloha.

2 ounces pineapple juice
1/2 teaspoon powdered sugar
2 ounces club soda
2 ounces dry white wine
Club soda

1. Pour the pineapple juice, powdered sugar, and club soda in a collins glass.
2. Stir.
3. Fill with crushed ice.
4. Add white wine.
5. Fill with club soda.
6. Stir.
7. Garnish with an orange or lemon peel spiral.

85. HOT SPRINGS COCKTAIL

Hot Springs, Arkansas. Home to thermal springs, gangster lore, and plenty of gambling. Oh, and Bill Clinton lived here once. No word on whether he inhaled these.

1 1/2 ounces white wine
1 tablespoon pineapple juice
1/2 teaspoon maraschino liqueur
Dash of orange bitters

1. Fill cocktail shaker with ice.
2. Add white wine, pineapple juice, maraschino liqueur, and bitters.
3. Shake.
4. Strain into a cocktail glass.

86. CREAMY DRIVER

Go, speed racer, go. This one's waiting for you in the winner's circle.

1 1/2 ounces vodka
1 egg yolk
4 ounces orange juice
1/2 teaspoon sugar

1. Fill cocktail shaker with ice.
2. Add vodka, egg yolk, orange juice, and sugar.
3. Shake.
4. Strain into a highball glass.

87. BUNNY MOTHER

Multiplying rabbits? Now we know what they're drinking.

1 1/2 ounces vodka
1 ounce orange juice
1 ounce lemon juice
1 teaspoon sugar
1/4 ounce grenadine
1/4 ounce Cointreau

1. Fill cocktail shaker with ice.
2. Add vodka, juices, sugar, grenadine, and Cointreau.
3. Shake.
4. Strain into a highball glass.
5. Fill with crushed ice.
6. Garnish with an orange slice and a cherry.

88. NECTARINE COOLER

Surely this nectarine was served on Mount Olympus to create a buzz at dawn.

2 ounces vodka
3 ounces orange juice
1 teaspoon sugar
Several pieces peeled ripe nectarine
Lemon-lime soda

1. Fill cocktail shaker with ice.
2. Add vodka, orange juice, sugar, and nectarine.
3. Shake.
4. Strain into a highball glass with ice.
5. Fill with lemon-lime soda.
6. Garnish with nectarine slice.

89. DUKE

A drink equally at home in the palace or in your personal fiefdom.

1 egg
1/2 ounce triple sec
1/4 ounce orange juice
1/2 ounce lemon juice
1/4 ounce maraschino liqueur
Champagne

1. Fill cocktail shaker with ice.
2. Add egg, triple sec, juices, and maraschino liqueur.
3. Shake.
4. Strain into a delmonico glass.
5. Fill with champagne.

90. GRAVEL GERTIE

Ridden hard, hung up wet. Need we say more about our old friend Gertie? We like her. A lot.

1 ounce vodka
1 ounce tomato juice
1 ounce clam juice
Dash of Tabasco sauce

1. Build vodka, juices, and Tabasco sauce into an old-fashioned glass with ice.
2. Stir.

91. MAD BULL

Early mornings have you seeing red? Charge after this one, Toro.

1 1/2 ounces aquavit
3/4 ounce lime juice
2 ounces tomato juice
1 ounce beef bouillon

1. Build vodka, juices, and beef bouillon into a highball with ice.
2. Sprinkle with celery salt.

92. FRENCH WENCH

There once was a wench from Par-ee. Who climbed on a horse next to me. She said with a grin as I tickled her chin, if you offer me drinks, I say "Oui."

2 ounces red Dubonnet
Ginger ale

1. Pour Dubonnet in a highball glass with ice.
2. Add ginger ale.
3. Garnish with lime squeeze.

93. MONDAY MORNING

This little elixir takes the sting out of the first day of the work week.

1 1/2 ounces Fernet Branca
1 1/2 ounces pineapple juice
Juice of 1 lime
Juice of 1 orange
Dash of absinthe

1. Fill cocktail shaker with ice.
2. Add Fernet Branca, juices, and absinthe.
3. Shake.
4. Strain into a cocktail glass.

LOUNGE LIZARDS' CLASSIC COCKTAILS—
Making Sinatra Proud

Hipsters in sharkskin suits. Crooners eyeing bombshells in tight satin evening dresses. A bygone era of nights in smoky clubs with cocktails that packed a punch. You don't have to roll the dice in Vegas, baby, to down drinks that would make the worst singer sound like Sinatra. Classic concoctions offer everyone the chance to unleash the swank and sass of their inner Rat Packer. Make any party a swinging affair. Plug in the Hi-Fi mood tunes and sip the stressful cares away in a cocktail of cool. There's a reason these definitive drinks have stood the test of time. Indulge.

94. GREYHOUND

Go Greyhound. Leave the driving to someone else.

1 1/4 ounces vodka
Grapefruit juice

1. Fill highball glass with ice.
2. Add vodka.
3. Fill with grapefruit juice.

95. GODFATHER

An offer no self-respecting swinger can refuse.

1 1/2 ounces scotch
3/4 ounce amaretto

1. Fill old-fashioned glass with ice.
2. Add scotch and amaretto.

96. TOM COLLINS

This drink is so good they named a glass after it.

2 to 2 1/2 ounces gin
1 to 2 teaspoons sugar
1/2 to 1 ounce lemon juice
Iced club soda

1. Fill cocktail shaker with ice.
2. Add gin, sugar, and lemon juice.
3. Shake.
4. Strain into a collins glass half-filled with ice.
5. Add soda.
6. Stir.
7. Garnish with lemon slice and/or orange slice and/or cherry. Serve with a straw.

97. JOHN COLLINS

Tom's low-profile cousin.

Juice of 1/2 lemon
1 teaspoon powdered sugar
2 ounces blended whiskey
Club Soda

1. Fill cocktail shaker with ice.
2. Add lemon, powdered sugar, and whiskey.
3. Strain into a collins glass.
4. Add several cubes of ice.
5. Fill with club soda.
6. Stir.
7. Garnish with lemon slice and/or orange slice and/or cherry. Serve with a straw.

98. VODKA COLLINS

The tipsy aunt Tom and John don't talk about.

Juice of 1/2 lemon
1 teaspoon powdered sugar
2 ounces vodka
Club Soda

1. Fill cocktail shaker with ice.
2. Add lemon, powdered sugar, and vodka.
3. Strain into a collins glass.
4. Add several cubes of ice.
5. Fill with club soda.
6. Stir.
7. Garnish with lemon slice and/or orange slice and/or cherry. Serve with a straw.

99. MINT JULEP

Quintessentially Southern. Consumed by many a Scarlett awaiting her Rhett.

12 mint leaves on stem
6 mint leaves on stem
1 teaspoon sugar
2 teaspoons water
2 1/2 ounces 86- or 100-proof bourbon

1. Tear the 12 mint leaves partially while leaving them on the stem.
2. Place them in a silver julep mug or 12-ounce glass with sugar and water.
3. Muddle or stir until sugar is completely dissolved.
4. Fill glass with cracked ice.
5. Add bourbon.
6. Stir until ice is partially dissolved.
7. Add more ice to rim.
8. Stir.
9. Tear the remainder of the mint leaves to release aroma and insert into ice with leaves on top.

100. WHITE RUSSIAN

The perfect nightcap to sip in an icy, abandoned dacha.

1 ounce coffee liqueur
2 ounces vodka
Milk or cream

1. Fill an old-fashioned glass with ice.
2. Add coffee liqueur and vodka.
2. Fill with milk or cream.

101. SIDECAR

Needless to say, this one is for passengers only.

Juice of 1/4 lemon
1 ounce triple sec
1 ounce brandy

1. Fill cocktail shaker with ice.
2. Add lemon, triple sec, and brandy.
3. Strain into cocktail glass.

102. MANHATTAN

Classic drink for a classic city.

1/4 ounce sweet vermouth
1 1/2 ounces blended whiskey

1. Fill cocktail shaker with ice.
2. Add vermouth and whisky.
3. Stir.
4. Strain into cocktail glass.
5. Serve with a cherry.

103. HARVEY WALLBANGER

Harvey is actually a pretty quiet guy—unless you forget to bring his drink. Don't test him.

1 ounce vodka
4 ounces orange juice
1/2 ounce Galliano

1. Fill collins glass with ice.
2. Add vodka and orange juice.
4. Float Galliano on top.

104. GIBSON

Fun Fact: This drink was named in honor of Charles Gibson, the artist who created the famed "Gibson Girls" images in the early 1900s.

2 ounces gin
1/4 ounce Rose's lime juice (or 1/2 ounce fresh lime juice for substitution)

1. Fill a cocktail shaker with ice.
2. Add gin and lime juice.
3. Shake.
4. Strain into chilled old-fashioned glass.
5. Garnish with skewered cocktail onions.

105. PINK LADY

Preferred cocktail for Rizzo, Frenchy, and all of you cool chick wannabees. It's the one that you want.

1 1/2 ounces dry gin
1 teaspoon sweet cream
1 teaspoon grenadine
1 egg white

1. Fill a cocktail shaker with ice.
2. Add gin, sweet cream, grenadine, and egg white.
3. Shake.
4. Strain into a cocktail glass.

106. OLD FASHIONED

A flapper's favorite, this one gained popularity in Prohibition-era speakeasies.

1 sugar cube
Dash of Angostura bitters
1 teaspoon water
2 ounces blended whiskey

1. Add sugar cube, bitters, and water in old-fashioned glass and muddle well.
2. Add whiskey.
3. Stir.
4. Add a twist of lemon peel and ice cubes.
5. Garnish with orange and lemon slices and a cherry.
6. Serve with a swizzle stick.

107. ROB ROY

Named for a red-haired Scottish outlaw, renowned for his daring prison breaks. Lift your glass and toast a true hero of the Highlands.

3/4 ounce sweet vermouth
1 1/2 ounces scotch

1. Fill a cocktail shaker with ice.
2. Add vermouth and scotch.
3. Stir.
4. Strain into a cocktail glass.

108. ABBEY COCKTAIL

Happy hour at the monastery.

1 1/2 ounces gin
Juice of 1/4 orange
Dash orange bitters

1. Fill a cocktail shaker with ice.
2. Add gin, orange juice, and bitters.
3. Shake.
4. Strain into cocktail glass.
5. Garnish with a cherry.

109. WHISKEY SOUR

The Popeye of drinks. It am what it am.

1 ounce whiskey
2 ounces sour mix

1. Fill a cocktail shaker with ice.
2. Add whiskey and sour mix.
3. Shake.
4. Strain into a sour glass.
5. Garnish with a cherry.

110. BLACK RUSSIAN

Order one of these and kiss your troubles Do svidaniya.

1 1/2 ounces vodka
3/4 ounce coffee liqueur

1. Fill an old-fashioned glass with ice cubes.
2. Add vodka and coffee liqueur.

111. SAZERAC

Some claim this was truly the first cocktail, made by a West Indian apothecary in New Orleans. New Orleans, birthplace of the cocktail? Go figure.

1/4 teaspoon absinthe
1/2 teaspoon sugar
1/4 teaspoon bitters (Peychaud's, if possible)
2 ounces bourbon

1. Swirl absinthe in a chilled old-fashioned glass until coated.
2. Add sugar, bitters, and one tablespoon water.
3. Stir until sugar dissolves.
4. Add large ice cube and bourbon.
5. Stir.
6. Garnish with a lemon peel.

112. GIMLET

A late nineteenth century concoction, the gimlet later spawned the Kamikaze and the Cosmopolitan. Admire the pedigree.

2 ounces gin
1/2 ounce Rose's lime juice

1. Fill a cocktail shaker with ice.
2. Add gin and lime juice.
3. Stir extremely well.
4. Strain into sugar-frosted rim chilled cocktail glass.
5. Garnish with lime wedge.

113. GIN AND TONIC

Half price for those wearing seer-sucker.

2 ounces gin
Tonic water

1. Fill highball glass with ice.
2. Add gin.
3. Fill with tonic water.
4. Stir.
5. Garnish with lime slice.

114. SCREWDRIVER

Depending on which way you turn this one, you'll either get tight or get loose.

1 1/2 ounces vodka
Orange juice

1. Fill highball glass with ice.
2. Add vodka.
3. Fill with orange juice.
4. Stir.

115. CAIPIRINHA

Used to be Brazil's best-kept secret but—luckily for us— the cat is out of the bag.

2 to 3 lime wedges
Dash of sugar
3 ounces Brazilian rum
1/2 ounce sour mix

1. Mash lime wedges with sugar in cocktail shaker.
2. Add ice, rum, and sour mix.
3. Shake.
4. Pour into highball glass.
5. Garnish with lime wedge.

116. BRONX

Raise a glass to the birthplace of Rat Packer Joey Bishop.

1 ounce gin
1/2 ounce dry vermouth
1/2 ounce sweet vermouth
Juice of 1/4 orange

1. Fill cocktail shaker with ice.
2. Add gin, vermouths, and juice.
3. Shake.
4. Strain into a cocktail glass.

117. RUM SWIZZLE

The most-treasured of all the pirate's booty.

Juice of 1 lime
1 teaspoon powdered sugar
2 ounces club soda
2 dashes of Angostura bitters
2 ounces rum

1. Fill a collins glass with shaved ice.
2. Add lime, powdered sugar, and club soda.
3. Stir with a swizzle stick.
4. Add bitters and rum.
5. Fill with club soda.
6. Serve with swizzle stick.

118. BLACK DEVIL

Sometimes, it's all about the olive.

2 ounces light rum
1/2 ounce dry vermouth

1. Fill cocktail shaker with ice.
2. Add rum and vermouth.
3. Stir.
4. Strain into cocktail glass.
5. Garnish with a black olive.

119. FRENCH RIVIERA

Take a liquid trip to the Cote d'Azur.

1 ounce rye whiskey
1/2 ounce apricot brandy
1 teaspoon fresh lemon juice

1. Fill cocktail shaker with ice.
2. Add whiskey, brandy, and lemon juice.
3. Shake.
4. Strain into a cocktail glass.
5. Garnish with a cherry.

120. GORDON COCKTAIL

Flash Gordon? Jeff Gordon? Commissioner Gordon? Gordon Sumner? All we know is, this one's our favorite.

2 ounces Gordon's gin
1/2 ounce sherry

1. Fill cocktail shaker with ice.
2. Add gin and sherry.
3. Stir.
4. Strain into a cocktail glass.

121. HONEY BEE

A little bit o' honey in every sip.

1/2 ounce honey
2 1/2 ounces dark rum
1/2 ounce lemon juice

1. Fill cocktail shaker with ice.
2. Add honey, rum, and lemon juice.
3. Shake.
4. Strain into cocktail glass.

122. LONDON FOG

Elementary, my dear Watson. We order another round.

1 ounce white crème de menthe
1 ounce anisette
Dash of Angostura bitters

1. Fill cocktail shaker with ice.
2. Add crème de menthe, anisette, and bitters.
3. Shake.
4. Strain into a cocktail glass.

123. INTERNATIONAL COCKTAIL

Quick! Call the U.N.

1 1/2 ounces cognac
splash of vodka
splash of anisette
1/3 ounce Cointreau

1. Fill cocktail shaker with ice.
2. Add cognac, vodka, anisette, and Cointreau.
3. Shake.
4. Strain into a cocktail glass.

124. ORANGE BLOSSOM

Fragrant, timeless, and truly special. Mix it for your favorite flower.

1 ounce gin
1/2 ounce triple sec
1 1/2 ounces orange juice

1. Fill cocktail shaker with ice.
2. Add gin, triple sec, and orange juice.
3. Shake.
4. Strain into a cocktail glass.

125. STINGER

Ouch! That's going to leave a mark.

1 1/2 ounces brandy
1/2 ounce white crème de menthe

1. Fill cocktail shaker with ice.
2. Add brandy and crème de menthe.
3. Stir.
4. Strain into a chilled cocktail glass.

126. NEGRONI

Camillo Negroni of Florence never wavered from this aperitif. Why should you?

1 ounce gin
1 ounce Campari
1 ounce sweet vermouth

1. Fill cocktail shaker with ice.
2. Add gin, Campari, and vermouth.
3. Stir.
4. Strain into a chilled cocktail glass.
5. Garnish with a twist of lemon.

127. ALEXANDER

Patriarch of the proud Alexander family of cocktails.

1 ounce crème de cacao
1 ounce gin
1 ounce heavy cream

1. Fill cocktail shaker with ice.
2. Add crème de cacao, gin, and cream.
3. Shake.
4. Strain into a chilled cocktail glass.
5. Garnish with nutmeg.

128. GIN RICKEY

Rickey, don't lose this recipe. You don't want to drink nothing else.

1 1/2 ounces gin
Juice of 1/2 lime
Club soda

1. Fill highball glass with ice.
2. Add gin and lime.
3. Fill with club soda.

129. LEAVE IT TO ME

...Not the Beaver. Ha. Just giving you the business.

1 ounce gin
1/2 ounce apricot brandy
1/2 ounce dry vermouth
3 dashes lemon juice
3 dashes grenadine

1. Fill cocktail shaker with ice.
2. Add gin, brandy, vermouth, lemon juice, and grenadine.
3. Shake.
4. Strain into a chilled cocktail glass.

130. GIN FIZZ

For those who like their gin on the softer side, this drink offers less of a kick.

1 1/2 ounces dry gin
1 tablespoon powdered sugar
3 ounces sour mix
1 ounce club soda

1. Fill cocktail shaker with ice.
2. Add gin, powdered sugar, and sour mix.
3. Shake.
4. Pour over ice into collins glass.
5. Add club soda.
6. Garnish with a cherry and an orange slice.

131. CLOVER CLUB

Where leprechauns grab a quiet nip after a long day at the end of the rainbow.

1 1/2 ounces dry gin
Juice of 1/2 lemon
2 teaspoons grenadine
1 egg white

1. Fill cocktail shaker with ice.
2. Add gin, lemon, grenadine, and egg white.
3. Shake.
4. Strain into a cocktail glass.

132. MARGUERITE

Marguerite, Marguerite...oh that life could be so sweet!

3/4 ounce dry vermouth
1 1/2 ounces dry gin
1/4 teaspoon curacao
Dash of orange bitters

1. Fill cocktail shaker with ice.
2. Add vermouth, gin, curacao, and bitters.
3. Stir.
4. Strain into a cocktail glass.
5. Garnish with an olive.

133. CLASSIC MARGARITA

Legend says Margarita Sames, a Dallas socialite who spent time in Acapulco, created this drink in the late 1940s for her international guests.

1 1/2 ounces tequila
1/2 ounce triple sec
1 1/2 ounces sour mix
Several dashes of lime juice

1. Fill cocktail shaker with ice.
2. Add tequila, triple sec, sour mix, and lime juice.
3. Shake.
4. Strain into a chilled salt-rimmed cocktail glass or an old-fashioned glass.

134. MONTE CARLO

For the race-car driving, Baccarat-playing, jet-setting super spy in all of us.

1 1/2 ounces rye whiskey
1/2 ounce Benedictine
3 or 4 dashes of Angostura bitters

1. Fill cocktail shaker with ice.
2. Add whiskey, Benedictine, and bitters.
3. Shake.
4. Pour into a chilled cocktail glass.

135. GOLDEN FIZZ

Plop, plop, fizz, fizz, oh what a relief this drink is.

1 ounce gin
2 ounces sour mix
1 egg yolk
1 ounce club soda

1. Fill cocktail shaker with ice.
2. Add gin, sour mix, egg yolk, and club soda.
3. Shake.
4. Strain into a collins glass filled with ice.
5. Top with club soda.

136. CUBA LIBRE

Originated near the end of the Spanish-American War. Translated, it means "free Cuba."

1 1/2 ounces light rum
6 ounces cola

1. Fill highball glass with ice.
2. Add rum and cola.
3. Stir.
4. Garnish with lime wedge.

137. DUBONNET COCKTAIL

This sedate cocktail predates Prohibition, and its base was once the preferred drink of the French Foreign Legion. Vive La France!

1 ounce gin or vodka
1 ounce red Dubonnet

1. Fill cocktail shaker with ice.
2. Add gin or vodka and Dubonnet.
3. Stir.
4. Strain into a chilled cocktail glass.

138. CASINO COCKTAIL

Pace yourself, sport, or you'll end up with snake eyes.

2 ounces gin
1/2 teaspoon lemon juice
1/4 teaspoon maraschino liqueur
2 dashes orange bitters

1. Fill cocktail shaker with ice.
2. Add gin, lemon juice, maraschino liqueur, and bitters.
3. Shake.
4. Strain into a chilled cocktail glass.
5. Serve with a cherry.

139. MILLIONAIRE

Enjoy this seven-figure drink even if you are on a blue-collar budget.

1 1/2 ounces bourbon
1/2 ounce Pernod
2 or 3 dashes curacao
2 or 3 dashes of grenadine
Half of an egg white

1. Fill cocktail shaker with ice.
2. Add bourbon, Pernod, curacao, grenadine, and egg white.
3. Shake.
4. Strain into a chilled cocktail glass.

140. BERMUDA ROSE

Delicate and dainty, but too many of these and you'll be lost in the Triangle.

1 1/4 ounces dry gin
1/4 ounce apricot liqueur
1/4 ounce grenadine

1. Fill cocktail shaker with ice.
2. Add gin, apricot liqueur, and grenadine.
3. Shake.
4. Strain into a cocktail glass.

141. BISHOP

Say Hail Mary three times, kneel, and pour.

Juice of 1/4 lemon
Juice of 1/4 orange
1 teaspoon of powdered sugar
Burgundy

1. Fill cocktail shaker with ice.
2. Add juices and powdered sugar.
3. Shake.
4. Strain into a highball glass.
5. Add two ice cubes.
6. Fill with burgundy.
7. Stir.
8. Garnish with lemon and orange twists.

142. CHINESE COCKTAIL

Ancient Chinese secret. See recipe below.

1 1/2 ounces Jamaican rum
1 tablespoon grenadine
1 tablespoon maraschino liqueur
1 tablespoon triple sec
Dash of Angostura bitters

1. Fill cocktail shaker with ice.
2. Add rum, grenadine, maraschino liqueur, triple sec, and bitters.
3. Shake.
4. Strain into a cocktail glass.

143. KENTUCKY COCKTAIL

Why you really had to carry him back to his old Kentucky home…

2 ounces bourbon
1 ounce pineapple juice

1. Fill cocktail shaker with ice.
2. Add bourbon and pineapple juice.
3. Shake.
4. Strain into a chilled cocktail glass.

144. MARY PICKFORD

1930's international film superstar, known as "America's Sweetheart" as much for her movie roles as for her romance with heartthrob Douglas Fairbanks. Pop in a DVD of Coquette *and drink up!*

1/2 ounce rum
1/2 ounce pineapple juice
1 teaspoon grenadine
6 drops maraschino liqueur

1. Fill cocktail shaker with ice.
2. Add rum, pineapple juice, grenadine, and maraschino liqueur.
3. Shake.
4. Strain into a cocktail glass.

145. SLOE GIN FIZZ

Sloe...bartenders crossing.

1 ounce sloe gin
2 ounces sour mix
Club soda

1. Fill cocktail shaker with ice.
2. Add sloe gin and sour mix.
3. Shake.
4. Strain into a chilled collins glass.
5. Fill with club soda.
6. Garnish with cherry.

146. RUM COLLINS

Tom, John, and Vodka's long-lost Caribbean cousin.

2 ounces light rum
1 teaspoon sugar syrup
1/2 ounce lime juice
Club soda

1. Fill collins glass with ice.
2. Add rum, sugar syrup, and lime juice.
3. Stir.
4. Fill with club soda.
5. Garnish with lime slice.

147. MINT COLLINS

Tom, John, Vodka, and Rum's cool older cousin.

2 ounces mint-flavored gin
1 teaspoon powdered sugar
Juice of 1/2 lemon
Club soda

1. Pour gin, powdered sugar, and lemon into collins glass.
2. Add several ice cubes.
3. Fill with club soda.
4. Stir.
5. Garnish with lemon, orange, and a cherry.

148. ALABAMA

Stars won't be the only things falling on Alabama after a few of these.

1 ounce brandy
1 ounce curacao
1/2 ounce lime juice
1/2 teaspoon sugar syrup

1. Fill cocktail shaker with ice.
2. Add brandy, curacao, lime juice, and sugar syrup.
3. Shake.
4. Strain into a chilled cocktail glass.
5. Garnish with an orange peel.

149. PHOEBE SNOW

Mysterious and enthralling, this cocktail leaves you wanting more.

1 1/4 ounces brandy
1 1/4 ounces red Dubonnet
1/4 teaspoon Pernod

1. Fill cocktail shaker with ice.
2. Add brandy, Dubonnet, and Pernod.
3. Shake.
4. Strain into a chilled cocktail glass.

150. GIN AND LIME

Ideal for sipping alfresco and watching the masses go by.

1 1/2 ounces gin
1/2 ounce fresh lime juice
1/2 ounce orange juice
1 teaspoon Rose's lime juice

1. Fill cocktail shaker with ice.
2. Add gin and juices.
3. Shake.
4. Strain into a chilled cocktail glass.
5. Garnish with a lime peel.

151. SALTY DOG

Let me drink your Salty Dog, or I won't be your gal at all...

2 ounces vodka
1/2 unsweetened grapefruit juice
1 teaspoon lemon juice

1. Fill cocktail shaker with ice.
2. Add vodka, grapefruit juice, and lemon juice.
3. Shake.
4. Strain into a chilled cocktail glass.
5. Sprinkle drink with several dashes of salt.

152. SINGAPORE SLING

First concocted at Raffle's Hotel in Singapore, which W. Somerset Maugham once claimed held "all the fables of the exotic East." Sweet and indulgent.

Juice of 1/2 lemon
1 teaspoon powdered sugar
2 ounces gin
Club soda
1/2 ounce cherry-flavored brandy

1. Fill cocktail shaker with ice.
2. Add lemon, powdered sugar, gin, club soda, and brandy.
3. Shake.
4. Strain into a collins glass.
5. Add ice cubes.
6. Fill with club soda.
7. Float cherry-flavored brandy on top.
8. Garnish with fruits in season and serve with a straw.

153. RUSTY NAIL

Before drinking, prepare a tetanus "shot."

3/4 ounce scotch
1/4 ounce Drambuie

1. Fill old-fashioned glass with ice.
2. Pour scotch.
3. Float Drambuie on top.

154. LONG ISLAND ICED TEA

Walk away from this one sober. I dare you.

1/2 ounce vodka
1/2 ounce gin
1/2 ounce light rum
1/2 ounce tequila
Juice of 1/2 lemon
1 dash cola

1. Fill highball glass with ice.
2. Pour vodka, gin, rum, tequila, and lemon in high-ball glass.
3. Add cola for cooler.
4. Garnish with a slice of lemon.

155. MOSCOW MULE

Born out of an abundance of ginger beer at Hollywood's Cock 'n' Bull, this one became huge in the 1950s. Kicks like crazy.

1 1/2 ounces vodka
Juice of 1/2 lime
Ginger beer

1. Pour vodka and lime juice into a copper mug or a collins glass.
2. Add ice cubes.
3. Fill with ginger beer.
4. Stir.
4. Add a twist of lemon peel.

156. KING COLE

You brought me a drink? Bless your merry old soul.

1 slice orange
1 slice pineapple
1/2 teaspoon powdered sugar
2 ounces blended whiskey
2 ice cubes

1. Muddle orange, pineapple, and powdered sugar in old-fashioned glass.
2. Add whiskey and ice cubes.
3. Stir well.

157. NEW YORK SOUR

All the bite of the big apple without the hassle.

Juice of 1/2 lemon
1 tablespoon powdered sugar
2 ounces blended whiskey
Claret

1. Fill cocktail shaker with ice.
2. Add lemon, powdered sugar, and whiskey.
3. Shake.
4. Strain into white wine glass, leaving half of inch from top.
5. Float claret.
6. Garnish with half-slice of lemon and a cherry.

158. NEW YORK COCKTAIL

Start spreading the news, I'm having one today.

Juice of 1 lime or 1/2 lemon
1 tablespoon powdered sugar
1 1/2 ounces blended whiskey
1/2 teaspoon grenadine

1. Fill cocktail shaker with ice.
2. Add lime or lemon juice, powdered sugar, whiskey, and grenadine.
3. Shake.
4. Strain into a cocktail glass.
5. Add a twist of lemon peel.

159. DAISY

After a few of these, Miss Daisy needed a driver.

2 ounces tequila
1 ounce lemon juice
2 teaspoons grenadine
Splash of club soda

1. Fill cocktail shaker with ice.
2. Add tequila, lemon juice, grenadine, and club soda.
3. Shake.
4. Strain into an old-fashioned glass.
5. Add ice.
6. Top with a splash of club soda.

160. AMERICAN BEAUTY

The desperately-needed cocktail of suburban husbands.

3/4 ounce brandy
3/4 ounce dry vermouth
1/2 ounce grenadine
3/4 ounce orange juice
1/2 ounce crème de menthe

1. Fill cocktail shaker with ice.
2. Add brandy, dry vermouth, grenadine, orange juice, and crème de menthe.
3. Shake.
4. Strain into a chilled cocktail glass.

161. BACARDI COCKTAIL

Okay, Smarty, drink some Bacardi. Call up your friends and have a little party.

1 1/2 ounces Bacardi light or gold rum
1/2 ounce lime juice
3 dashes grenadine

1. Fill cocktail shaker with ice.
2. Add rum, lime juice, and grenadine.
3. Shake.
4. Strain into a chilled cocktail glass.

162. BETWEEN THE SHEETS

This drink is a pleasure...indulge.

3/4 ounce brandy
3/4 ounce triple sec
3/4 ounce light rum
3/4 ounce sour mix

1. Fill cocktail shaker with ice.
2. Add brandy, triple sec, rum, and sour mix.
3. Shake.
4. Strain into an old-fashioned glass with ice.

163. CARROLL COCKTAIL

As Lewis Carroll said: Down the rabbit hole. Drink me!

1 1/2 ounces brandy
3/4 ounce sweet vermouth

1. Fill cocktail shaker with ice.
2. Add brandy and vermouth.
3. Stir.
4. Strain into a chilled cocktail glass.
5. Garnish with a cherry.

164. FUZZY NAVEL

Less painful than a belly button piercing.

1 1/2 ounces peach schnapps
6 ounces orange juice

1. Fill highball glass with ice.
2. Add peach schnapps and orange juice.
3. Stir.

165. SCARLETT O'HARA

As God as my witness, I'll never be thirsty again.

1 1/2 ounces Southern Comfort
1 1/2 ounces cranberry juice
Juice of 1/2 fresh lime

1. Fill cocktail shaker with ice.
2. Add Southern Comfort and juices.
3. Shake.
4. Strain into a deep-shell champagne saucer.

166. DESERT COOLER

Fun fact: The Desert Cooler was created at Las Vegas' famed Desert Inn, built in 1950. Who owned it at one time? Billionaire Howard Hughes.

1 1/2 ounces Southern Comfort
Pineapple-grapefruit juice

1. Fill collins glass with ice.
2. Add Southern Comfort.
3. Fill with juice.
4. Garnish with orange slice and cherry.

167. RED LION

Invented in the 1930s by an enterprising Brit, who cleverly took England's national emblem and claimed it for his own.

1 1/2 ounces gin
1 1/2 ounces Grand Marnier
3/4 ounce fresh orange juice
3/4 ounce fresh lemon juice

1. Fill cocktail shaker with ice.
2. Add gin, Grand Marnier, and juices.
3. Shake.
4. Strain into an old-fashioned glass with ice.
5. Garnish with lemon or orange peel.

168. HARLEM COCKTAIL

Perfect for your own personal night at the Apollo.

1 1/2 ounces gin
1 ounce pineapple juice
1/2 teaspoon maraschino liqueur

1. Fill cocktail shaker with ice.
2. Add gin, pineapple juice, and maraschino liqueur.
3. Shake.
4. Strain into a chilled cocktail glass.
5. Garnish with two pineapple chunks on toothpick across glass.

169. PINK GIN

Fashionable in mid-nineteenth century Britain, it spread worldwide with the help of the roving British Navy. A no-nonsense way of getting your daily gin requirement.

2 ounces gin
2 dashes of Angostura bitters

1. Fill cocktail shaker with ice.
2. Add gin and bitters.
3. Stir.
4. Strain into a rocks glass with ice.

170. BRONX SILVER

Despite the name, this one is hardly second best.

1 ounce gin
1/2 ounce dry vermouth
3/4 ounce orange juice
1/2 ounce sweet vermouth
1 egg white

1. Fill cocktail shaker with ice.
2. Add gin, vermouths, orange juice, and egg white.
3. Shake.
4. Strain into a cocktail glass.
5. Garnish with an orange slice.

171. SILVER FIZZ

The right cocktail for a twenty-fifth wedding anniversary.

2 ounces dry gin
1 teaspoon powdered sugar
Juice of 1/2 lemon
1 egg white
Club soda

1. Fill cocktail shaker with ice.
2. Add gin, powdered sugar, lemon juice, and egg white.
3. Shake.
4. Strain into a highball glass with ice.
5. Fill with club soda.

172. CLASSIC COCKTAIL

Drinks come and go, but the perfect mix of sweet and strong has kept this one popular for decades. A must.

1 1/2 ounces brandy
1/4 ounce Cointreau
1/4 ounce maraschino liqueur
1 teaspoon lemon juice

1. Fill cocktail shaker with ice.
2. Add brandy, Cointreau, maraschino liqueur, and lemon juice.
3. Shake.
4. Strain into a chilled cocktail glass.

173. SOUTHSIDE

This drink was once popular with the notorious gangsters of Chicago's old Southside. Think speakeasies, big deals, and bathtub gin.

1 1/2 ounces gin
Juice of 1/2 lemon
1 teaspoon powdered sugar
2 sprigs fresh mint

1. Fill cocktail shaker with ice.
2. Add gin, lemon, powdered sugar, and mint.
3. Shake.
4. Strain into a cocktail glass.

174. DAIQUIRI

Fun fact: The daiquiri became popular at early twentieth century Cuban hurricane watch parties.

2 ounces light rum
1 ounce lime juice
1 teaspoon sugar

1. Fill cocktail shaker with ice.
2. Add rum, lime juice, and sugar.
3. Shake.
4. Strain into a champagne saucer.
5. Garnish with a lime slice.

175. MARTINEZ

Possible fore-father of the more famous martini. Created in California in the 1800s. A favorite among gold miners.

2 ounces gin
3 ounces dry vermouth
3 or 4 drops maraschino liqueur
3 or 4 drops Angostura bitters

1. Fill cocktail shaker with ice.
2. Add gin, vermouth, maraschino liqueur, and bitters.
3. Shake.
4. Strain into an old-fashioned glass filled with ice.

176. MELBA

What is this mystery ingredient called Swedish punch? A mixture of spices, tea, lemon, sugar, and rum with wine added after a few months of steeping.

1/2 ounce Swedish punch
1/2 ounce rum
Juice of 1/4 lemon
2 dashes absinthe
2 dashes grenadine

1. Fill cocktail shaker with ice.
2. Add Swedish punch, rum, lemon juice, absinthe, and grenadine.
3. Shake.
4. Strain into a cocktail glass.

177. DELMONICO

A drink named for the historic New York City restaurant that made it famous.

3/4 ounce gin
1/2 ounce dry vermouth
1/2 ounce sweet vermouth
1/2 ounce brandy

1. Fill cocktail shaker with ice.
2. Add gin, vermouths, and brandy.
3. Stir.
4. Strain into a cocktail glass.
5. Garnish with lemon twist.

178. MOJITO

James Bond's preferred drink while capering in Cuba.

2 1/2 ounces light rum
1 tablespoon sugar syrup
8 mint sprigs
Club soda
1 lime

1. Put the mint leaves and cooled sugar syrup into a highball glass.
2. Using a spoon, muddle mint leaves with sugar syrup for about 20-30 seconds.
3. Cut the lime in half and remove the seeds.
4. Squeeze the juice from both halves into the glass.
5. Add one-half of the lime to the glass.
6. Pour in rum.
7. Stir.
8. Add ice.
9. Top with club soda.
10. Garnish with a mint sprig.

179. AMERICANO

Another favorite of James Bond; he drinks it in the first Bond book Casino Royale.

1 ounce Campari
1 ounce sweet vermouth
3 ounces club soda

1. Fill highball glass with ice
2. Add Campari, vermouth, and club soda.
3. Stir.

180. DEVIL'S TAIL

Lucifer's liquid lightning.

1 1/2 ounces light rum
1 ounce vodka
1 1/2 ounces apricot-flavored brandy
1 1/2 teaspoons grenadine
1 tablespoon lime juice
4 ounces crushed ice

1. Combine rum, vodka, brandy, grenadine, lime juice, and ice in a blender.
2. Blend at low speed.
3. Pour into a champagne flute.
4. Garnish with a lime peel.

181. MISSISSIPPI MULE

Johnny Reb's favorite drink. Watch out for the kick.

1 1/2 ounces gin
1 teaspoon crème de cassis
1 teaspoon lemon juice

1. Fill cocktail shaker with ice.
2. Add gin, crème de cassis, and lemon juice.
3. Shake.
4. Strain into an old-fashioned glass with ice.

182. NAPOLEON

Able was I, ere I saw Elba.

2 ounces gin
1/4 ounce red Dubonnet
1 ounce orange curacao
Dash of Angostura bitters

1. Fill cocktail shaker with ice.
2. Add gin, Dubonnet, curacao, and bitters.
3. Stir.
4. Strain into a cocktail glass.
5. Garnish with a lemon twist.

183. PETER PAN

For the boy who never grew up but still has legal I.D.

3/4 ounce gin
3/4 ounce dry vermouth
3/4 ounce orange juice
2 dashes of Angostura bitters

1. Fill cocktail shaker with ice.
2. Add gin, vermouth, orange juice, and bitters.
3. Shake.
4. Strain into a cocktail glass.

184. PRESBYTERIAN COCKTAIL

A sure way to liven up the church picnic.

1 1/2 ounces bourbon
Splash of club soda
Splash of ginger ale

1. Build in a highball glass.
2. Garnish with a lime twist.

185. THUNDER AND LIGHTNING

The way this hits you is frightening. You better knock on wood.

1 1/2 ounces brandy
1 egg yolk
1 teaspoon sugar
Pinch of cayenne pepper

1. Fill cocktail shaker with ice.
2. Add brandy, egg yolk, sugar, and cayenne pepper.
3. Shake.
4. Strain into a cocktail glass.

186. WILL ROGERS COCKTAIL

Will Rogers never met a man he didn't like. Drink these, hug the guy on the next bar stool.

1 1/2 ounces gin
1/2 ounce dry vermouth
1/2 ounce orange juice
1/4 ounce orange curacao

1. Fill cocktail shaker with ice.
2. Add gin, vermouth, orange juice, and curacao.
3. Shake.
4. Strain into a cocktail glass.

187. CHARLESTON

Don the fringe flapper dress, pearls, and feather boa and start gamboling.

1/2 ounce gin
1/2 ounce Kirsch
1/2 ounce dry vermouth
1/2 ounce sweet vermouth
1/4 ounce maraschino liqueur
1/4 ounce orange curacao

1. Fill cocktail shaker with ice.
2. Add gin, Kirsch, vermouths, maraschino liqueur, and curacao.
3. Stir.
4. Strain into a cocktail glass.

188. ORIENTAL COCKTAIL

Serve these to guests and let them pretend they are traveling on the Orient Express.

1 ounce blended whiskey
1/2 ounce sweet vermouth
1/2 ounce triple sec
Juice of 1/2 lime

1. Fill cocktail shaker with ice.
2. Add whiskey, vermouth, triple sec, and lime juice.
3. Shake.
4. Strain into a cocktail glass.

189. DEMPSEY COCKTAIL

Just try and go fifteen rounds with this heavy weight.

1 ounce gin
1 ounce apple brandy
1/4 ounce pastis
1/4 ounce grenadine

1. Fill cocktail shaker with ice.
2. Add gin, apple brandy, pastis, and grenadine.
3. Stir.
4. Strain into a cocktail glass.

190. MULE'S HIND LEG

Grab this one when you can. It's got quite a kick but it's worth the ride.

1/2 ounce gin
1/2 ounce apple brandy
2 teaspoons Benedictine
2 teaspoons apricot brandy
2 teaspoons maple syrup

1. Fill cocktail shaker with ice.
2. Add gin, apple brandy, Benedictine, apricot brandy, and maple syrup.
3. Shake.
4. Strain into an old-fashioned glass filled with ice.

191. TORPEDO COCKTAIL

Sink another drink; it'll give you time to think.

1 1/2 ounces apple brandy
3/4 ounce brandy
1 to 2 dashes gin

1. Fill cocktail shaker with ice.
2. Add brandies and gin.
3. Shake.
4. Strain into a chilled cocktail glass.

192. NEW ORLEANS BUCK

What the locals call you if you get naked on Bourbon Street.

1 1/2 ounces light rum
1/2 ounce fresh lime juice
1/2 ounce orange juice
2 dashes Angostura bitters
Ginger ale

1. Fill cocktail shaker with ice.
2. Add rum, juices, and bitters.
3. Shake.
4. Strain into a highball glass half-filled with ice.
5. Top with ginger ale.
6. Stir.
7. Garnish with a lime slice.

193. OPERA

The preferred choice after the fat lady sings.

1 1/2 ounces gin
1/2 ounce red Dubonnet
1/2 ounce maraschino liqueur

1. Fill cocktail shaker with ice.
2. Add gin, Dubonnet, and maraschino liqueur.
3. Stir.
4. Strain into a cocktail glass.

CHAMPAGNE CONCOCTIONS—
Park Avenue Potions

Cole Porter said, "I get no kick from champagne." But what did he know? Champagne fizzes with dizzying expectations and golden giddiness. Put simply: champagne makes people happy. Often associated with the beautiful and famous, champagne cocktails can be decadently expensive and devilishly delightful, especially when mixed with lavish liqueurs. So get the party started with a little champagne. Even if it's not a vintage Rothschild, bubbly inevitably transforms the most humdrum Herbert or Harriet into a shooting star.

194. CLASSIC CHAMPAGNE COCKTAIL

Dorothy Parker said it best: "Three be the things I shall attain: envy, content, and sufficient champagne."

1 sugar cube
2 dashes Angostura bitters
Chilled champagne

1. Place sugar and bitters in a chilled champagne flute.
2. Top with champagne.
3. Garnish with a lemon peel.

195. CHAMPAGNE CORNUCOPIA

Forget the flute, pass the horn of plenty. Make that plenty of bubbly.

1 ounce cranberry juice
2 scoops rainbow sherbet
1 ounce vodka
3/4 ounce peach schnapps
1 ounce champagne

1. Pour cranberry juice into an oversized red wine glass.
2. Pour rainbow sherbet, vodka, and peach schnapps into a blender.
3. Blend until smooth.
4. Pour mixture over cranberry juice.
5. Layer champagne on top.
6. Garnish with an orange slice.

196. BELLINI

Champagne and peaches! A dynamite duo, baby.

1 fresh peach
Chilled brut champagne

1. Puree peach in a blender.
2. Pour into champagne glass.
3. Add chilled champagne.

197. BELLINI PUNCH

Come quickly I'm tasting stars—the immortal words of the man himself...Dom Perignon.

Fresh peaches
Iced brut champagne
1 tablespoon lemon juice
Sugar

1. In a blender, puree enough peaches to cover the bottom of a punch bowl.
2. Pour the peach mixture into a punch bowl.
3. Add approximately three times as much champagne to peach mixture.
4. Add lemon juice and sugar to taste.
5. Stir.

198. IMPERIAL FIZZ

Conquer the empire. One glass at a time.

1 ounce bourbon
1/2 ounce lemon juice
1/2 teaspoon sugar
Chilled champagne

1. Fill cocktail shaker with ice.
2. Add bourbon, lemon juice, and sugar.
3. Shake.
4. Strain into a chilled champagne glass.
5. Fill with champagne.

199. FROZEN BIKINI

Icy and tingly in all the right places.

2 ounces vodka
1 ounce peach schnapps
3 ounces peach nectar
2 ounces orange juice
Splash of fresh lemon juice
1 ounce chilled champagne
4 ounces crushed ice

1. Pour vodka, peach schnapps, peach nectar, juices, and ice into a blender.
3. Blend until smooth.
4. Pour into a goblet.
5. Top with champagne.

200. CHAMBORD ROYALE SPRITZER

Be a part of the court even if you don't own a crown.

1 1/2 ounces Chambord
Chilled champagne
Club soda

1. Pour Chambord into a wine glass.
2. Add splash of champagne.
3. Fill with club soda.

201. CHAMPAGNE CUP

My cup runneth over. Give me a bigger one.

4 teaspoons powdered sugar
6 ounces club soda
1 ounce triple sec
2 ounces brandy
16 ounces chilled champagne

1. Fill a pitcher with ice.
2. Add powdered sugar, club soda, triple sec, and brandy.
3. Add champagne.
4. Stir.
5. Decorate with fruits in season and cucumber rind on side of pitcher.
6. Top with mint.
7. Serve in red wine glasses.
(Serves 6)

202. MIMOSA

This classic brunch drink is perfect for anytime of day; enjoy it at breakfast, lunch, or dinner.

3 ounces chilled champagne
3 ounces chilled orange juice

1. Pour champagne and orange juice into champagne flute.

203. CARIBBEAN CHAMPAGNE

Isaac can't make these fast enough on the Pacific Princess.

1/2 teaspoon light rum
1/2 teaspoon banana liqueur
Dash of orange bitters
4 ounces chilled brut champagne
1 banana slice

1. Pour rum, banana liqueur, and bitters into a chilled champagne glass.
2. Add champagne.
3. Stir gently.
4. Float banana slice on top.

204. CHAMPAGNE FRAISE

Remember the first time someone dropped a strawberry in your champagne? Delicious.

1/2 teaspoon strawberry liqueur
1/2 teaspoon Kirsch
4 ounces chilled brut champagne
1 large strawberry

1. Pour strawberry liqueur and Kirsch into a chilled champagne glass.
2. Swirl the glass, coating with strawberry liqueur and Kirsch.
3. Top with champagne.
4. Float strawberry on top.

205. TINTORETTO

A delightful and unexpected "pair" of flavors.

1 pear
Chilled champagne
Dash of pear brandy

1. Puree pear in blender.
2. Pour 1/2 ounce pear puree into a champagne glass.
3. Top with champagne.
4. Add pear brandy.

206. VALENCIA

A bubbly citrus bonanza.

2 ounces apricot brandy
1 ounce orange juice
2 to 3 dashes orange bitters
Chilled champagne

1. Fill cocktail shaker with ice.
2. Add apricot brandy, orange juice, and bitters.
3. Shake.
4. Strain into a goblet.
5. Top with champagne.

207. SPARKLING WINE POLONAISE

A teaser that you can't skirt.

1 teaspoon blackberry liqueur
1 teaspoon blackberry brandy
1/2 teaspoon cognac
3 ounces chilled dry sparkling wine
Sugar

1. Moisten champagne glass with blackberry liqueur.
2. Sugar frost rim.
3. Add blackberry brandy, cognac, and sparkling wine.
4. Gently stir.

208. SPARKLING WINE JULEP

For the Frenchman at the Derby who shuns bourbon.

1 mint sprig
1 tablespoon sugar syrup
1 1/2 ounces brandy
3 ounces chilled dry sparkling wine

1. Pour sugar syrup and mint sprig into champagne glass.
2. Crush mint in sugar syrup.
3. Fill glass with crushed ice.
4. Add brandy.
5. Fill with sparkling wine.
6. Gently stir.
7. Garnish with a mint sprig.

209. CHAMPAGNE MANHATTAN

Step One: Don top hat and tails. Step two: Hit the town. Step three: Leave an empty bottle of champagne at every stop.

1 ounce Canadian whiskey
1/4 ounce sweet vermouth
Dash of Angostura bitters
3 ounces chilled brut champagne
1 brandied cherry

1. Fill cocktail shaker with ice.
2. Add whiskey, vermouth, and bitters.
3. Stir.
4. Strain into a chilled champagne glass.
5. Top with champagne.
6. Float brandied cherry on top.

210. CHAMPAGNE NORMANDE

Lord Maynard Keynes said, "My only regret is that I did not drink more champagne." Don't be like him.

1 teaspoon Calvados
1/2 teaspoon sugar
Dash of Angostura bitters
4 ounces chilled brut champagne

1. Pour Calvados, sugar, and bitters into chilled champagne glass.
2. Stir.
3. Top with champagne.
4. Stir gently.

211. CHAMPAGNE NOYAUX

Don't hold back. Go nuts.

1/2 ounce crème de noyaux
1 teaspoon lime juice
1 large toasted almond
4 ounces chilled brut champagne
Lime slice

1. Pour crème de noyaux and lime juice into a chilled champagne glass.
2. Add the almond.
3. Top with champagne.
5. Float a lime slice on top.

212. SAVOY SPRINGTIME

I'm stomping at the Savoy with a glass of champagne in my hand. Life couldn't be better.

1/4 ounce gin
1/4 ounce Cointreau
1/4 ounce fresh orange juice
Chilled champagne

1. Pour gin, Cointreau, and orange juice into a champagne glass.
2. Top with champagne.
3. Stir gently.

213. KING'S PEG

A favorite of the Versailles crowd way back when.

2 1/2 ounces cognac
Chilled champagne

1. Fill wine glass with ice cubes.
2. Add cognac.
3. Top with champagne.

214. MOSCOW MIMOSA

What all the well-heeled Muscovites will be drinking this season.

3 ounces chilled champagne
3 ounces orange juice
1/2 ounce vodka

1. Pour champagne, orange juice, and vodka into wine glass.
2. Stir gently.

215. ROYAL SCREW

A drink fit for a king, a queen, and a castle full of concubines.

2 ounces cognac
2 ounces orange juice
Chilled champagne

1. Pour cognac into a champagne glass.
2. Add orange juice.
3. Stir gently.
4. Top with champagne.

216. ROYAL PEACH FREEZE

Peaches and champagne never tasted so majestic.

1 1/2 ounces champagne
2 ounces peach schnapps
2 ounces orange juice
1/2 ounce Rose's lime juice
3 ounces crushed ice

1. Pour champagne, peach schnapps, juices, and ice into a blender.
2. Blend until smooth.
3. Pour into a goblet.

217. SPARKLING GALLIANO

"Champagne, if you are seeking the truth, is better than a lie detector." So said Graham Greene; try this and see if you agree.

1/2 ounce Galliano
1/2 teaspoon lemon juice
4 ounces chilled brut champagne
Cucumber peel

1. Pour Galliano and lemon juice into a chilled champagne glass.
2. Top with champagne.
3. Garnish with a cucumber peel.

218. CHAMPAGNE OLD-FASHIONED

A trio of classic perennials that never goes out of style.

1/2 ounce Grand Marnier
Dash of orange bitters
Chilled brut champagne

1. Pour Grand Marnier and bitters into an old-fashioned glass with ice.
2. Top with champagne.
3. Garnish with a cherry and an orange slice.

219. CHARTREUSE CHAMPAGNE

Lime green bubbly for our favorite Irish holiday.

1/2 teaspoon green Chartreuse
1/2 teaspoon cognac
4 ounces chilled brut champagne

1. Pour green Chartreuse, cognac, and champagne into a chilled champagne glass.
2. Stir gently.
3. Garnish with twisted lemon peel.

220. ORANGE CHAMPAGNE

Knock, knock. Who's there? Orange. Orange who? Orange you glad you ordered another glass of this?

Spiraled orange peel
2 teaspoons curacao
4 ounces chilled brut champagne

1. Drop the spiraled orange peel into chilled champagne glass.
2. Add curacao and champagne.
3. Stir gently.

221. CHERRY CHAMPAGNE

My cherie amour. This tastes great, so pour me some more.

1/2 ounce iced cherry liqueur
4 ounces chilled brut champagne
1/2 pitted cherry

1. Pour cherry liqueur into a chilled champagne glass.
2. Fill with champagne.
3. Float cherry on top.

222. MELBA CHAMPAGNE

A delicate dessert that delights from head to toe.

1/2 ounce raspberry brandy
4 ounces chilled brut champagne
1 fresh raspberry
Raspberry sherbet

1. Pour raspberry brandy into a chilled champagne glass.
2. Add champagne and fresh raspberry.
3. Use a melon baller to scoop a single ball of sherbet.
4. Float sherbet on top.

223. GULF STREAM

A drink that goes straight to your head. You might need a co-pilot for this one.

1 ounce blue curacao
3 ounces champagne
1/2 ounce light rum
1/2 ounce brandy
6 ounces lemonade
1 ounce lime juice
3 ounces crushed ice
Sugar

1. Pour curacao, champagne, light rum, brandy, lemonade, lime juice, and ice into a blender.
2. Pour into a sugar-rimmed parfait glass.
3. Garnish with a whole strawberry.

224. ARISE MY LOVE

And bring me the bottle of fizzy.

1 teaspoon crème de menthe
Chilled champagne

1. Pour crème de menthe into a champagne flute.
2. Top with champagne.

225. STOCKHOLM 75

Fun fact: In 1901, Stockholm hosted the awarding of the first Nobel prizes.

3/4 ounce citrus vodka
3/4 ounce sugar syrup
3/4 ounce lemon juice
5 ounces chilled champagne
Sugar

1. Fill cocktail shaker with ice.
2. Add vodka, sugar syrup, and lemon juice.
3. Shake.
4. Strain into a sugar-rimmed oversized cocktail glass.
5. Top with champagne.

226. NIJINSKI BLINI

Lord Byron said: "A woman should never be eating or drinking, unless it be lobster salad and champagne." Sign me up!

1 ounce vodka
2 ounces pureed peaches
1/2 ounce lemon juice
Splash of peach schnapps
Splash of chilled champagne

1. Pour vodka, peach puree, lemon juice, peach schnapps, and champagne into champagne flute.
2. Stir gently.

227. SCOTCH ROYALE

Hey there, Macbeth: I know that champagne gives you a kick, but let's keep the kilt on next time.

1 sugar cube
1 1/2 ounces scotch
Dash of Angostura bitters
Chilled champagne

1. Place sugar cube in a champagne flute.
2. Add scotch and bitters.
3. Fill with champagne.

228. TYPHOON

Typhoon season is usually a cause for alarm except when this libation blows in.

1 ounce gin
1/2 ounce anisette
1 ounce lime juice
Chilled champagne

1. Fill cocktail shaker with ice.
2. Add gin, anisette, and lime juice.
3. Shake.
4. Strain into a collins glass with ice.
5. Top with champagne.

229. DIAMOND FIZZ

Diamonds are a girl's best friend, especially when they're paired with bubbly.

Juice of 1/2 lemon
1 teaspoon powdered sugar
2 ounces gin
Chilled champagne

1. Fill cocktail shaker with ice.
2. Add lemon juice, powdered sugar, and gin.
3. Shake.
4. Strain into a highball glass with ice.
5. Fill with champagne.
6. Stir.

230. FRENCH 75

Fun fact: Named in honor of a World War I French field gun. Indulge and make love, not war.

Juice of 1 lemon
2 teaspoons powdered sugar
2 ounces gin
Chilled champagne

1. Pour lemon juice, powdered sugar, and gin into a collins glass.
2. Stir.
3. Add ice.
4. Fill with champagne.
5. Stir.
6. Garnish with a lemon or an orange slice and a cherry.
7. Serve with straws.

231. LUXURY COCKTAIL

Champagne wishes, caviar dreams…buy me a yacht and hear me scream.

3 ounces brandy
2 dashes orange bitters
3 ounces chilled champagne

1. Fill a cocktail shaker with brandy, champagne, and bitters.
2. Stir.
3. Pour into a champagne flute.

232. AMERICANA

President Dwight D. Eisenhower on America: "Some people wanted champagne and caviar when they should have had beer and hot dogs." You know whose side we're on.

1/4 ounce Tennessee whiskey
1/2 teaspoon sugar
1 to 2 dashes Angostura bitters
Chilled champagne
Peach slice

1. Pour whiskey, sugar, and bitters into a collins glass.
2. Stir until sugar dissolves.
3. Fill with champagne.
4. Add peach slice.

233. LONDON SPECIAL

Taking the posh down a peg or two, Clement Attlee once said, "The House of Lords is like a glass of champagne that has stood for five days." Don't keep this drink waiting; bottoms up!

Orange peel
1 sugar cube
2 dashes of Angostura bitters
Chilled champagne

1. Drop orange peel into champagne flute.
2. Add sugar cube and bitters.
3. Fill with champagne.
4. Stir.

234. BLACK VELVET

An Irish favorite: one part pub, one part castle.

One part Guinness (preferably on draft)
One part champagne

1. Combine equal amounts of Guinness and champagne in a chilled collins glass.
2. Stir.

235. CHICAGO

Sure to warm you up on the windiest of days.

1 1/2 ounces brandy
Dash of curacao
Dash of Angostura bitters
Chilled brut champagne
Sugar

1. Fill cocktail shaker with ice.
2. Add brandy, curacao, and bitters.
3. Shake.
4. Strain into a sugar-rimmed goblet or wine glass.
5. Fill with champagne.

236. CONCORDE

The Captain has turned on the "Drinking" sign. Please feel free to move about the cabin.

2 ounces cognac
2 ounces chilled pineapple juice
Champagne

1. Fill cocktail shaker with ice.
2. Add cognac and pineapple juice.
3. Stir.
4. Strain into a champagne glass with cracked ice.
5. Fill with champagne.

237. DEATH IN THE AFTERNOON

Parlez-vous francais? The French refer to a climax as "le petit mort" or "the little death."

1 1/2 ounces Pernod
Chilled champagne

1. Pour Pernod into a chilled champagne glass.
2. Fill with champagne.

238. EVE

Drink deeply from the Tree of Knowledge. Fig leaf optional.

1/2 teaspoon Pernod
1 tablespoon cognac
2 teaspoons sugar
2 teaspoons curacao
Chilled pink sparkling wine

1. Pour Pernod into a large wine glass.
2. Swirl to coat sides of glass with Pernod.
3. Add cognac.
4. In a bowl, combine sugar and curacao until sugar dissolves.
5. Add mixture to wine glass.
6. Stir.
7. Add ice cubes.
8. Fill with sparkling wine.

239. FRENCH LIFT

A drink popularized by Pierre Wonka. Fizzy lifting French drink, indeed.

3 ounces chilled dry sparkling wine
1/2 ounce grenadine
2 ounces Perrier water
3 or 4 fresh blueberries

1. Pour sparkling wine into a champagne glass.
2. Add grenadine.
3. Fill with Perrier water.
4. Float blueberries on top.

240. FROBISHER

Named for a famous adventurer. Have a couple of these and find out where they'll take you.

2 ounces gin
3 dashes Angostura bitters
Chilled champagne

1. Pour gin and bitters into highball glass with ice.
2. Stir.
3. Fill with champagne.
4. Garnish with a lemon twist.

241. PRINCE OF WALES

Strong enough for a king, but made for a prince.

1 ounce Madeira
1 ounce brandy
3 or 4 drops curacao
2 dashes Angostura bitters
Chilled champagne

1. Fill cocktail shaker with ice.
2. Add Madeira, brandy, curacao, and bitters.
3. Shake.
4. Strain into champagne glass.
5. Fill with champagne.
6. Garnish with an orange slice.

242. AIRMAIL

Always delivers, right on time.

1 ounce white rum
1/2 ounce lime juice
1/2 ounce honey syrup
3 ounces champagne

1. Fill cocktail shaker with ice.
2. Add rum, lime juice, and honey syrup.
3. Shake.
4. Strain into chilled champagne glass.
5. Top with champagne.

243. CHAMPAGNE BUCK

A *few glasses of this concoction and you'll want to dance in the snow "buck" naked.*

1/2 ounce gin
1/4 ounce cherry brandy
1/4 ounce orange juice
Chilled champagne
Orange peel

1. Build gin, cherry brandy, and orange juice into a highball glass.
2. Fill with champagne.
3. Add orange peel.

244. BARBOTAGE OF CHAMPAGNE

"When her guests were awash with champagne and with gin, she was recklessly sober, as sharp as a pin."
—William Plomer

Dash of Angostura bitters
1/2 teaspoon sugar
Dash of lemon juice
Chilled champagne
Orange peel

1. Build bitters, sugar, and lemon juice in a collins glass.
2. Fill the glass half-full with crushed ice.
3. Fill with champagne.
4. Add orange peel.

245. CHAMPAGNE COBBLER

A snow cone for the posh kids.

1/4 ounce lemon juice
1/4 ounce orange curacao
Champagne

1. Fill a double old-fashioned glass two-thirds full with shaved ice.
2. Add lemon juice and curacao.
3. Stir.
4. Fill with champagne.
5. Garnish with an orange slice.

246. CHAMPAGNE COOLER

Drink this while enjoying your balcony view of the city scape on a steamy summer night.

1/2 ounce brandy
1/2 ounce Cointreau
Champagne
Mint sprig

1. Pour brandy and Cointreau into a collins glass with ice.
2. Fill with champagne.
3. Add mint sprig.

247. LAST THOUGHT COCKTAIL

Ensures that the night's final ruminations are warm and fuzzy. Need us to tuck you in?

1 ounce brandy
1 ounce champagne

1. Fill a cocktail shaker with brandy and champagne.
2. Stir.
3. Strain into a cocktail glass.

248. CHAMPAGNE NUT COCKTAIL

Sometimes you feel like a nut. Sometimes you feel like a rich nut.

1/2 ounce crème de noyaux
1/2 ounce crème de cacao
Champagne
1 almond

1. Layer crème de noyaux and crème de cacao in a cocktail glass.
2. Fill with champagne.
3. Add almond.

249. CHAMPAGNE SIDECAR

Careful with that crystal flute—dangerous curves ahead!

1/4 ounce lemon juice
1/4 ounce brandy
1/4 ounce Cointreau
Champagne

1. Fill cocktail shaker with ice.
2. Add lemon juice, brandy, and Cointreau.
3. Shake.
4. Strain into a cocktail glass.
5. Fill with champagne.

250. CHAMPAGNE SOUR

Not as bitter as the name suggests. But what champagne drink is?

1/2 ounce lemon juice
1/2 teaspoon sugar
Chilled champagne

1. Pour lemon juice and sugar in a sour glass.
2. Fill with champagne.
3. Garnish with a lemon slice or a cherry.

251. CUCUMBER CHAMPAGNE

Sure to get you pickled.

1 ounce Benedictine
1/2 ounce lemon juice
Champagne

1. Pour Benedictine and lemon juice in a collins glass with ice.
2. Fill with champagne.
3. Garnish with lemon peel.

252. SOYER AU CHAMPAGNE COCKTAIL

"How about a nightcap on the company. My company."
                    —*James Bond,* The Spy Who Loved Me

1 tablespoon vanilla ice cream
1/4 ounce maraschino liqueur
1/4 ounce orange curacao
1/4 ounce brandy
Chilled champagne

1. Put vanilla ice cream in a chilled champagne glass.
2. Add maraschino liqueur, curacao, and brandy.
3. Fill with champagne.
4. Garnish with an orange slice and a cherry.

253. WALSH CHAMPAGNE COCKTAIL

Mrs. Walsh never touches champagne. Unless she's thirsty.

1 teaspoon sugar
1 mint sprig
1 lemon twist
Champagne

1. Build sugar, mint sprig, and lemon twist in a collins glass with ice.
2. Fill with champagne.
3. Float a cherry on top.

254. CHAMPAGNE COMFORT

Silver screen icon Bette Davis nailed it when she said: "There comes a time in every woman's life when the only thing that helps is a glass of champagne."

Splash of Southern Comfort
2 dashes Angostura bitters
Champagne
Peach slice

1. Pour Southern Comfort and bitters in a champagne glass.
2. Fill with champagne.
3. Add a peach slice.

255. CHAMPAGNE ISLAND

Where fantasies really do come true. The plane! The plane!

Splash of orange curacao
2 dashes Angostura bitters
Chilled champagne

1. Pour curacao and bitters into a chilled cocktail glass.
2. Fill with champagne.
3. Garnish with a twist of lemon.

256. CHAMPAGNE GREENBAUM

Bartender's gonna set you up with the Spirit in the Sky.

1 1/2 ounces vodka
3/4 ounce melon liqueur
Dash of Rose's lime juice
Chilled champagne

1. Layer vodka, melon liqueur, lime juice, and champagne in a champagne flute.

257. CHAMPAGNE NAPOLEON

The General once said, "I drink champagne when I win, to celebrate…and I drink champagne when I lose, to console myself."

3/4 ounce Mandarine Napoleon
Splash of orange juice
Chilled champagne

1. Pour Mandarine Napoleon into a champagne flute.
2. Add orange juice.
3. Fill with champagne.

258. VIRTUAL REALITY

Sometimes, even better than the real thing.

1/3 ounce Calvados
1 ounce gin
3/4 ounce grenadine
3/4 ounce lemon juice
Chilled champagne

1. Fill cocktail shaker with ice.
2. Add Calvados, gin, grenadine, and lemon juice.
3. Shake.
4. Strain into a highball glass with ice.
5. Top with champagne.

259. PICK ME UP

Off the floor, that is.

1 ounce cognac
2/3 ounce orange juice
1/3 ounce grenadine
Chilled champagne

1. Pour cognac, orange juice, and grenadine into a champagne flute.
2. Fill with champagne.
3. Garnish with an orange slice and a cherry.

260. KIR ROYALE

Founding Father Benjamin Franklin's wise words: "He who drinks fast pays slow."

6 ounces champagne
Splash of crème de cassis

1. Pour champagne into champagne flute.
2. Add splash of crème de cassis.

261. KIR IMPERIAL

Purple, the color of royalty.

3/4 ounce raspberry liqueur
Champagne

1. Pour raspberry liqueur in champagne flute.
2. Fill with champagne.

262. CHAMPS-ELYSEES

Puts extra sparkle in the City of Lights.

2/3 ounce Cointreau
2/3 ounce strawberry liqueur
Chilled champagne

1. Pour Cointreau and strawberry liqueur into a
   champagne flute.
2. Fill with champagne.
3. Garnish with small strawberry.

263. CHAMPAGNE SUGARPOP

"Champagne is the only wine that leaves a woman beautiful after drinking it." So saith Madame de Pompadour. Don't argue with her.

1 sugar cube
2 dashes Angostura bitters
1 ounce cognac
Chilled champagne

1. Place sugar cube in a champagne flute.
2. Add bitters and cognac.
3. Fill with champagne.

264. RITZ FIZZ

Dressed up like a million-dollar trouper? Accessorize with this!

Dash of amaretto
Dash of blue curacao
Dash of lemon juice
Champagne

1. Add the dashes of amaretto, curacao, and lemon juice in a champagne flute.
2. Fill with champagne.

265. ROULETTE

Where she stops, nobody knows. Except the bartender.

1 ounce blue curacao
Chilled champagne

1. Pour curacao into a champagne flute.
2. Fill with champagne.
3. Garnish with a mint sprig.

266. POMME FIZZ

An apple a day, you say? Just one? Perish the thought!

1/2 ounce vermouth
1/2 ounce apple juice concentrate
2 ounces champagne

1. Fill cocktail shaker with ice.
2. Add vermouth and apple juice concentrate.
3. Shake.
4. Strain into a champagne glass.
5. Top with champagne.
6. Garnish with an apple chip.

267. CHAM CHAM

Note the absence of "pagne" and "bord." That's not an accident.

5 ounces champagne
1/2 ounce Chambord
Raspberries

1. Pour champagne into a champagne glass.
2. Add Chambord to taste.
3. Float raspberries on top.

268. SLAMMER ROYALE

Aptly named.

6 ounces tequila
4 ounces champagne

1. Pour tequila and champagne into a cocktail shaker.
2. Stir.
3. Pour into shot glasses.
4. Slam glasses on table to create fizz.
(Serves 5)

269. PUSH

Hey barkeep—push another one of these my way.

1/2 ounce apricot brandy
1/2 ounce amaretto
3 ounces pineapple juice
Chilled champagne

1. Fill cocktail shaker with ice.
2. Add apricot brandy, amaretto, and pineapple juice.
3. Stir.
4. Strain into a collins glass with ice.
5. Fill with champagne.
6. Garnish with a lime wheel and cherry.

270. MONTE CARLO

Odds are you'll like this one.

1 1/2 ounces gin
3/4 ounce crème de menthe
3/4 ounce lemon juice
Champagne

1. Fill cocktail shaker with ice.
2. Add gin, crème de menthe, and lemon juice.
3. Shake.
4. Strain into a highball glass with ice.
5. Fill with champagne.

271. APPLE STRUDEL

Tell Grandma you're sneaking off to the kitchen for some of this. She'll be none the wiser.

1 1/2 ounces vodka
1/2 ounce honey liqueur
1/2 ounce blackberry puree
Dash of vanilla syrup
2 ounces apple juice
Champagne

1. Fill cocktail shaker with ice.
2. Add vodka, honey liqueur, blackberry puree, vanilla syrup, and apple juice.
3. Shake.
4. Strain into a collins glass with ice.
5. Top with champagne.

272. LEMONHEAD

Sweet, fizzy, and tart, like your favorite candy in a glass.

1/2 fresh lemon
1 teaspoon powdered sugar
1 teaspoon water
2 1/2 ounces champagne

1. Squeeze lemon into a chilled cocktail shaker.
2. Add sugar and water to lemon.
3. Stir.
4. Pour into a cocktail glass.
5. Fill cocktail glass with shaved ice.
6. Add champagne.
7. Stir.

273. 90210 ICED TEA

All the rage on Rodeo Drive.

1 ounce sour mix
1 ounce gin
1 ounce white rum
1 ounce tequila
1 ounce Tia Maria
1 ounce vodka
Chilled champagne

1. Pour sour mix, gin, white rum, tequila, Tia Maria, and vodka into a zombie glass.
2. Fill with champagne.

274. BORDEAUX BITTER

The best of France and Italy, in the palm of your hand.

1 ounce Campari
Champagne

1. Pour Campari and champagne into deep-saucer champagne glass.
2. Stir.

275. DUBONNET FIZZ

A *splendid combination of flavors, sure to liven the gathering.*

1 ounce orange juice
2 ounces Dubonnet
Champagne

1. Fill cocktail shaker with ice.
2. Add orange juice and Dubonnet.
3. Shake.
4. Strain into an old-fashioned glass.
5. Fill with champagne.

276. CORPSE REVIVER

Sure to jolt the most reticent party guest back to life.

2 dashes of grenadine
2/3 ounce lemon juice
2/3 ounce orange juice
2/3 ounce brandy
Champagne

1. Fill cocktail shaker with ice.
2. Add grenadine, juices, and brandy.
3. Shake.
4. Strain into an old-fashioned glass.
5. Top with champagne.

277. FONTANA

Sip on this while basking on a sun-drenched Italian piazza. Or just pretend you are.

1 ounce orange juice
1 ounce Campari
1/2 ounce Cointreau
1/2 ounce Grand Marnier
Champagne

1. Fill cocktail shaker with ice.
2. Add orange juice, Campari, Cointreau, and Grand Marnier.
3. Shake.
4. Strain into an old-fashioned glass.
5. Top with champagne.
6. Garnish with shredded lemon peel.

278. FRENCH 90

"Gentlemen, in the little moment that remains to us between the crisis and the catastrophe, we may as well drink a glass of champagne." —Paul Claudell, French playwright

2 ounces sour mix
1 ounce brandy
Champagne

1. Fill cocktail shaker with ice.
2. Add sour mix and brandy.
3. Stir.
4. Strain into a collins glass with ice.
5. Fill with champagne.

279. LE PETIT FIZZ

It's not the size of the fizz that matters, it's what you do with it that counts.

1 ounce blue curacao
1/2 ounce vodka
Champagne
Lime slice

1. Pack a margarita glass with crushed ice.
2. Pour blue curacao into the center of the glass.
3. Add vodka.
4. Top with champagne.
5. Squeeze lime wedge on top and drop in.

280. SILVER REIGN

Although equally apt to make one dance, this drink should not be confused with the Prince album of a slightly different name.

1 1/3 ounces bourbon
1 ounce champagne
1 ounce Drambuie

1. Pour bourbon, champagne, and Drambuie into an old-fashioned glass with ice.
2. Stir.

281. 78 CAMARO

Much like the automobile: loud and dirty, yet strangely appealing.

3/4 ounce Yukon Jack
3/4 ounce rum
3/4 ounce apricot brandy
1 ounce pineapple juice
Champagne

1. Fill cocktail shaker with ice.
2. Add Yukon Jack, rum, apricot brandy, and pineapple juice.
3. Shake.
4. Strain into a highball glass.
5. Top with champagne.

282. ATHEIST'S BEST

Enjoyed by many a lazy non-believer on Sunday mornings.

1 1/2 ounces vodka
3/4 ounce cherry juice
3/4 ounce lemon juice
3 ounces extra dry champagne

1. Fill cocktail shaker with ice.
2. Add vodka and juices.
3. Shake.
4. Strain into a cocktail glass.
5. Top with champagne.

283. A GOOD NIGHT KISS

If it's done right, it lingers on the lips just a bit.

Drop of Angostura bitters
1 sugar cube
4 ounces champagne
Splash of Campari

1. Put one drop of bitters on a sugar cube.
2. Drop into a champagne flute.
3. Add champagne.
4. Splash with Campari.

284. THE CAROLINA

Nothing could be finer than to drink a Carolina in the morning. Or anytime.

2 ounces Strega
2 ounces champagne

1. Pour Strega into a chilled wine glass.
2. Add champagne.
3. Stir gently.

285. AMBROSIA

The drink of toga-wearing gods with expensive tastes.

1 ounce apple jack
1 ounce brandy
Dash of triple sec
Juice of 1 lemon
Chilled champagne

1. Fill cocktail shaker with ice.
2. Add apple jack, brandy, triple sec, and lemon juice.
3. Shake.
4. Strain into a highball glass with ice.
5. Fill with champagne.
6. Stir lightly.

286. FRENCH PIRATE

Cheers to Jean LaFitte, the Gentleman Pirate of New Orleans!

1/2 ounce orange curacao
1 ounce dark rum
Champagne

1. Pour curacao into champagne flute.
2. Add rum.
3. Top with champagne.

287. ORIGINAL SIN

Harder to resist than that first bite of the apple.

3/4 ounce triple sec
1 1/2 ounces brandy
1 1/2 ounces cherry liqueur
Splash of sour mix
Dash of grenadine
6 ounces champagne

1. Fill a hurricane glass with crushed ice.
2. Add triple sec, brandy, cherry liqueur, sour mix, and grenadine.
3. Stir.
4. Top with champagne.
5. Garnish with orange, lemon, and lime slices.

MARTINI MADNESS—
Bond and Babe Drinks

Before Bradshaw, Carrie Bradshaw, there was Bond, James Bond, asking for his chosen drink, shaken not stirred. Smooth and suave, not to mention sexy as sin, James Bond was the quintessential martini drinker; in his first twenty films, the super spy drank eighteen. Bond owned the drink until a sex writer from Manhattan wooed the young and hip masses with fruitful neon twists on the classic. Soon, *Sex and the City* wannabees were teetering in expensive stilettos and ordering designer 'tinis in sleek bars from coast to coast. If ever a cocktail personified sex and status, it's the martini in all of its glorious renditions from past to present.

288. ORIGINAL MARTINI

Simple, classic, elegant. Your dad definitely wants one. Make it a double.

1 1/2 ounces gin
Dry vermouth to taste

1. Fill cocktail shaker with ice.
2. Add gin and vermouth.
3. Stir.
4. Strain into a martini glass.
5. Garnish with an olive.

289. VESPER MARTINI

Fear not, noble churchgoer—this is not a mischievous addition to your church potluck, but a libation that pays homage to James Bond's leggy love interest in Casino Royale.

3 ounces gin
1 ounce vodka
1/2 ounce Lillet blonde

1. Fill cocktail shaker with ice.
2. Add gin, vodka, and Lillet blonde.
3. Shake.
4. Strain into a chilled martini glass.
5. Garnish with a slice of lemon peel.

290. VODKA MARTINI

Drink of choice for a certain British secret agent. Order this, and you have a license to swill.

1 1/2 ounces vodka
Dash dry vermouth

1. Fill cocktail shaker with ice.
2. Add vodka and vermouth.
3. Stir.
4. Strain into a chilled martini glass.
5. Garnish with an olive.

291. ALGONQUIN

Best enjoyed while seated at a round table, arguing literature with your crowd's Dorothy Parker.

1 1/2 ounces whiskey
1 ounce dry vermouth to taste
1 ounce pineapple juice

1. Fill cocktail shaker with ice
2. Add whiskey, vermouth, and pineapple juice.
3. Shake.
2. Strain into a chilled martini glass.

292. BLACK AND WHITE MARTINI

The perfect accompaniment for the man who prefers a martini that matches his tuxedo.

3 ounces vanilla-flavored vodka
1 ounce crème de cacao

1. Fill cocktail shaker with ice.
2. Add vodka and crème de cacao.
3. Shake.
4. Strain into a chilled martini glass.
5. Garnish with black and white licorice candies.

293. CABARET MARTINI

Mix them up, pop in the Liza video, practice your Fosse moves. Tuxedo tap pants? A must.

3 ounces gin
1 1/2 ounces red Dubonnet
4 dashes Angostura bitters
4 dashes Pernod

1. Fill cocktail shaker with ice.
2. Add gin, Dubonnet, bitters, and Pernod.
3. Shake.
4. Strain into a chilled martini glass.
5. Garnish with a lime twist.

294. COLONY CLUB MARTINI

Perfect for the hidden British expatriate in all of us.

3 ounces gin
1 teaspoon Pernod
4 dashes orange bitters

1. Fill cocktail shaker with ice.
2. Add gin, Pernod, and bitters.
3. Shake.
4. Strain into a chilled martini glass.
5. Garnish with an orange twist.

295. DEEP SEA MARTINI

Passing this one up would be unfathomable. Enjoy with a viewing of Jaws or, if you're parental, the 500th viewing of Finding Nemo.

3 ounces gin
1 ounce dry vermouth
1/2 teaspoon Pernod
Dash orange bitters

1. Fill cocktail shaker with ice.
2. Add gin, vermouth, Pernod, and bitters.
3. Stir.
4. Strain into a chilled martini glass.

296. DUSTY MARTINI

Ideal for long walks with the son of a preacher man.

2 ounces gin
Dash dry vermouth
Scotch

1. Fill cocktail shaker with an ice cube.
2. Add gin and vermouth.
3. Stir.
4. Strain into a chilled martini glass rimmed with scotch.
5. Garnish with a lemon twist.

297. FARE THEE WELL MARTINI

A nice touch for long, lingering goodbyes with your paramour. Mix well, and he might have to stay longer.

3 ounces gin
1/2 ounce dry vermouth
1/2 ounce sweet vermouth
Dash Cointreau

1. Fill cocktail shaker with ice.
2. Add gin, vermouths, and Cointreau.
3. Stir.
4. Strain into a chilled martini glass.

298. FDR'S MARTINI

Fireside Chats are much more pleasant with a pitcher of these nearby. Make this drink your New Deal.

1 ounce gin
1/2 ounce vermouth
1 teaspoon olive brine

1. Fill cocktail shaker with ice.
2. Add gin, vermouth, and olive brine.
3. Stir.
4. Rub a lemon twist around the rim of a chilled martini glass.
5. Strain into the glass.
6. Garnish with an olive.

299. FIFTY-FIFTY VODKA MARTINI

Even Steven. Dutch. You get the idea.

2 ounces vodka
2 ounces dry vermouth

1. Fill cocktail shaker with ice.
2. Add vodka and vermouth.
3. Stir.
4. Strain into a chilled martini glass.
5. Garnish with an olive.

300. GREAT CAESAR'S MARTINI

Must surely have been the favorite drink of Perry White, Clark Kent's editor at The Daily Planet. Order this one loudly with three exclamation points. (!!!)

3 ounces vodka
1/2 ounce dry vermouth

1. Fill cocktail shaker with ice.
2. Add vodka and vermouth with cracked ice.
3. Shake.
4. Strain into a martini cocktail glass.
5. Garnish with an anchovy-stuffed olive.

301. IMPERIAL MARTINI

Drink this and watch a magic crown appear above your head. Really!

3 ounces gin
1 ounce dry vermouth
1/2 teaspoon maraschino liqueur
4 dashes Angostura bitters

1. Fill cocktail shaker with ice.
2. Add gin, vermouth, maraschino liqueur, and bitters.
3. Stir.
4. Strain into a chilled martini glass.

302. HOT AND DIRTY MARTINI

Ladies—when ordering this one, add a low, husky purr to your voice. Shrinks your bar tab instantly.

3 ounces pepper vodka
1/2 ounce dry vermouth
1 teaspoon olive brine

1. Fill cocktail shaker with ice.
2. Add vodka, vermouth, and olive brine.
3. Shake.
4. Strain into a chilled martini glass.
5. Garnish with an olive stuffed with pickled jalapeno pepper.

303. LONDON MARTINI

I do say, old bean, let's bend our elbows and toast Mother England! There's a good chap! (Bowler hats sold separately.)

3 ounces gin
1/2 teaspoon maraschino liqueur
4 dashes orange bitters
1/2 teaspoon sugar

1. Fill cocktail shaker with ice.
2. Add gin, maraschino liqueur, bitters, and sugar.
3. Stir.
4. Strain into a chilled martini glass.
5. Garnish with a lemon twist.

304. LOW TIDE MARTINI

Cape Cod in a martini glass. Who needs planes, trains, and automobiles?

3 ounces vodka
1/2 ounce dry vermouth
1 teaspoon clam juice

1. Fill cocktail shaker with ice.
2. Add vodka, vermouth, and clam juice.
3. Shake.
4. Strain into a chilled martini glass.
5. Garnish with an olive stuffed with smoked clam and a lemon twist.

305. OPAL MARTINI

A liquefied birthstone for October babies. Taste this and you'll wish for another when you blow out the candles.

3 ounces gin
1/2 ounce triple sec
1 ounce fresh orange juice
1/4 teaspoon sugar

1. Fill cocktail shaker with ice
2. Add gin, triple sec, orange juice, and sugar.
3. Shake.
4. Strain into a chilled martini glass.

306. PALL MALL MARTINI

Toss-off this fact to impress a date: the Pall Mall Martini is named for a London thoroughfare in the St. James district, home to Marlborough House. If your date asks a follow-up question, make a toast and change the subject.

2 ounces gin
1/2 ounce dry vermouth
1/2 ounce sweet vermouth
1 teaspoon white crème de menthe
Dash orange bitters

1. Fill cocktail shaker with ice.
2. Add gin, vermouths, crème de menthe, and bitters.
3. Stir.
4. Strain into a chilled martini glass.

307. DEAN MARTINI

Rat Packers of the World, unite! Raise a toast to swingin' daddy-o's everywhere.

3 ounces vodka or gin (Bartender's choice)
Splash red sweet vermouth

1. Fill cocktail shaker with ice.
2. Add vodka or gin and vermouth.
3. Stir.
4. Strain into a chilled martini glass.
5. Garnish with an orange wheel.

308. SICILIAN MARTINI

Truly an offer he can't refuse. Just don't ask him about the family business.

1 1/2 ounces gin
1/4 ounce dry vermouth
1/2 ounce dry Marsala

1. Fill cocktail shaker with ice.
2. Add gin, vermouth, and Marsala.
3. Stir briskly.
4. Strain into a chilled martini glass.
5. Twist lemon over drink and drop into the glass.

309. RUDE COSMOPOLITAN

This one has a surprising bite, as if Jose Cuervo took a wrong turn at Albuquerque and ended up in your glass.

1 1/4 ounces tequila
1/4 ounce Grand Marnier
Juice from whole lime
1 ounce cranberry juice

1. Fill cocktail shaker with ice.
2. Add tequila, Grand Marnier, and juices.
3. Shake.
4. Strain into a chilled martini glass.
5. Garnish with an orange peel.

310. GOLF MARTINI

So, this must explain golfer's fashion choices.

4 ounces gin
1 ounce dry vermouth
4 dashes Angostura bitters

1. Fill cocktail shaker with ice.
2. Add gin, vermouth, and bitters.
3. Shake.
4. Strain into a chilled martini glass.
5. Garnish with an olive.

311. VELVET BUNNY MARTINI

Remember your favorite stuffed animal from childhood while this warms you before bedtime.

1 1/2 ounces vodka
Dash banana liqueur
Dash black sambuca

1. Fill cocktail shaker with ice.
2. Add vodka, banana liqueur, and sambuca.
3. Shake.
4. Strain into a chilled martini glass.
5. Garnish with banana slices.

312. PRINCESS MARTINI

She'll feel like royalty when you present Her Highness with this libation. Make it a double and she just might knight you.

1 1/2 ounces vodka
Dash strawberry liqueur

1. Fill cocktail shaker with ice.
2. Add vodka and strawberry liqueur.
3. Shake.
4. Strain into a chilled martini glass.
5. Squeeze slice of orange over the glass and drop in.

313. NEW ORLEANS MARTINI

Iko, Iko! Shake off the workday voodoo with this taste of the Big Easy.

3 ounces vanilla vodka
1/2 ounce dry vermouth
1/2 ounce Pernod
Dash Angostura bitters

1. Fill cocktail shaker with ice.
2. Add vodka, vermouth, Pernod, and bitters.
3. Shake.
4. Strain into a chilled martini glass.
5. Garnish with mint sprig.

314. LEAP YEAR

This is The Official Drink of February 29th, but we urge you to throw caution to the wind—make 'em on July 5th. Or May 13th.

2 ounces gin
1/2 ounce sweet vermouth
1/2 ounce Grand Marnier
1/4 teaspoon lime juice

1. Fill cocktail shaker with ice.
2. Add gin, vermouth, Grand Marnier, and lime juice.
3. Shake.
4. Strain into a chilled martini glass.

315. PALM BEACH MARTINI

A favorite among wealthy Florida socialites.

3 ounces gin
1 teaspoon sweet vermouth
2 ounces grapefruit juice

1. Fill cocktail shaker with ice.
2. Add gin, vermouth, and grapefruit juice.
3. Shake.
4. Strain into a chilled martini glass.

316. PARK AVENUE MARTINI

When Eva Gabor told Eddie Arnold, "Darling, I love you, but give me Park Avenue," she surely had this one in mind. Mix, sip, and ponder what the commoners are doing today.

3 ounces gin
1/2 ounce sweet vermouth
1/2 ounce dry vermouth

1. Fill cocktail shaker with ice.
2. Add gin and vermouths.
3. Shake.
4. Strain into a chilled martini glass.

317. WARSAW

Surely the preferred choice of famous Poles like Lech Walesa and Count Pulaski.

1 1/2 ounces gin
1 ounce apple brandy
1 ounce sweet vermouth
1 teaspoon yellow Chartreuse

1. Fill cocktail shaker with ice.
2. Add gin, apple brandy, vermouth, and Chartreuse.
3. Shake.
4. Strain into a chilled martini glass.

318. JOURNALIST

Stop the presses! This smooth libation will make even the most reluctant source spill the beans.

2 ounces gin
1 teaspoon dry vermouth
1 teaspoon sweet vermouth
1 teaspoon triple sec
1 teaspoon lime juice
Dash Angostura bitters

1. Fill cocktail shaker with ice.
2. Add gin, vermouths, triple sec, and lime juice.
3. Shake.
4. Strain into a chilled martini glass.

319. ICEBERG

A nice accompaniment to your Titanic viewing parties. Garnish with Kleenex.

2 ounces gin
Dash white crème de menthe

1. Fill cocktail shaker with ice.
2. Add gin and crème de menthe.
3. Shake.
4. Strain into a chilled martini glass.
5. Garnish with fresh mint.

320. SMOKY MARTINI

They say smoke gets in your eyes, but this goes straight to your head.

3 ounces gin
1/2 ounce dry vermouth
1 teaspoon scotch

1. Fill cocktail shaker with ice.
2. Add gin, vermouth, and scotch.
3. Stir.
4. Strain into a chilled martini glass.
5. Garnish with lemon twist.

321. THIRD DEGREE MARTINI

For loosening the tongues of uncooperative suspects. Mix, administer, repeat as needed.

3 ounces gin
1 ounce dry vermouth
1/2 ounce Pernod

1. Fill cocktail shaker with ice.
2. Add gin, vermouth, and Pernod.
3. Shake.
4. Strain into a chilled martini glass.

322. BLENTON

As James Thurber said, "One martini is all right. Two are too many, and three are not enough."

1 1/2 ounces gin
3/4 ounce dry vermouth
Dash Angostura bitters

1. Fill cocktail shaker with ice.
2. Add gin, vermouth, and bitters.
3. Stir.
4. Strain into a chilled martini glass.

323. BLOODHOUND

Turn the tables on this canine detective—pursue doggedly.

1 ounce gin
1/2 ounce dry vermouth
1/2 ounce sweet vermouth
1/2 ounce strawberry liqueur

1. Fill cocktail shaker with ice.
2. Add gin, vermouths, and strawberry liqueur.
3. Shake.
4. Strain into a chilled martini glass.
5. Drop a whole strawberry into glass.

324. FINO MARTINI

As Bob Hope said in The Cat and the Canary: *"Let's all drink gin and make wry faces."*

2 ounces gin
1/2 ounce fino sherry

1. Fill cocktail shaker with ice.
2. Add gin and sherry.
3. Stir.
4. Strain into a chilled martini glass.
5. Garnish with olive or lemon twist.

325. FLYING DUTCHMAN

Legend is that this drink's namesake is a ghostly sea captain, doomed to sail the seas for all eternity. Can't be all bad. At least he's got this tasty concoction to keep him company.

Curacao
2 ounces gin
1/4 ounce dry vermouth

1. Pour enough curacao into prechilled cocktail glass to coat sides.
2. Twirl glass and coat with curacao.
3. Fill cocktail shaker with ice.
4. Add gin and vermouth.
5. Stir.
6. Strain into glass.

326. MARSALA MARTINI

Marsala—Italy's answer to sherry —makes this martini an adventurous departure from the standard. Bongiorno!

3/4 ounce gin
3/4 ounce dry vermouth
3/4 ounce dry Marsala

1. Fill cocktail shaker with ice.
2. Add gin, vermouth, and Marsala.
3. Stir.
4. Strain into a chilled martini glass.
5. Twist lemon above drink and drop in.

327. DUTCH MARTINI

Got a date who hates going Dutch? Change her mind with these.

2 ounces Dutch genever gin
1/2 ounce dry vermouth

1. Fill cocktail shaker with ice.
2. Add gin and vermouth.
3. Stir.
4. Strain into a chilled martini glass.
5. Twist lemon above drink and drop in.

328. PERFECT

Once you taste one of these, you'll quickly grasp the name.

1 1/2 ounces gin
1/2 ounce dry vermouth
1/2 ounce sweet vermouth

1. Fill cocktail shaker with ice.
2. Add gin and vermouths.
3. Stir.
4. Strain into a chilled martini glass.
5. Garnish with olive or lemon.

329. PAISLEY MARTINI

A blatant, and highly effective, attempt to attract the attention of thirsty hippies everywhere.

2 1/4 ounces gin
1/4 ounce dry vermouth
1 teaspoon scotch

1. Fill cocktail shaker with ice.
2. Add gin, vermouth, and scotch.
3. Stir.
4. Strain into a chilled martini glass.

330. RACQUET CLUB MARTINI

"Biff? Muffy? Shall I order us a round? Fabulous..."

2 ounces gin
1/2 ounce dry vermouth
2 dashes orange bitters

1. Fill cocktail shaker with ice.
2. Add gin, vermouth, and bitters.
3. Shake until outside of shaker is completely frosted.
4. Strain into a cold martini glass.

331. MORRO

Be like Little Orphan Annie and order "to."

1 ounce gin
1/2 ounce golden rum
1/2 ounce lime juice
1/2 ounce pineapple juice
Sugar

1. Fill cocktail shaker with ice.
2. Add gin, rum, and juices.
3. Shake.
4. Strain into a sugar-rimmed chilled martini glass.

332. POMPANO

Fun fact: Pompano racetrack in south Florida features nighttime horse racing. Giddyup!

1 ounce gin
1/2 ounce dry vermouth
1 ounce grapefruit juice
4 dashes orange bitters

1. Fill cocktail shaker with ice.
2. Add gin, vermouth, grapefruit juice, and bitters.
3. Shake.
4. Strain into a chilled cocktail or old-fashioned glass.
5. Garnish with an orange slice.

333. ST. LO

Named for the patron saint of the vertically challenged.

1 1/2 ounces gin
1/2 ounce Calvados
1/2 ounce lemon juice
1 teaspoon sugar

1. Fill cocktail shaker with ice.
2. Add gin, Calvados, lemon juice, and sugar.
3. Shake.
4. Strain into a chilled martini glass.

334. PRINCETON

Adventurous Ivy Leaguers will enjoy this concoction. Sis boom bah!

1 1/4 ounces gin
3/4 ounce dry vermouth
1/2 ounce lime juice

1. Fill cocktail shaker with ice.
2. Add gin, vermouth, and lime juice.
3. Shake.
4. Strain into a cocktail glass.

335. RED CLOUD

So named for the pleasant fog that envelops the drinker's brain.

1 1/2 ounces gin
1/2 ounce apricot liqueur
1/2 ounce lemon juice
1 teaspoon grenadine
Dash Angostura bitters

1. Fill cocktail shaker with ice.
2. Add gin, apricot liqueur, lemon juice, grenadine, and bitters.
3. Shake.
4. Strain into a cocktail glass.

336. LAVA LAMP MARTINI

An unusually tasty byproduct of "60s Night" at the country club.

Splash raspberry liqueur
Splash honey
3 ounces vodka

1. Mix raspberry liqueur and honey in a shot glass.
2. Fill cocktail shaker with ice.
3. Add vodka.
4. Shake.
5. Strain into a martini glass.
6. Spoon in raspberry liqueur and honey mixture.

337. SECRET MARTINI

Don't tell anyone about this one. Keep the recipe to yourself and indulge in covert actions.

3 ounces gin
1 ounce Lillet Blonde
2 dashes Angostura bitters

1. Fill cocktail shaker with ice.
2. Add gin, Lillet Blonde, and bitters.
3. Stir.
4. Strain into a chilled martini glass.

338. MONTMARTRE

The ideal locule for consuming this drink? The tallest point in Paris, of course.

1 1/2 ounces gin
1/2 ounce sweet vermouth
1/2 ounce triple sec

1. Fill cocktail shaker with ice.
2. Add gin, vermouth, and triple sec.
3. Shake.
4. Pour into an old-fashioned glass filled with ice.

339. MOULIN ROUGE

Can you make zees drink? Oui! Everybody can-can!

1 1/2 ounces sloe gin
1/2 ounce sweet vermouth
3 dashes Angostura bitters

1. Fill cocktail shaker with ice.
2. Add sloe gin, vermouth, and bitters.
3. Shake.
4. Strain into a chilled martini glass.

340. HELLFIRE CLUB MARTINI

Emma Peel surely downed one of these after escaping the Hellfire Club's sinister clutches.

1 1/2 ounces pepper vodka
1/2 ounce dry vermouth

1. Fill cocktail shaker with ice.
2. Add pepper vodka and dry vermouth.
3. Stir.
4. Strain into a chilled martini glass.
5. Garnish with a jalapeno pepper and a dash of cayenne pepper.

341. DIPLOMAT

The martini strong enough to solve the world's problems. Share liberally.

2 ounces dry vermouth
1 ounce sweet vermouth
2 dashes maraschino liqueur

1. Fill cocktail shaker with ice.
2. Add vermouths and maraschino liqueur.
3. Stir.
4. Strain into a chilled martini glass.
5. Garnish with an orange peel twist.

342. TRUFFLE MARTINI

Raise a glass to toast the tireless work of our porcine brethren, who have selflessly sniffed out underground truffle troves for generations.

3 1/2 ounces cognac
Splash lime juice
Splash Grand Marnier
7 paper-thin slices black truffle

1. Fill cocktail shaker with ice.
2. Add cognac, lime juice, and Grand Marnier and 2 slices of black truffle.
3. Shake.
4. Strain into a chilled martini glass.
5. Garnish with remaining five slices of black truffle.

343. POMEGRANATE MARTINI

Persephone, heroine of Greek mythology, was banished to Hades for eating an other-worldly pomegranate. Lucky you—she took the fall, you get the drink.

2 ounces fresh squeezed pomegranate juice
2 ounces vodka
1/4 ounce sugar syrup

1. Fill cocktail shaker with ice.
2. Add pomegranate juice, vodka, and sugar syrup.
3. Shake.
4. Strain into a chilled martini glass.

344. COWBOY MARTINI

A refreshing respite for cowpunchers both urban and rural. Saddle up!

2 ounces gin
1/2 ounce dry vermouth
Dash sugar syrup

1. Fill cocktail shaker with ice.
2. Add gin, vermouth, and sugar syrup.
3. Shake.
4. Strain into a chilled martini glass.
5. Garnish with a floating mint sprig.

345. COSMOPOLITAN

The drink that made Sex in the City *chicks teeter in their Jimmy Choos. Fruity and light, drink a few and get ready to hear all about your friend's Mr. Big.*

2 ounces lemon-flavored vodka
1 ounce triple sec
1 ounce cranberry juice
1/2 ounce lime juice

1. Fill cocktail shaker with ice.
2. Add vodka, triple sec, cranberry juice, and lime juice.
3. Shake.
4. Strain into a chilled martini glass.
5. Garnish with a lime slice.

346. FLIRTINI

Sure to make you think the bartender is cute enough to deserve a wink or two.

1/2 ounce raspberry vodka
1/2 ounce Cointreau
Splash lime juice
Splash pineapple juice
Splash cranberry juice
5 raspberries
Brut champagne

1. Muddle raspberries in bottom of slightly chilled cocktail glass.
2. Fill cocktail shaker with ice.
2. Add vodka, Cointreau, and juices.
3. Shake.
4. Strain into a chilled martini glass.
5. Top with champagne.
6. Garnish with a mint sprig.

347. WEMBLEY MARTINI

Perhaps the reason soccer hooligans often riot at Wembley is that the bartender has run out of this tasty treat? A promising theory.

3 ounces gin
1/2 ounce dry vermouth
1 teaspoon apricot brandy
1 teaspoon Calvados

1. Fill cocktail shaker with ice.
2. Add gin, vermouth, apricot brandy, and Calvados.
3. Shake.
4. Strain into a chilled martini glass.
5. Garnish with a lemon twist.

348. NEWBURY

Like the British town and Boston street of the same name, the Newbury is sweet, posh, and delicious. Perfect for the parched Anglophile.

1 1/2 ounces gin
1 ounce sweet vermouth
1/4 teaspoon triple sec

1. Fill cocktail shaker with ice.
2. Add gin, vermouth, and triple sec.
3. Shake.
4. Strain into a chilled martini glass.
5. Garnish with a lemon twist.

349. BLUE MARTINI

The perfect hand candy for the air traveler with a window seat.

3 ounces vodka
1/2 ounce blue curacao
Dash Angostura bitters

1. Half-fill cocktail shaker with ice.
2. Add vodka, curacao, and bitters.
3. Shake.
4. Strain into a chilled martini glass.
5. Garnish with an olive.

350. GIRLIE MARTINI

Careful there, mister—order a "couple of girlies" too loudly, and your barmates may eye you with suspicion. Proceed with caution.

Splash dry vermouth
4 ounces vodka
3 ounces chilled champagne
Dash maraschino liqueur

1. Coat inside of martini glass with dry vermouth.
2. Fill cocktail shaker with ice.
3. Add vodka, champagne, and maraschino liqueur.
4. Stir.
5. Strain into the martini glass.
6. Garnish with an olive and a cherry.

351. SOHO

The decadent way to end a day of shopping and art gallery exploration.

2 ounces vodka
1/2 ounce vanilla vodka
1/2 ounce orange curacao
Dash orange bitters

1. Fill cocktail shaker with ice.
2. Add vodkas, orange curacao, and bitters.
3. Shake.
4. Strain into a martini glass.
5. Garnish with a flamed orange peel.

352. LONG KISS GOODNIGHT MARTINI

Like its namesake, this one is sweet and leaves you wanting more. Much more.

1/2 ounce vanilla vodka
1 ounce vodka
1/2 ounce white crème de cacao
Shaved white chocolate

1. Freeze a martini glass with white chocolate on rim.
2. Fill cocktail shaker with ice
3. Add vodkas and crème de cacao.
4. Shake lightly.
5. Strain into the glass.
6. Garnish with a chocolate kiss.

353. ST. TROPEZ

While this drink won't give you that perfect St. Tropez tan, you can hear the ocean if you hold the empty glass over your ear.

2 ounces vodka
1/2 ounce maraschino liqueur
3 ounces peach juice

1. Fill cocktail shaker with vodka, maraschino liqueur, and peach juice.
2. Add ice.
3. Stir.
4. Strain into a chilled martini glass.

354. BLUE LAGOON

So you weren't lucky enough to be shipwrecked with a young Brooke Shields? Join the club. Drown your sorrows while cursing the name of Christopher Atkins.

2 ounces vodka
1/4 ounce blue curacao
3 ounces pineapple juice

1. Fill cocktail shaker with vodka, curacao, and pineapple juice.
2. Add ice.
3. Shake.
4. Strain into a chilled martini glass.

355. GIN AND SIN

Want to really ruffle the petticoats of your teetotaling Aunt Gladys? Offer her one of these aptly named combinations, and watch her scurry for the safety of her Prohibition League meeting.

1 1/2 ounces gin
1 ounce orange juice
1 ounce lemon juice
1/2 teaspoon grenadine

1. Fill cocktail shaker with ice.
2. Add gin, juices, and grenadine.
3. Shake.
4. Strain into a chilled martini glass.

356. SPECIAL SWEET MARTINI

Make it for the girl in your life. Claim you invented it and named it after her. We won't tell.

Dash of orange bitters
1/2 ounce gin
1/2 ounce sweet vermouth

1. Fill cocktail shaker with ice.
2. Add bitters, gin, and vermouth.
3. Shake.
4. Strain into a chilled martini glass.

357. MEDIUM MARTINI

If Starbucks was a bar, this one would be called a "Grande."

1/4 ounce dry vermouth
1/2 ounce sweet vermouth
1/3 ounce dry gin

1. Fill cocktail shaker with ice.
2. Add vermouths and gin.
3. Shake.
4. Strain into a chilled martini glass.

358. PINK PUPPY

Roll over and fetch this one whenever possible. If you bring me one, I promise to scratch your tummy.

1 1/2 ounces vodka
1 1/2 ounces gin
4 1/2 ounces grapefruit juice

1. Fill cocktail shaker with ice.
2. Add vodka, gin, and grapefruit juice.
3. Shake.
4. Strain into a chilled martini glass.
5. Garnish with a cherry.

359. PALME D'OR

This drink shares its name with the big prize from the Cannes Film Festival. Mix one up and pretend to strut down the red carpet.

1 1/2 ounces vodka
3/4 ounces lemon juice
2 teaspoons lime cordial

1. Fill cocktail shaker with ice.
2. Add vodka, lemon juice, and lime cordial.
3. Shake.
4. Strain into a chilled martini glass.
5. Garnish with twist of lemon and a cherry.

360. RAZMOPOLITAN

It's the raspberry that makes this drink so sinfully delicious. But don't down too many and razz the patrons.

2 1/4 ounces raspberry vodka
1 1/8 ounces triple sec
1 1/2 ounces cranberry juice
3/4 ounce lime juice
1 teaspoon caster sugar

1. Fill cocktail shaker with ice.
2. Add vodka, triple sec, juices, and sugar.
3. Shake.
4. Strain into a chilled martini glass.
5. Twist lime peel above glass and drop in.

361. SILVER BULLET

If the Lone Ranger ever left one of these behind, Tonto would have questioned the Masked Man's sanity.

1 1/2 ounces gin
Splash scotch

1. Fill cocktail shaker with ice.
2. Add gin and scotch.
3. Shake.
4. Strain into a chilled martini glass.

(This drink may also be stirred and served on the rocks.)

362. MARTINI NOIR

Drink this at the beginning of a beautiful friendship, preferably with a feisty—yet compliant—gun moll.

2 ounces vodka
1 ounce Chambord

1. Fill cocktail shaker with ice.
2. Add vodka and Chambord.
3. Shake.
4. Strain into a chilled martini glass.
5. Garnish with lemon twist.

363. CREOLE MARTINI

My great-uncle Boudreaux claims that this drink makes him handsome, funny, and a really great dancer.

2 ounces gin
1/4 ounce dry vermouth

1. Fill cocktail shaker with ice.
2. Add gin and vermouth.
3. Stir.
4. Strain into a chilled martini glass.
5. Garnish with jalapeño pepper.

364. THE FIGGY

Get jiggy with the figgy.

2 ounces vodka
1/4 ounce fig vodka
1/4 ounce maraschino liqueur
1 ounce half and half

1. Pour vodkas, maraschino liqueur, and cream into cocktail shaker.
2. Fill cocktail shaker with ice.
3. Let stand for five seconds.
4. Shake.
4. Strain into a chilled martini glass.
5. Garnish with dark chocolate kiss and a fig slice.

365. SAKETINI

A few of these will have you singing like Aretha Franklin, to the tune of "Respect." "Saketini-saketini-saketini-saketini..."

1 1/2 ounces sake
1 1/2 ounces gin

1. Fill cocktail shaker with ice.
2. Add sake and gin.
3. Shake.
4. Strain into a chilled martini glass.
5. Garnish with an olive.

366. MILKY WAY MARTINI FOR TWO

Bob had a problem. He was thirsty, AND he had missed dessert. Milky Way Martini to the rescue!

6 ounces vanilla vodka
1 Milky Way candy bar
1 tablespoon sweet chocolate shavings

1. Slice Milky Way candy bar into pieces.
2. Place candy bar slices in microwaveable bowl and heat until melted.
3. Fill cocktail shaker with ice.
4. Add vodka.
5. Shake.
6. Spoon 1 teaspoon melted candy bar in bottom of each chilled cocktail glasses.
7. Strain vodka into the glasses.
8. Garnish with chocolate shavings.

367. CHOCOLATE ORANGE DROP FOR TWO

Overheard near the ski lodge fireplace, "Baby, this drink is just like you, sweet, but with a kick."

3 ounces orange vodka
1 ounce chocolate vodka
1 ounce Cointreau
1 1/2 ounces white chocolate liqueur

1. Fill cocktail shaker with ice.
2. Add vodkas, Cointreau, and white chocolate liqueur.
3. Shake.
4. Strain into two chilled martini glasses.
5. Garnish with chocolate orange slices.

368. WHITEOUT MARTINI FOR TWO

No mistake here. Make this drink for your favorite secretary.

4 ounces vanilla vodka
1 ounce white crème de cacao
2 ounces white chocolate liqueur

1. Fill cocktail shaker with ice.
2. Add vodka.
3. Shake.
4. Add white crème de cacao and white chocolate liqueur.
5. Swirl shaker for one minute.
6. Rest shaker for one minute.
7. Strain into two frozen martini glasses.
8. Dust with coconut flakes.

369. MINT PATTY MARTINI

All this great taste and fresh breath, too? What a country!

3 ounces pepper vodka
2 ounces white crème de menthe
1 Starlight mint
1 ounce dark chocolate liqueur
1 tablespoon peppermint schnapps

1. Fill cocktail shaker with ice.
2. Add pepper vodka, crème de menthe, and Starlight mint.
3. Let shaker stand for one minute.
4. Shake.
5. Add dark chocolate liqueur.
6. Shake.
7. Strain into two chilled martini glasses.
8. Top each glass with half of the peppermint schnapps.

370. GIMLET LIMETINI

Can't get your date to pucker up? Order a couple of these, and it'll be next stop: Smoochville, Population: 2.

4 ounces key lime vodka
1/2 teaspoon dry vermouth
1 teaspoon bottled water
1 lime

1. Fill cocktail shaker with ice.
2. Add vodka.
3. Stir.
4. Add vermouth and water.
5. Squeeze in half of lime.
6. Stir.
7. Strain into a chilled martini glass.
8. Garnish with lime twist.

371. LEMON DROP MARTINI

Lemon Drop, Lemon Drop, Oh Lemon-Lemon Drop...easy to make and the chicks dig it.

1 1/2 ounces citrus vodka
1 teaspoon sugar
1/4 of a lemon

1. Slice 1/4 lemon into wedges.
2. Fill cocktail shaker with ice.
3. Add lemon wedges.
4. Add vodka and sugar.
5. Shake.
6. Strain into sugar-rimmed chilled martini glass.
7. Garnish with a lemon twist.

372. EURO-COSMO

No, this is not the poor man's Parisian astronaut or that dance-a-teria round the way. But it is a taste sensation.

1 1/2 ounces vodka
1/2 ounce Cointreau
1/4 ounce lime juice
1 ounce cranberry juice

1. Fill cocktail shaker with ice.
2. Add vodka, Cointreau, lime juice, and cranberry juice.
3. Shake.
4. Strain into a chilled martini glass.
5. Garnish with an orange slice.

373. MELONTINI

Livens up the traditional gin martini with a welcomed fruity flavor.

2 ounces gin
Dash melon liqueur

1. Fill cocktail shaker with ice.
2. Add gin and melon liqueur.
3. Shake.
4. Strain into a chilled martini glass.

374. FRENCHMAN'S FOLLY

Pierre is being too humble—if this libation is a mistake, sacre bleu!

4 ounces gin
3 ounces dry vermouth
1 ounce lemonade
1 ounce water

1. Fill cocktail shaker with ice.
2. Add gin, vermouth, lemonade, and water.
3. Shake.
4. Strain into a chilled martini glass.

375. UPTOWN GIN MARTINI

You know those sharp-looking guys at the corner table, who always look like they have it all together? This is what they're drinking.

1 1/2 ounces gin
1/8 ounce dry vermouth
1/4 ounce olive juice
Dash Angostura bitters

1. Fill cocktail shaker with ice.
2. Add gin, vermouth, olive juice, and bitters.
3. Shake.
4. Strain into a chilled martini glass.

376. ROSE PETAL MARTINI

Big Moe behind the bar will not make you one of these. Don't ask him.

2 ounces vodka
Dash rose water

1. Fill cocktail shaker with ice.
2. Add vodka and rose water.
3. Stir 10 times.
4. Strain into a chilled martini glass.
5. Garnish with rose petals.

377. GYPSY

A drink so good, even nomads will stick around.

1 1/2 ounces sweet vermouth
1 1/2 ounces gin

1. Fill cocktail shaker with ice.
2. Add vermouth and gin.
3. Stir.
4. Strain into a chilled martini glass.
5. Garnish with cherry.

378. AFTERBURNER

Ahh...sweet mother alcohol with a healthy dose of Vitamin C. Scurvy, begone!

1 1/2 ounces triple sec
3 ounces vodka
3/4 ounce grapefruit juice

1. Fill cocktail shaker with ice.
2. Add triple sec, vodka, and grapefruit juice.
3. Shake.
4. Strain into a chilled martini glass.
5. Garnish with a strawberry slice.

379. BOUNTY MARTINI

Please pardon the reference to a paper towel slogan, but this drink is indeed the "quicker picker upper." Ouch.

1 1/2 ounces red vodka
1 1/2 ounces vanilla vodka
2 1/4 ounces cream of coconut
Dash sugar syrup
Six drops orange bitters

1. Muddle vodkas, cream of coconut, sugar syrup, and bitters in cocktail shaker.
2. Add ice.
3. Shake.
4. Strain into a chilled martini glass.
5. Garnish with fresh strawberries.

380. EGG CUSTARD MARTINI

One word: Flan-tastic!

3 ounces vodka
1 1/2 ounces Warnicks advocaat
3/4 ounce vanilla vodka
3/4 ounce bourbon
1/8 ounce sugar syrup

1. Fill cocktail shaker with ice.
2. Add vodka, Warnicks advocaat, vanilla vodka, bourbon, and sugar syrup.
3. Stir.
4. Strain into a chilled martini glass.
5. Dust with nutmeg.

381. HIGH ROLLER

If you order this in a casino, the pit boss comps you all sorts of free stuff. Really. Give it a whirl.

1 1/2 ounces dry vermouth
1 1/2 ounces gin
3/4 ounce triple sec
3/4 ounce apricot brandy

1. Fill cocktail shaker with ice.
2. Add vermouth, gin, triple sec, and apricot brandy.
3. Stir.
4. Strain into a chilled martini glass.
5. Garnish with a cherry.

382. JASMINE

Preferably served in a magic lamp on a flying carpet.

1 1/2 ounces gin
3/4 Campari
3/4 ounce triple sec
Dash sugar syrup

1. Fill cocktail shaker with ice.
2. Add gin, Campari, triple sec, and sugar syrup.
3. Shake.
4. Strain into a chilled martini glass.
5. Garnish with lemon peel.

383. KNICKERBOCKER

Hard to get much more old school than this one. Good any-where, but especially in a dark, wood-paneled haunt.

1 1/2 ounces gin
1/4 teaspoon sweet vermouth
3/4 ounce dry vermouth

1. Fill cocktail shaker with ice.
2. Add gin and vermouths.
3. Stir.
4. Strain into a chilled martini glass.
5. Garnish with a lemon peel.

384. MANGOTINI

The libidinous taste of mango combined with the spirit-lifting effects of vodka.

1 1/2 ounces mango vodka
3/4 ounce triple sec
Splash mango juice

1. Fill cocktail shaker with ice.
2. Add vodka, triple sec, and mango juice.
3. Shake.
4. Strain into a chilled martini glass.
5. Garnish with a mango slice.

385. ORANGE COSMO

A flavorful burst that cries for a second round.

2 ounces vodka
1 ounce Grand Marnier
1/4 ounce lime juice
1 ounce cranberry juice

1. Fill cocktail shaker with ice.
2. Add vodka, Grand Marnier, and juices.
3. Shake.
4. Strain into a chilled martini glass.
5. Garnish with an orange peel.

386. PRINCE EDWARD MARTINI

First cigars, now a martini. Are there any vices that Prince Edward didn't endorse? My kind of guy.

3 ounces gin
1/2 ounce Drambuie

1. Fill cocktail shaker with ice.
2. Add gin and Drambuie.
3. Shake.
4. Strain into a chilled martini glass.
5. Garnish with a lemon twist.

387. QUEEN ELIZABETH MARTINI

Royally delicious. God Save The Queen!

3 ounces gin
1/2 ounce dry vermouth
2 teaspoons Benedictine

1. Fill cocktail shaker with ice.
2. Add gin, vermouth, and Benedictine.
3. Shake.
4. Strain into a chilled martini glass.

388. CHOCOLATE MARTINI

The perfect gateway drink for beginning lushes. It's the candy cigarette of the alcohol world.

1 1/2 ounces vodka
3/4 ounce white crème de cacao
Cocoa powder

1. Fill cocktail shaker with ice.
2. Add vodka and crème de cacao.
3. Shake.
4. Strain into a cocoa powder-rimmed chilled martini glass.
5. Garnish with a chocolate kiss—tip up—in the glass.

AFTER DINNER DREAMS—
Turn Your Lamp Down Low

andles twinkle in a plush den. The smooth Reverend Al Green plays on the stereo. Hey, don't pull out the tequila. No way. That's not the liquor of choice after a romantic meal or on a rainy Sunday night after a most pleasurable weekend. Lay back and relax some more. Think romance. Think seduction. Oh yeah, that's it. Now you're talking. A Brandy Alexander. Delish. A Grasshopper? Creamy green devils sure to make you lose your mind. A Golden Cadillac? Is that what you drive? Silly me, you mean the drink. I'll take one. Then another. If you're lucky.

389. BLUE ANGEL

Ever wonder why those Air Force stunt pilots defy death for your viewing pleasure? It's because they get to sip these little Top Guns when they return to the hangar.

1/2 ounce blue curacao
1/2 ounce parfait amour
1/2 ounce brandy
1/2 ounce lemon juice
1/2 ounce cream

1. Fill cocktail shaker with ice.
2. Add curacao, parfait amour, brandy, lemon juice, and cream.
3. Shake.
4. Strain into a cocktail glass.

390. GOLDEN DREAM

Sip a few of these and slip into a fantastic sleep.

1 ounce Galliano
1/2 ounce triple sec
1 tablespoon orange juice
1 tablespoon light cream

1. Fill cocktail shaker with ice.
2. Add Galliano, triple sec, orange juice, and cream.
3. Shake.
4. Strain into a cocktail glass.

391. BANANA SLIP

What would Freud say about this one?

1 1/2 ounces crème de banana
1 1/2 ounces Irish cream liqueur

1. Layer crème de banana and Irish Cream in a cordial glass.

392. CRÈME DE CACAO NIGHTCAP

Just what a nightcap should be: sweet, silky, and smooth. Be sure to brush before turning in.

1/4 cup cream
2 teaspoons sugar
1 tablespoon crème de cacao
10 ounces milk
4 ounces crème de cacao
2 ounces brandy
3 tablespoons sugar
Powdered cocoa

1. Beat cream until whipped.
2. Stir in 2 teaspoons sugar and 1 tablespoon crème de cacao.
3. Store in refrigerator.
4. Heat milk, 4 ounces crème de cacao, brandy, and sugar until hot.
5. Pour into 4 small goblets.
6. Top with whipped cream, sugar, and crème de cacao mixture.
7. Sprinkle cocoa on top.
(Serves 4)

393. CHOCOLATE ORANGE FRAPPE

A sinful liquid bonbon to be indulged in slowly.

3/4 ounce crème de cacao
3/4 ounce orange juice
1 teaspoon Galliano

1. Pour crème de cacao, orange juice, and Galliano into cocktail shaker.
2. Stir without ice.
3. Pour over crushed ice in deep saucer champagne glass.

394. FOXY LADY

A throwback to the days of disco balls, satin hot pants, and glitter eyeshadow. Let's pretend it's 1976 again.

1 ounce amaretto
1/2 ounce crème de cacao
1 ounce heavy cream

1. Fill cocktail shaker with ice.
2. Add amaretto, crème de cacao, and heavy cream.
3. Shake.
4. Strain into a cordial glass.

395. FLYING GRASSHOPPER

Higher octane for high-performing grasshoppers.

3/4 ounce crème de menthe
3/4 ounce crème de cacao
3/4 ounce vodka

1. Fill cocktail shaker with ice.
2. Add crème de menthe, crème de cacao, and vodka.
3. Stir.
4. Strain into a cordial glass.

396. CAPRI

A magical concoction like the dreamy island that bears its name.

3/4 ounce crème de cacao
3/4 ounce crème de banana
3/4 ounce light cream

1. Fill cocktail shaker with ice.
2. Add crème de cacao, crème de banana, and cream.
3. Shake.
4. Strain into a cordial glass.

397. SUISSESSE

A popular drink in Switzerland and France. The Swiss and French know what time it is. Suissesse time.

1 1/2 ounces Pernod
1/2 ounce anisette
1/4 ounce cream
1/2 ounce egg white

1. Fill cocktail shaker with ice.
2. Add Pernod, anisette, cream, and egg white.
3. Shake.
4. Strain into a chilled cocktail glass.

398. COFFEE GRAND MARNIER

No better drink than this one to sip while prattling about life's little nuisances.

1/2 ounce coffee liqueur
1/2 ounce Grand Marnier
1/2 ounce orange juice

1. Pour coffee liqueur, Grand Marnier, and orange juice into cocktail shaker.
2. Pour over crushed ice in deep saucer champagne glass.
3. Garnish with orange slice.

399. MIXED MOCHA FRAPPE

All the taste of coffee with all the discernment of full-bodied liqueurs.

3/4 ounce coffee liqueur
1/4 ounce white crème de menthe
1/4 ounce crème de cacao
1/4 ounce triple sec
Sugar

1. Pour coffee liqueur, crème de menthe, crème de cacao, and triple sec into cocktail shaker.
2. Stir without ice.
3. Fill sugar-rimmed deep saucer champagne glass with crushed ice.
4. Pour mixture over ice.

400. SAMBUCA FRAPPE

Mix two and slip into something silky. Enjoy a night full of secrets.

1 ounce sambuca
1/2 ounce coffee liqueur

1. Pour sambuca and coffee liqueur into cocktail shaker.
2. Stir without ice.
3. Fill deep saucer champagne glass with crushed ice.
4. Pour mixture over ice.

401. DUTCH VELVET

If the Dutch masters had partaken in this, they might have discovered the beauty of velvet as a canvas.

1/2 ounce chocolate mint liqueur
1/2 ounce banana liqueur
2 ounces cream

1. Fill cocktail shaker with ice.
2. Add chocolate mint liqueur, banana liqueur, and cream.
3. Shake.
4. Strain into a chilled cocktail glass.
5. Garnish with shaved chocolate.

402. DUTCH COFFEE

Don't let the evening end without this one.

1 1/2 ounces Vandermint liqueur
Hot coffee

1. Pour Vandermint liqueur into a coffee mug.
2. Add hot coffee.
3. Top with whipped cream.

403. VELVET KISS

A kiss is just a kiss unless it's lined with velvet.

1 ounce gin
1/2 ounce banana liqueur
1/2 ounce pineapple juice
1 ounce heavy cream

1. Fill cocktail shaker with ice.
2. Add gin, banana liqueur, pineapple juice, and heavy cream.
3. Shake.
4. Strain into a chilled cocktail glass.

404. MILLIONAIRE'S COFFEE

Rich, just like the name suggests. A nightcap for high rollers and those who can only dream.

1/2 ounce coffee liqueur
1/2 ounce Irish cream liqueur
1/2 ounce Grand Marnier
1/2 ounce Frangelico
Hot coffee

1. Pour coffee liqueur, Irish cream liqueur, Grand Marnier, and Frangelico into a deep coffee mug.
2. Add hot coffee.
3. Top with whipped cream.

405. CADIZ

Fun fact: Cadiz, Spain is thought by many to be the oldest city in Europe.

3/4 ounce sherry
3/4 ounce blackberry liqueur
1/2 ounce triple sec
1/2 ounce cream

1. Fill cocktail shaker with ice.
2. Add sherry, blackberry liqueur, triple sec, and cream.
3. Shake.
4. Strain into a chilled old-fashioned glass.

406. PEACH MELBA

Dessert in a glass never tasted so good. Take a pass on the cheesecake and indulge in this.

1 ounce peach schnapps
1/2 ounce black raspberry liqueur
3 ounces cream

1. Fill cocktail shaker with ice.
2. Add peach schnapps, black raspberry liqueur, and heavy cream.
3. Shake.
4. Strain into a chilled old-fashioned glass.
5. Garnish with a peach slice.

407. PANAMA COCKTAIL

Tastes best when you're wearing a white suit and a big straw hat.

1 ounce crème de cacao
1 ounce light cream
1 ounce brandy

1. Fill cocktail shaker with ice.
2. Add crème de cacao, cream, and brandy.
3. Shake.
4. Strain into a cocktail glass.

408. LOVER'S KISS

Gentlemen: Check your shirt collars for tell-tale traces of this sweet treat. Dead giveaway.

1/2 ounce amaretto
1/2 ounce cherry brandy
1/2 ounce crème de cacao
1 ounce cream

1. Fill cocktail shaker with ice.
2. Add amaretto, cherry brandy, crème de cacao, and cream.
3. Shake.
4. Strain into a parfait glass.
5. Top with whipped cream, chocolate shavings, and a cherry.

409. BRANDY ALEXANDER

Drink and dessert, all in one glass. The best of the Alexander family.

1/2 ounce crème de cacao
1/2 ounce brandy
1/2 ounce heavy cream

1. Fill cocktail shaker with ice.
2. Add crème de cacao, brandy, and heavy cream.
3. Shake.
4. Strain into a cocktail glass.

410. GARZA'S NIGHTCAP

Tossing and turning? Tiptoe into the kitchen and toss back one of these hot milk treasures.

6 ounces milk
1 ounce coffee liqueur
1 teaspoon powdered sugar

1. Heat milk on stove.
2. Add sugar and coffee liqueur.
3. Pour into a coffee mug.
4. Dust with nutmeg.

411. SHERRIED COFFEE

A touch of sherry never hurt anyone.

1 1/4 ounces sherry
1 1/4 ounces coffee liqueur
2 teaspoons cream

1. Fill cocktail shaker with ice.
2. Add sherry and coffee liqueur.
3. Shake.
4. Strain into a chilled old-fashioned glass.
5. Float cream on top.

412. COFFEE GRASSHOPPER

How Jiminy Cricket ends his day.

3/4 ounce coffee liqueur
3/4 ounce white crème de menthe
3/4 ounce cream

1. Fill cocktail shaker with ice.
2. Add coffee liqueur, white crème de menthe, and cream.
3. Shake.
4. Strain into a chilled cocktail glass.

413. PINK ALMOND

Don't reach for that pretty bowl of pastel almonds at the next wedding reception. Choose this instead.

1/2 ounce crème de noyaux
1/2 ounce orgeat
1 ounce blended whiskey
1/2 ounce Kirsch
1/2 ounce lemon juice

1. Fill cocktail shaker with ice.
2. Add crème de noyaux, orgeat, blended whiskey, Kirsch, and lemon juice.
3. Shake.
4. Strain over ice in a chilled old-fashioned glass.
5. Garnish with lemon slice.

414. MOCHA MINT

Like that ice cream you loved as a child—plus the added bonus that comes with adulthood.

3/4 ounce coffee liqueur
3/4 ounce crème de menthe
3/4 ounce crème de cacao
Sugar

1. Fill cocktail shaker with ice.
2. Add coffee liqueur, crème de menthe, and crème de cacao.
3. Shake.
4. Moisten cocktail glass rim with coffee liqueur.
5. Dip rim in sugar.
4. Strain mixture into glass.

415. ALL-WHITE FRAPPE

Nighttime blizzards are more fun when sharing one of these under the covers.

1/2 ounce anisette
1/4 ounce white crème de menthe
1/2 ounce crème de cacao
1 teaspoon lemon juice

1. Pour anisette, crème de menthe, crème de cacao, and lemon juice into cocktail shaker.
2. Stir without ice.
3. Pour over crushed ice in deep saucer champagne glass.

416. COFFEE ALEXANDER

What the Alexander family drinks by moonlight.

1 ounce brandy
1 ounce coffee liqueur
1 ounce cream

1. Fill cocktail shaker with ice.
2. Add brandy, coffee liqueur, and cream.
3. Shake.
4. Pour into a cocktail glass.

417. ANGEL'S WING

Legend has it that an angel becomes mortal if his wings are cut off. Conversely, if the bartender doesn't cut you off too soon, you'll feel heavenly.

1/3 ounce crème de cacao
1/3 ounce brandy
1/3 ounce cream

1. Layer crème de cacao, brandy, and cream in a cordial glass.

418. ANGEL'S TIP

"Psst...listen, pal. If you want my advice, I'd bet on the Big Guy."

3/4 ounce crème de cacao
1/4 ounce cream

1. Layer crème de cacao and cream in a cordial glass.
2. Top with cherry.

419. ANGEL'S KISS

Served by Charlie to his crime-fighting heroines.

1/4 ounce crème de cacao
1/4 ounce crème de yvette
1/4 ounce brandy
1/4 ounce cream

1. Layer crème de cacao, crème de yvette, brandy, and cream in a cordial glass.

420. ANGEL'S DELIGHT

Put the shine back in your halo with this luscious cocktail.

1/4 ounce grenadine
1/4 ounce triple sec
1/4 ounce crème de yvette
1/4 ounce cream

1. Layer grenadine, triple sec, crème de yvette, and cream in a cordial glass.

421. PEPPERMINT TWIST

Let's twist again like we did last winter.

1 1/2 ounces peppermint schnapps
1/2 ounce white crème de cacao
3 scoops vanilla ice cream

1. Pour peppermint schnapps, crème de cacao, and vanilla ice cream into blender.
2. Mix low speed.
3. Pour into large parfait glass.
4. Garnish with mint sprig and peppermint candy stick.
5. Serve with a straw.

422. QUAALUDE

While under its influence, please refrain from driving or operating heavy machinery.

1 ounce vodka
1 ounce Frangelico
1 ounce coffee liqueur
Splash milk

1. Fill old-fashioned glass with ice.
2. Add vodka, Frangelico, coffee liqueur, and milk.

423. TOASTED ALMOND

Finally: A signature drink for drunken nut jobs everywhere.

1 1/2 ounces coffee liqueur
1 ounce amaretto
1 1/2 ounces cream

1. Fill old-fashioned glass with ice.
2. Add coffee liqueur, amaretto, and cream.

424. BANANA BANSHEE

Much less frightening than its name would indicate. Nothing spooky here, but you just might scream...with delight.

1 ounce crème de banana
1/2 ounce crème de cacao
1/2 ounce light cream

1. Fill cocktail shaker with ice.
2. Add crème de banana, crème de cacao, and cream.
3. Shake.
4. Strain into a chilled cocktail glass.

425. DIANA

Ideal for bringing out your inner princess, or huntress if you prefer mythology.

1 1/2 ounces white crème de menthe
3/4 ounce brandy

1. Pour crème de menthe into an old-fashioned glass.
2. Add crushed ice.
3. Float brandy on top.

426. FRENCH DREAM

Pepé Le Pew's go-to drink. For when he is playing hard to get, no?

1 1/2 ounces Irish cream liqueur
1/2 ounce raspberry liqueur
2 ounces half and half
4 ounces ice cubes

1. Pour Irish cream liqueur, raspberry liqueur, half and half, and ice cubes into a blender.
2. Blend at low speed for 30 seconds.
3. Pour into a parfait glass.

427. IRISH COFFEE

No blarney—this is an outstanding end to the evening.

1 1/2 ounces Irish whiskey
Hot coffee

1. Pour Irish whiskey into coffee mug.
2. Add hot coffee.
3. Top with whipped cream, if desired.

428. IRISH ANGEL

She had wings of green and flaming red hair when she appeared to Paddy and whispered sweet nothings in his ear.

3/4 ounce Irish whiskey
1/4 ounce crème de cacao
1/4 ounce white crème de menthe
1 1/2 ounces heavy cream

1. Fill cocktail shaker with ice.
2. Add whiskey, crème de cacao, crème de menthe, and cream.
3. Shake.
4. Strain into a chilled cocktail glass or in old-fashioned glass with ice.

429. IRISH NIGHTCAP

When in Ireland, do as the Irish do.

4 ounces hot milk
1 1/2 ounces Irish whiskey
1 teaspoon sugar

1. Pour hot milk into coffee mug.
2. Add whiskey and sugar.
3. Stir.

430. BANK HOLIDAY

What the Brits drink on their holidays from work.

1/2 ounce bourbon
1/2 ounce Galliano
1/2 ounce crème de cacao
1/2 ounce brandy
1 to 2 ounces sweet cream

1. Fill cocktail shaker with ice.
2. Add bourbon, Galliano, crème de cacao, brandy, and sweet cream.
3. Shake.
4. Strain into a cocktail glass.

431. PRINCESS MARY

Before bedtime, don a tiara and sip one of these.

1/3 ounce dry gin
1/3 ounce crème de cacao
1/3 ounce cream

1. Fill cocktail shaker with ice.
2. Add gin, crème de cacao, and cream.
3. Shake.
4. Strain into a cordial glass.

432. GOLDEN CADILLAC

Boss Lady likes them pink, but you'll like them golden. Crush velvet seats, indeed.

1 ounce Galliano
1 ounce white crème de cacao
2 ounces heavy cream

1. Fill cocktail shaker with ice.
2. Add Galliano, crème de cacao, and cream.
3. Shake.
4. Strain into a chilled cocktail glass.

433. RUSSIAN BEAR

For decades, smaller countries cowered in the Russian Bear's shadow. Feel the power of the Motherland in the palm of your hand.

1 ounce vodka
1/2 ounce crème de cacao
1/2 ounce cream

1. Fill cocktail shaker with ice.
2. Add vodka, crème de cacao, and cream.
3. Shake.
4. Strain into a chilled cocktail glass.

434. COFFEE COOLER

For sultry summer nights that are too good to end.

4 ounces cold coffee
1 1/2 ounces vodka
1 ounce cream
1 ounce coffee liqueur
1 teaspoon sugar
1 small scoop coffee ice cream

1. Fill cocktail shaker with ice.
2. Add coffee, vodka, cream, coffee liqueur, and sugar.
3. Shake.
4. Strain into a tall glass.
5. Add coffee ice cream.

435. BANANA RUM FRAPPE

Add beach chair, sand, setting sun on the horizon. Repeat as needed.

1/2 ounce banana liqueur
1/2 ounce light rum
1/2 ounce orange juice

1. Pour banana liqueur, rum, and orange juice into cocktail shaker.
2. Stir without ice.
3. Pour over crushed ice in deep saucer champagne glass.

436. BANANA APRICOT FRAPPE

Nobody says no to a second one of these, even when it's time to say good night.

3/4 ounce brandy
1/2 ounce apricot-flavored brandy
1/4 ounce crème de noyaux

1. Pour brandies and crème de noyaux into cocktail shaker.
2. Stir without ice.
3. Pour over crushed ice in deep saucer champagne glass.

437. CHARTREUSE COGNAC FRAPPE

A glowing mix of herbal flavors and a strong brandy base.

3/4 ounce yellow Chartreuse
3/4 ounce cognac

1. Pour Chartreuse and cognac into cocktail shaker.
2. Stir without ice.
3. Pour over crushed ice in deep saucer champagne glass.

438. PINK SQUIRREL

Don't miss out on this one—it'll have you hopping from tree to tree.

1 ounce crème de noyaux
1 ounce crème de cacao
3/4 ounce cream

1. Fill cocktail shaker with ice.
2. Add crème de noyaux, crème de cacao, and cream.
3. Shake.
4. Strain into chilled sugar-rimmed cocktail glasses.

439. RUSSIAN COFFEE

Warm enough to ward off even the worst Siberian winter nights.

3/4 ounce coffee liqueur
3/4 ounce vodka
3/4 ounce cream
1/3 cup crushed ice

1. Pour coffee liqueur, vodka, cream, and crushed ice into a blender.
2. Blend low for 15 seconds.
3. Pour into chilled deep saucer champagne glass.

440. DULCET

dul cet [adj] : Sweet to the taste, pleasing to the ear. Never was a truer definition written.

1 ounce vodka
1/2 ounce curacao
1/2 ounce anisette
1/2 ounce apricot liqueur
1 teaspoon lemon juice
1/2 brandied apricot

1. Fill cocktail shaker with ice.
2. Add vodka, curacao, anisette, apricot liqueur, and lemon juice.
3. Shake.
4. Strain into chilled old-fashioned glass on ice.
5. Drop in brandied apricot half.

441. GRASSHOPPER

In Aesop's fable, the Grasshopper languished while the busy Ant prepared for winter. Little did the Ant know about the Grasshopper's secret hooch stash.

3/4 ounce crème de cacao
3/4 ounce crème de menthe
3/4 ounce cream

1. Fill cocktail shaker with ice.
2. Add crème de cacao, crème de menthe, and cream.
3. Shake.
4. Strain into chilled cocktail glass.

442. CREAM PUNCH

This will keep you awake for that late-night argument and then dull the pain.

2 ounces cognac
1/4 teaspoon sugar
2 ounces cream
1/4 ounce lemon juice
1/4 ounce dark rum

1. Fill cocktail shaker with ice.
2. Add cognac, sugar, cream, lemon juice, and rum.
3. Shake.
4. Strain into chilled cocktail glass.
5. Dust with nutmeg.

443. CALM VOYAGE

For the traveler who knows no timetable.

1/2 ounce Galliano
1/2 ounce passion fruit syrup
2 teaspoons lemon juice
1/2 ounce light rum
1/2 egg
1/3 cup crushed ice

1. Pour Galliano, passion fruit syrup, lemon juice, rum, egg half, and crushed ice into a blender.
2. Blend at low speed for 15 seconds.
3. Pour into a chilled deep saucer champagne glass.

444. ST. LOUIS COCKTAIL

Fun fact: With its prominent and well-known arch, St. Louis is sometimes known as the "Gateway to the West." Wonder if travelers took this with them?

1/2 peach or apricot
Southern Comfort

1. Place peach or apricot into deep saucer champagne glass.
2. Add finely cracked ice.
3. Fill with Southern Comfort.
4. Serve with a spoon.

445. CAPPUCCINO COCKTAIL

Ideal to mix and place on the bedside table, to sip while enjoying a good read.

3/4 ounce coffee flavored brandy
3/4 ounce vodka
1 ounce cream

1. Fill cocktail shaker with ice.
2. Add brandy, vodka, and cream.
3. Shake.
4. Strain into chilled cocktail glass.

446. MOONLIGHT MADNESS

What the "Werewolves of London" drink with their big bowls of beef chow mein.

1/2 ounce Frangelico
1/2 ounce crème de cacao
1 ounce vodka
Splash of cream

1. Fill cocktail shaker with ice.
2. Add Frangelico, crème de cacao, vodka, and cream.
3. Shake.
4. Strain into chilled cocktail glass.

447. SAVOY HOTEL

Really gets you stomping.

1/3 ounce dark crème de cacao
1/3 ounce Benedictine
1/3 ounce brandy

1. Layer dark crème de cacao, Benedictine, and brandy into a pousse café glass.

448. KING ALPHONSE

Ahhh...it's good to be the king!

2 ounces coffee liqueur
1 ounce cream

1. Pour coffee liqueur into a cordial glass.
2. Float cream on top.
      —OR—
1. Fill an old-fashioned glass with ice.
2. Add coffee liqueur.
3. Top with cream.
4. Stir.

449. KREMLIN COCKTAIL

A favorite of KGB agents after a long day of wiretapping.

1 ounce vodka
1 ounce crème de cacao
1 ounce cream

1. Fill cocktail shaker with ice.
2. Add vodka, crème de cacao, and cream.
3. Shake.
4. Strain into an old-fashioned glass with ice.

450. PANDA BEAR

When the zookeeper isn't looking, the pandas love to sneak a few of these.

1 ounce amaretto
1/2 ounce crème de cacao
1/2 ounce dark crème de cacao
5 ounces vanilla ice cream
1/4 ounce chocolate syrup
2 to 3 dashes vanilla extract

1. Pour amaretto, crème de cacao, dark crème de cacao, vanilla ice cream, chocolate syrup, and vanilla extract into a blender.
2. Blend until smooth.
3. Pour into a chilled goblet.

451. VELVET HAMMER

Smooth but hard-hitting. A sinful delight disguised as an innocent milk shake.

1 tablespoon crème de cacao
1 1/2 ounces vodka
1 tablespoon light cream

1. Fill cocktail shaker with ice.
2. Add crème de cacao, vodka, and cream.
3. Shake.
4. Strain into a cocktail glass.

452. CRICKET

When administered properly, it will make you (and your paramour) rub your legs together. Chirping optional.

1 ounce crème de cacao
1 ounce crème de menthe
1 ounce cream
Dash of brandy

1. Fill cocktail shaker with ice.
2. Add crème de cacao, crème de menthe, cream, and brandy.
3. Shake.
4. Strain into a chilled deep-saucer champagne glass.

453. GOOD AND PLENTY

Drink some Now, save some for Later. If you can stand it.

3/4 ounce ouzo
3/4 ounce anisette

Pour ouzo and anisette into a brandy snifter.

454. B & B

As comfortable as a good bed & breakfast, with none of the curious breakfast companions.

1/2 ounce Benedictine
1/2 ounce brandy

1. Pour Benedictine into a cordial glass.
2. Float brandy on top.

455. DIRTY MOTHER

She was filthy, but she told a mean bedtime story.

1 1/2 ounces brandy
3/4 ounce coffee liqueur

1. Fill old-fashioned glass with ice.
2. Add brandy and coffee liqueur.
3. Stir.

456. ADRIENNE'S DREAM

As the poet Anne Sexton said, "In a dream you are never eighty."

2 ounces brandy
1/2 ounce peppermint schnapps
1/2 ounce crème de cacao
1/2 ounce lemon juice
1/2 teaspoon sugar
1 ounce club soda

1. Fill cocktail shaker with ice.
2. Add brandy, peppermint schnapps, crème de cacao, lemon juice, and sugar.
3. Shake.
4. Strain into a collins glass.
5. Add ice.
6. Fill with club soda.
7. Garnish with mint sprig.

457. ALMOND JOY

Sometimes you feel like a nut...and sometimes you feel like one of these.

1 ounce cream of coconut
1 ounce amaretto
1 ounce dark crème de cacao
2 ounces cream

1. Fill cocktail shaker with ice.
2. Add crème of coconut, amaretto, dark crème de cacao, and cream.
3. Shake.
4. Strain into a highball glass filled with ice.

458. AUNT JEMIMA

All the sweetness of syrup without pancakes.

1/2 ounce brandy
1/2 ounce crème de cacao
1/2 ounce Benedictine

1. Layer ingredients in a pony glass.

459. BIG BLUE SKY

Best consumed while flat on one's back, cloud-gazing.

1/2 ounce light rum
1/2 ounce blue curacao
1/2 ounce cream of coconut
2 ounces pineapple juice
3 ounces crushed ice

1. Pour rum, curacao, cream of coconut, pineapple juice, and crushed ice into a blender.
2. Blend at low speed for 30 seconds or until smooth.
3. Pour into goblet.

460. SICILIAN KISS

Receiving a kiss from a Sicilian has been a death sentence in many a gangster movie. This smooch is much less deadly.

1 1/2 ounces Southern Comfort
1/2 ounce amaretto

1. Fill an old-fashioned glass with ice.
2. Add Southern Comfort and amaretto.
3. Stir.

461. BLACK LACE

Delicate with a subtle hint of frill.

1/2 of a lemon
2 ounces sambuca
1 ounce crème de banana
1 ounce peach schnapps

1. Fill cocktail shaker with ice.
2. Squeeze lemon into shaker.
3. Add sambuca, crème de banana, and peach schnapps.
4. Shake.
5. Strain into a chilled cocktail glass.

462. BLACK MONK

Communion never tasted so good.

1 1/4 ounce B&B
Coffee

1. Fill a sugar-rimmed coffee mug with B&B and coffee.
2. Top with whipped cream.

463. CAFÉ ALPINE

No need to travel all the way to the ski slopes to enjoy this minty mug—heat one up anytime.

Coffee
1 ounce peppermint schnapps

1. Pour coffee into a mug.
2. Add peppermint schnapps.
3. Top with whipped cream.

464. CAFÉ ROYALE

Coffee fit for a king.

1 sugar cube
Brandy
Coffee

1. Soak sugar cube in a spoon with brandy.
2. Light the sugar cube aflame.
3. When flame dies, drop brandied cube into coffee.

465. HOT NUTTY IRISHMAN

Quite possibly one of the greatest drink names ever. It's also delicious.

3/4 ounce Irish cream liqueur
3/4 ounce Frangelico
3/4 ounce coffee

1. Fill coffee mug with Irish cream liqueur, Frangelico, and coffee.
2. Top with whipped cream.
3. Garnish with a cherry.

466. GODMOTHER

Finish this by midnight or turn into a pumpkin.

1 1/2 ounces vodka
3/4 ounce amaretto

1. Fill an old-fashioned glass with ice.
2. Pour vodka and amaretto.

467. CARA SPOSA

*Fun fact: "Cara sposa" is an aria from Handel's Rinaldo,
in which the title character laments the kidnapping of a
lost love.*

1 ounce coffee liqueur
1 ounce curacao
1/2 ounce cream
1/3 cup crushed ice

1. Pour coffee liqueur, curacao, cream, and crushed
   ice into a blender.
2. Blend at low speed for 15 to 30 seconds or until
   smooth.
3. Pour into a chilled deep-saucer champagne glass.

468. ORANGE COMFORT

Who knew Southern Comfort could taste any better?

1/2 ounce Southern Comfort
1/2 ounce anisette
3/4 ounce orange juice
1/2 ounce lemon juice

1. Fill cocktail shaker with ice.
2. Add Southern comfort, anisette, orange juice, and lemon juice.
3. Shake.
4. Strain into a chilled cocktail glass.
5. Garnish with an orange slice.

469. ORACABESSA

Named for a Jamaican city, this strong beverage is a delicious night treat.

1 ounce banana liqueur
1/2 ounce lemon juice
1/2 ounce 151-proof rum

1. Fill cocktail shaker with ice.
2. Add banana liqueur, lemon juice, and rum.
3. Shake.
4. Strain into an old-fashioned glass filled with ice.
5. Garnish with banana and lemon slices.

470. BIRD OF PARADISE

Fun fact: There are more than forty different members of this avian family, thirty-five of which reside in New Guinea.

3/4 ounce tequila
3/4 ounce crème de cacao
1/2 ounce amaretto
1 ounce cream

1. Fill cocktail shaker with ice.
2. Add tequila, crème de cacao, amaretto, and cream.
3. Shake.
4. Strain into a cocktail glass.

471. PARISIAN BLONDE

As intoxicating as Brigitte Bardot. As alluring as Catherine Deneuve.

1 ounce light rum
3/4 ounce curacao
3/4 ounce cream

1. Fill cocktail shaker with ice.
2. Add light rum, curacao, and cream.
3. Shake.
4. Strain into a cocktail glass.

472. BLACK-EYED SUSAN

Susan says she walked into a door, but she left out the part about drinking immediately prior.

2 ounces Grand Marnier
1/2 ounce white crème de menthe
1/2 ounce brandy

1. Fill cocktail shaker with ice.
2. Add Grand Marnier, white crème de menthe, and brandy.
3. Shake.
4. Strain into a chilled cocktail glass.

473. CAFÉ THEATRE

Serve these, and it'll be "standing room only" at your house.

1/2 ounce Irish cream liqueur
1/2 ounce crème de cacao
Hot coffee
Dash Frangelico
Dash dark crème de cacao

1. Pour Irish cream liqueur and crème de cacao into a coffee mug.
2. Add coffee until mug is almost filled.
3. Add Frangelico and dark crème de cacao.
4. Top with whipped cream.
5. Garnish with cinnamon stick.

474. BLUE CARNATION

The only drink that looks good on a lapel.

1/2 ounce crème de cacao
1/2 ounce blue curacao
2 ounces cream

1. Fill cocktail shaker with ice.
2. Add crème de cacao, blue curacao, and cream.
3. Shake.
4. Strain into a chilled cocktail glass.

475. CLIMAX

When the rest of the evening goes badly, at least there's this to look forward to.

1/2 ounce crème de cacao
1/2 ounce amaretto
1/2 ounce triple sec
1/2 ounce vodka
1/2 ounce banana liqueur
1 ounce cream

1. Fill cocktail shaker with ice.
2. Add crème de cacao, amaretto, triple sec, vodka, banana liqueur, and cream.
3. Shake.
4. Strain into a chilled cocktail glass.

476. CUPID'S KISS

Pucker up, baby—here comes the winged one, and he wants some sugar.

1/2 ounce crème de noyaux
1/4 ounce crème de cacao
1 ounce cream

1. Fill cocktail shaker with ice.
2. Add crème de noyaux, crème de cacao, and cream.
3. Shake.
4. Strain into a tulip glass.
5. Garnish with a strawberry.

477. FESTIVAL

You get all the fun of a carnival, without being hassled by the carnies.

3/4 ounce dark crème de cacao
1 tablespoon apricot brandy
1 teaspoon grenadine
3/4 ounce heavy cream

1. Fill cocktail shaker with ice.
2. Add dark crème de cacao, apricot brandy, grenadine, and cream.
3. Shake.
4. Strain into an old-fashioned glass with ice.

478. XYLOPHONE

Finally: The reward for all those summers at band camp.

1 ounce tequila
1/2 ounce crème de cacao
1/2 ounce sugar syrup
1 ounce cream
3 ounces of ice

1. Pour tequila, crème de cacao, sugar syrup, cream, and ice into a blender.
2. Blend until smooth.
3. Pour into goblet.
4. Garnish with a cherry.

479. EVERGLADES SPECIAL

Bonus: Keeps the gators away.

1 ounce light rum
1 ounce crème de cacao
1 ounce light cream
2 teaspoons coffee liqueur

1. Fill cocktail shaker with ice.
2. Add rum, crème de cacao, cream, and coffee liqueur.
3. Shake.
4. Strain into a chilled cocktail glass.
5. Add ice.

480. EL MAGNIFICO

Magnificent, indeed. Mix it for your favorite Italian lover.

1 ounce vanilla liqueur
1 ounce curacao
1 ounce cream
3 ounces cracked ice

1. Pour vanilla liqueur, curacao, cream, and ice into a blender.
2. Blend until smooth.
3. Pour into a chilled cocktail glass.

481. WHITE ELEPHANT

Fun fact: In the story of Buddha, the white elephant is associated with fertility and knowledge.

1/2 ounce vodka
1/2 ounce crème de cacao
2 ounces cream

1. Fill cocktail shaker with ice.
2. Add vodka, crème de cacao, and cream.
3. Shake.
4. Strain into a chilled cocktail glass.

482. ITALIAN DELIGHT

A *real Roman treasure.*

1 ounce amaretto
1/2 ounce orange juice
1 1/2 ounces cream

1. Fill cocktail shaker with ice.
2. Add amaretto, orange juice, and cream.
3. Shake.
4. Strain into a chilled stemmed glass.
5. Garnish with a cherry.

483. WHITE HEART

Mix *this one up for the icy hearted date du jour, and see your fortunes improve dramatically.*

1/2 ounce sambuca
1/2 ounce crème de cacao
2 ounce cream

1. Fill cocktail shaker with ice.
2. Add sambuca, crème de cacao, and cream.
3. Shake.
4. Strain into a chilled stemmed glass.

484. FROSTBITE

Like a childhood snowstorm for adults—sweet and nippy, all the way out to your fingers and toes.

11/2 ounces white tequila
1/2 ounce crème de cacao
2 to 3 dashes blue curacao
2 ounces cream

1. Fill cocktail shaker with ice.
2. Add white tequila, crème de cacao, blue curacao, and cream.
3. Shake.
4. Strain into a frosted sour glass.
5. Add ice.

485. GOLDEN SLIPPER

Make plenty for Cinderella and her crazy stepsisters.

1 ounce apricot brandy
1 ounce yellow Chartreuse
1 egg yolk

1. Fill cocktail shaker with ice.
2. Add apricot brandy, Chartreuse, and egg yolk.
3. Shake.
4. Strain into a chilled cocktail glass.

486. RENAISSANCE COCKTAIL

So you're a Renaissance Man, eh? Mix me one of these and prove it.

1/2 ounce gin
1/2 ounce dry sherry
1 tablespoon cream

1. Fill cocktail shaker with ice.
2. Add gin, sherry, and cream.
3. Shake.
4. Strain into a chilled cocktail glass.
5. Dust with nutmeg

487. WIDOW'S DREAM

For those still in mourning, this makes for some solid woolgathering.

2 ounces Benedictine
1 ounce heavy cream
1 egg

1. Fill cocktail shaker with ice.
2. Add Benedictine, heavy cream, and egg.
3. Shake.
4. Strain into a chilled cocktail glass.

488. NIGHTCAP

Bedtime never tasted so relaxing.

3/4 ounce brandy
3/4 ounce curacao
3/4 ounce anisette
1 egg yolk

1. Fill cocktail shaker with ice.
2. Add brandy, curacao, anisette, and egg yolk.
3. Shake.
4. Strain into a chilled cocktail glass.

6

BAHAMA MAMA TROPICAL DRINKS—
Hula 'Til It Hurts

Tiki torches and grass huts. Tiny paper umbrellas and coconut shells. Wicked blue concoctions that conjure up images of tranquil aqua seas. Creamy dreamy frozen treats just right for a sandy day at the beach. Tanned cabana boys in a palm fringed paradise with supermodel look-a-likes bathing in sun-drenched St. Tropez. Grab the pineapple juice, blue curacao, and rum and get ready to play beach blanket bingo on a private island getaway. With these fruity fantasies, Frankie and Annette won't be the only beach bunnies mastering the limbo and the watusi.

489. MAI TAI

The queen of tropical libations.

1 ounce dark rum
Dash of orgeat
1 1/2 ounces sour mix
1/2 ounce heavy rum
Squeeze of lime

1. Fill a large old-fashioned glass with crushed ice.
2. Add a cherry and a slice of pineapple.
3. Pour dark rum, orgeat, and sour mix.
4. Stir.
5. Float heavy rum on top.
6. Squeeze lime on top.
7. Garnish with mint sprig and an orchid, if available.

490. FROZEN DAIQUIRI

A few of these on a tropical island and Stella won't be the only one getting her groove back.

1/2 ounce fresh lime juice
1 teaspoon sugar
2 ounces light rum
1/2 cup crushed ice

1. Pour lime juice, sugar, rum, and ice into a blender.
2. Blend for 15 seconds on low speed.
3. Pour into chilled deep-saucer champagne glass.

Note: This drink can be made to taste more "rummy" by floating a layer of rum on top.

491. PIÑA COLADA

Fun fact: Rupert Holmes—creator of the 1979 number one hit song "Piña Colada"—once said he didn't even drink them. But you can.

2 ounces coconut milk or cream
2 ounces pineapple juice
1 1/2 ounces light rum

1. Fill cocktail shaker with ice.
2. Add coconut milk, pineapple juice, and rum.
3. Shake.
4. Strain into a blender half-filled with crushed ice.
5. Blend.
6. Serve in a hurricane glass.
7. Garnish with a pineapple spear, a cherry and/or shredded coconut.

492. BLUE HAWAII

Where dreams come true, so sayeth the King.

1 ounce light rum
1 ounce pineapple juice
1 ounce sour mix
Dash cream
Dash blue curacao
3 ounces crushed ice

1. Pour rum, pineapple juice, sour mix, cream, and curacao into a blender.
2. Blend.
3. Garnish with tropical fruit.

493. BARRACUDA BITE

Call this one the tiger of the sea.

1 1/2 ounces 150-proof rum
1 1/2 ounces vodka
1/2 ounce lime juice
1 ounce grenadine

1. Combine rum, vodka, lime juice, and grenadine in a cocktail shaker.
2. Shake lightly.
3. Pour into a zombie glass with ice.

494. CHI CHI

Drink three. Say Aloha, Gracie.

2 ounces pineapple juice
2 ounces coconut cream
1 1/2 ounces vodka
1 teaspoon shredded coconut

1. Fill cocktail shaker with ice.
2. Add pineapple juice, coconut cream, vodka, and shredded coconut.
3. Shake.
4. Strain into a tall glass.
5. Garnish with pineapple spear and a cherry.

495. FIJI BLACKOUT

A drink built for two to sip as Tiki torches flicker. Dare to drink it solo and you will certainly experience a blackout of your own.

1 1/2 ounces lime juice
1 ounce light maple syrup
4 ounces dark rum

1. Pour lime juice, maple syrup, and rum into cocktail shaker.
2. Stir.
3. Pour in two champagne glasses filled with finely crushed ice.

(Serves 2)

496. HULA MILKMAID

Eight hula maids a'shakin...and a monkey in a palm tree.

1 teaspoon sugar
1 1/2 ounces brandy, whiskey, or rum
8 ounces milk

1. Fill a cocktail shaker with scoop of ice.
2. Add sugar, liquor of choice, and milk.
3. Shake.
4. Strain into a chilled highball glass.
5. Dust with nutmeg.

497. HULA HULA

Even the straitlaced can't refuse a little grass skirt action after one of these delectable devils.

1 1/2 ounces gin
1 ounce orange juice
1/4 teaspoon sugar

1. Fill cocktail shaker with ice.
2. Add gin, orange juice, and sugar.
3. Shake.
4. Strain into a cocktail glass.

498. HAWAIIAN TORCH

Take a sip or two and you'll limbo like a limber Lucy.

1 teaspoon pineapple juice
1 teaspoon lemon juice
2 ounces whiskey
Club soda

1. Pour juices and whiskey into a highball glass with a few ice cubes.
2. Stir.
3. Fill with club soda.

499. SOUTH SEAS SLEEPER

Throw away the relaxation compact discs and tune in to a most ambient delight.

1 ounce dark rum
2 ounces light rum
1/2 teaspoon honey
Juice of one lime

1. Fill cocktail shaker with ice.
2. Add rums, honey, and lime.
3. Shake.
4. Strain into a chilled cocktail glass.

500. ZOMBIE SLEEPWALKER

Legend has it that naval men would drink these and then proceed to stumble to the plank after lights out. The result: honorable discharge.

1 ounce dark rum
1 ounce light rum
1 ounce Jamaican rum
4 dashes cherry brandy
4 dashes apricot brandy
Dash papaya juice
Juice of 1/2 lime
1/2 ounce 150-proof rum

1. Pour all rums, brandies, papaya, and lime juices in a zombie glass with cracked ice.
2. Top with 150-proof rum.
3. Stir.
4. Garnish with a cherry and an orange slice.
5. Serve with a long straw.

501. PLANTER'S PUNCH

Welakaho! Translation: Whoopee!

Juice of 2 limes
2 teaspoons powdered sugar
2 ounces club soda
2 dashes of Angostura bitters
2 1/2 ounces light rum
Dash of grenadine

1. Mix lime juice, powdered sugar, and club soda in a collins glass.
2. Add ice cubes.
3. Stir until glass frosts.
4. Add bitters and rum.
5. Stir.
6. Top with grenadine.
7. Garnish with lemon, pineapple, orange slice, and a cherry.
8. Serve with a straw.

502. COCONUT CANNON BALL

The drink of choice for tropical monkeys before a cross-country jungle race.

2 ounces gin or vodka
2 ounces coconut milk
1 ounce lemon juice
1 teaspoon sugar
Dash curacao

1. Mix liquor of choice, coconut milk, lemon juice, sugar, and curacao in a cocktail shaker.
2. Shake.
3. Serve in a coconut shell.

503. SCORPION

An enchantingly potent venom.

1 ounce light rum
1 ounce brandy
1 ounce sour mix
3 ounces orange juice
Dash Angostura bitters
2 ounces crushed ice

1. Mix light rum, brandy, sour mix, orange juice, and bitters in a blender filled with crushed ice.
2. Blend.
3. Serve into a collins glass.

504. NEPTUNE'S NUPTIAL

I take this mermaid to be my lawful wedded fish.

1 ounce gin
1 ounce whiskey
1 ounce crème de menthe
Juice of one lemon

1. Fill cocktail shaker with ice.
2. Add gin, whiskey, crème de menthe, and lemon.
3. Shake well.
4. Strain into a chilled cocktail glass.

505. HAWAIIAN CARESS

A gentle touch after a long day of sightseeing on Maui.

2 ounces Bacardi rum
2 ounces pineapple juice
5 drops maraschino liqueur
1 teaspoon grenadine

1. Pour rum, pineapple juice, maraschino liqueur, and grenadine in a cocktail shaker.
2. Stir.
3. Strain into an old-fashioned glass with crushed ice.

506. YO HO HO

And a bottle of rum for the pirate with the black eye patch, please.

Juice of 1/2 lime
1 1/2 ounces light rum
Cola soda

1. Squeeze lime juice into a zombie glass.
2. Drop in lime.
3. Add rum.
4. Add three ice cubes.
5. Stir gently.

507. PASSIONATE RUMMY

Fun fact: The earliest form of gin rummy can be traced to the mid-nineteenth century Mexican card game called Conquian. Don't drink too many of these while playing or you just might lose your hand...

4 1/2 ounces passion fruit nectar
1 1/2 ounces lemon juice
1 1/2 ounce sugar syrup
7 1/2 ounces light rum

1. Pour passion fruit nectar, lemon juice, sugar syrup, and light rum in a cocktail shaker.
2. Stir well until blended.
3. Pour over cracked ices in deep-saucer champagne glasses.

(Serves 4)

508. SEA SERPENT'S MILK

Ever wonder if there is an underwater chapter of the La Leche League?

1 1/2 ounces brandy
1/2 ounce cream

1. Pour brandy in a cordial glass.
2. Float cream on top.

509. LEI OF THE HOUR

And the award goes to: insert your best lover's name here.

1 ounce crème de cacao
1 ounce brandy
1 ounce cream

1. Layer in above order in a cordial glass.

510. MERMAID'S DELIGHT

The little mermaid's drink of choice on her 21st birthday.

1 ounce crème de menthe
1 ounce cream

1. Layer in above order in a cordial glass.

511. SOUTH SEA SIREN

"Come to me, and indulge in my nightcap," whispers the South Sea Siren. Don't be shy. Dive in.

1 ounce crème de menthe
1 ounce crème de cacao

1. Layer in above order in a cordial glass.

512. WHISPERING REEF

Hey, Fred. Did that reef just whisper to me? No, Barney. That's your conscience telling you to lay off the gin.

1 ounce dry gin
1 ounce crème de menthe
2 ounces pineapple juice

1. Fill cocktail shaker with cracked ice.
2. Add gin, crème de menthe, and pineapple juice.
3. Shake.
4. Strain into a chilled cocktail glass.

513. MISTY ISLAND

The scene of many a torrid romance. Drink and frolic.

Juice of 1/2 lemon
1 teaspoon sugar
1 1/2 ounces dry gin
Club soda

1. Fill cocktail shaker with cracked ice.
2. Add lemon, sugar, and gin.
3. Shake.
4. Strain into a chilled highball glass.
5. Fill with cold club soda.
6. Stir.
7. Garnish with mint sprigs.

514. BLUE DEVIL

Just because it's blue doesn't mean it's gentle. This devil wears a disguise.

1 1/2 ounces gin
1/2 ounce blue curacao
1/2 ounce lemon juice

1. Fill cocktail shaker with ice.
2. Add gin, curacao, and lemon juice.
3. Shake.
4. Strain into a chilled cocktail glass.
5. Garnish with a lemon slice.

515. BAHAMA MAMA

Forget the PTA! This drink will make any soccer mom want to sign up for hula classes.

1/2 ounce dark rum
1/2 ounce coconut liqueur
1/4 ounce 151-proof rum
1/4 ounce coffee liqueur
Juice of half lemon
4 ounces pineapple juice

1. Pour rums, liqueurs, and juices in a cocktail shaker.
2. Stir gently.
3. Pour into a highball glass with cracked ice.

516. FOG CUTTER

A misnomer: This is hardly the cocktail to make you see clearly.

1 1/2 ounces light rum
1/2 ounce brandy
1/2 ounce gin
1 ounce orange juice
3 tablespoon lemon juice
1 1/2 ounces orgeat syrup
1 teaspoon sweet sherry

1. Fill cocktail shaker with ice.
2. Add rum, brandy, gin, juices, and orgeat syrup.
3. Shake.
4. Strain into a collins glass with ice.
5. Top with sherry.

517. HAVANA COCKTAIL

The perfect accompaniment for that cigar smuggler. You know who you are.

1 1/2 ounces pineapple juice
1/2 teaspoon lemon juice
1/4 ounce light rum

1. Fill cocktail shaker with ice.
2. Add pineapple juice, lemon juice, and rum.
3. Shake.
4. Strain into a cocktail glass.

518. CRYSTAL BLUE PERSUASION

A drink for lazy days by the pool that will make life appear exactly as desired.

1/2 ounce Hypnotiq
1/2 ounce orange vodka
1/2 ounce vanilla vodka
1/4 ounce blue curacao
2 to 3 ounces pineapple juice
Sugar

1. Fill cocktail shaker with ice.
2. Add Hypnotiq, vodkas, curacao, and pineapple juice.
3. Shake.
4. Strain into a blue sugar-rimmed chilled martini glass.
5. Garnish with an orange twist or a blue rock candy swizzle stick.

*Created by Stephanie Caruthers, Trio's, Little Rock, Ark.

519. HURRICANE

Blows in fast, leaves a deadly aftermath.

1 ounce dark rum
1 ounce light rum
1/2 ounce Galliano
3/4 ounce lime juice
1 ounce passion fruit syrup
1 1/2 ounces orange juice
1 1/2 ounces pineapple juice
Dash Angostura bitters

1. Fill cocktail shaker with ice.
2. Add rums, Galliano, lime juice, passion fruit syrup, juices, and bitters.
3. Shake.
4. Strain into a hurricane glass filled with ice.
5. Garnish with tropical fruit.

520. MIAMI

The consummate companion for the bling bling of South Beach.

1 1/2 ounces light rum
1/2 ounce white crème de menthe
Dash of lemon juice

1. Fill cocktail shaker with ice.
2. Add rum, white crème de menthe, and lemon juice.
3. Shake.
4. Strain into a cocktail glass.

521. PASSION DAIQUIRI

Brings out the passion in even the stoniest curmudgeon.

1 1/2 ounces light rum
Juice of 1 lime
1 teaspoon powdered sugar
1 tablespoon passion fruit juice

1. Fill cocktail shaker with ice.
2. Add rum, lime juice, powdered sugar, and passion fruit juice.
3. Shake.
4. Strain into a cocktail glass.

522. RUM RICKEY

If you don't like this one, you've got some splainin' to do.

Juice of 1/2 lime
1/2 ounces light rum
Club soda

1. Pour lime juice and rum in a highball glass with ice.
2. Fill with club soda.
3. Stir.
4. Garnish with lime wedge.

523. SANTIAGO COCKTAIL

Make like an old Chilean bartender and share this with guests.

1/2 teaspoon powdered sugar
1/4 teaspoon grenadine
Juice of 1 lime
1 1/2 ounces light rum

1. Fill cocktail shaker with ice.
2. Add powdered sugar, grenadine, lime juice, and rum.
3. Shake.
4. Strain into a cocktail glass.

524. TAHITI CLUB

Not to be confused with Club Med, but feel free to indulge and disrobe.

2 ounces light rum
1 tablespoon lemon juice
1 tablespoon lime juice
1 tablespoon pineapple juice
1/2 teaspoon maraschino liqueur

1. Fill cocktail shaker with ice.
2. Add rum, juices, and maraschino liqueur.
3. Shake.
4. Strain into an old-fashioned glass with ice.
5. Garnish with a lemon slice.

525. TROPICA COCKTAIL

Take your baby and nestle in the nearest Tiki hut with a couple of these tropical tipples.

1 1/4 ounces light rum
5 ounces pineapple juice
2 ounces grapefruit juice
Dash grenadine

1. Pour rum, juices, and grenadine in a collins glass with ice.
2. Stir.
3. Garnish with a pineapple wedge.

526. ZOMBIE

Let your eyes roll back in your head and get ready for some voodoo loving. Only one per customer, please.

1 ounce unsweetened pineapple juice
Juice of 1 lime
Juice of 1 small orange
1 teaspoon powdered sugar
1/2 ounce apricot brandy
2 1/2 ounces light rum
1 ounce Jamaican rum
1 ounce passion fruit syrup, if desired
1 ounce 151-proof rum
1/2 cup crushed ice

1. Pour all juices, powdered sugar, apricot brandy, rums, and passion fruit syrup in a blender.
2. Blend at low speed for 1 minute.
3. Strain into a frosted highball glass.
4. Garnish with a pineapple stick and a cherry.
5. Float 151-proof rum on top.

527. WIKI WAKI WOO

Watch out for that wave, dude.

1/2 ounce vodka
1/2 ounce rum
1/2 ounce 151-proof rum
1/2 ounce tequila
1/2 ounce triple sec
1 ounce amaretto
1 ounce orange juice
1 ounce pineapple juice
1 ounce cranberry juice

1. Pour all ingredients in a cocktail mixer filled with ice.
2. Stir.
3. Pour into a hurricane glass.
4. Garnish with an orange slice and a cherry.

528. EAST INDIA COCKTAIL

Don't dare take a flask of these on your elephant ride. You just might end up hugging the trunk.

1 1/2 ounces brandy
1/2 teaspoon pineapple juice
1/2 teaspoon triple sec
1 teaspoon Jamaican rum
Dash Angostura bitters

1. Fill cocktail shaker with ice.
2. Add brandy, pineapple juice, triple sec, rum, and bitters.
3. Shake.
4. Strain into a cocktail glass.
5. Garnish with a lemon peel and a cherry.

529. FROZEN BANANA DAIQUIRI

Mix these with a wild and crazy tropical shirt and let it all hang out at the next company picnic.

1 1/2 ounces light rum
1/2 ounce lime juice
1 ounce banana liqueur
1/4 sliced banana
1 teaspoon sugar
1/2 ounce cream
1/2 cup crushed ice

1. Pour ingredients in blender.
2. Blend until smooth.
3. Pour into oversized wine glass.
4. Garnish with lime wedge.

530. MERMAID'S CHOICE

This magical potion will turn any mermaid from her fishy ways.

1 ounce brandy
1 ounce orange juice
1 ounce dry vermouth
Dash crème de menthe

1. Fill cocktail shaker with ice.
2. Add brandy, orange juice, vermouth, and crème de menthe.
3. Shake.
4. Strain into a cocktail glass.

531. BANANA MANGO

A wondrous concoction of tropical flavors sure to ease your cares away.

1 1/2 ounces light rum
1/4 ounce banana liqueur
1/2 ounce mango nectar
1/2 ounce lime juice

1. Fill cocktail shaker with ice.
2. Add rum, banana liqueur, mango nectar, and lime juice.
3. Shake.
4. Strain into a chilled old-fashioned glass with ice.

532. CONCH SHELL

Unlike its namesake, this drink does not blow.

4 ounces light rum
1/2 ounce lime juice

1. Fill cocktail shaker with ice.
2. Add rum and lime juice.
3. Shake.
4. Strain into a double old-fashioned glass with ice.

533. GAUGUIN

Fun fact: This depressed post-Impressionist French painter once worked as a stock broker. No wonder there's a drink named after him.

2 ounces light rum
1/2 ounce passion fruit syrup
1/2 ounce lemon juice
4 ounces lime juice
1/3 cup crushed ice

1. Pour all ingredients into a blender.
2. Blend for 15 seconds on low speed.
3. Pour into a chilled deep-saucer champagne glass.
4. Garnish with a cherry.

534. ISLE OF THE BLESSED COCONUT

In this episode: You and your friends get drunk. Again. Tune in for more next week. Same time. Same channel.

1 1/2 ounces light rum
1/2 ounce cream of coconut
1/2 ounce lime juice
1/4 ounce lemon juice
1/4 ounce orange juice
1/2 teaspoon sugar
1/3 cup crushed ice

1. Pour all ingredients into a blender.
2. Blend for 15 seconds on low speed.
3. Pour into a chilled deep-saucer champagne glass.
4. Garnish with a toasted coconut slice.

535. ICE PALACE

Cool as an ice queen's abode.

1 ounce light rum
1/2 ounce Galliano
1/2 ounce apricot brandy
2 ounces pineapple juice
1/4 ounce lemon juice

1. Fill cocktail shaker with ice.
2. Add rum, Galliano, apricot brandy, and juices.
3. Shake.
4. Strain into a collins glass over ice.
5. Garnish with a cherry and an orange slice.

536. SAN JUAN

After you taste this, you'll be a loyal and avid supporter of Puerto Rican statehood.

1 1/2 ounces light rum
1 ounce grapefruit juice
1 teaspoon cream of coconut
2 teaspoons lime juice
1/3 cup crushed ice
2 teaspoons 151-proof rum

1. Pour all ingredients into a blender.
2. Blend for 15 seconds on low speed.
3. Pour into chilled deep-saucer champagne glass.
4. Float 151-proof rum on top.

537. HAWAIIAN EYE

The official drink of Hawaiian private investigators. Don't tell Jack Lord.

1 1/2 ounces bourbon
1 ounce coffee liqueur
1 ounce heavy cream
1/2 ounce vodka
1/2 ounce banana liqueur
1 teaspoon Pernod
1 egg white
3 ounces cracked ice

1. Pour all ingredients into a blender.
2. Blend for 15 seconds.
3. Pour into chilled highball glass.
4. Garnish with a cherry and a pineapple slice.

538. ACAPULCO

Elvis said when in Acapulco, bossa nova, baby.

1 3/4 ounces rum
1/4 ounce triple sec
1 egg white
1/2 ounce lime juice

1. Fill cocktail shaker with ice.
2. Add rum, triple sec, egg white, and lime juice.
3. Shake.
4. Strain into an old-fashioned glass with ice.
5. Garnish with mint leaves.

539. COCO LOCO

The only good reason to be caught buying whole coconuts at the grocery store.

1 whole coconut in shell
1 ounce tequila
1 ounce rum
1 ounce gin
1/2 ounce grenadine
1 lemon slice

1. Cut a hole in the top of the coconut, leaving juice inside.
2. Pour tequila, rum, gin, and grenadine into coconut cup.
3. Add several ice cubes.
4. Stir.
5. Squeeze a lemon slice into the coconut.
6. Drop in the lemon.
7. Serve with long straw.

540. BARBARY COAST COCKTAIL

Arrrgh. Pour me another said the pirate to the barkeep.

1/2 ounce dry gin
1/2 ounce rum
1/2 ounce crème de cacao
1/2 ounce scotch
1/2 ounce cream

1. Fill cocktail shaker with ice.
2. Add gin, rum, crème de cacao, scotch, and cream.
3. Shake.
4. Strain into a cocktail glass.

541. CHIQUITA COCKTAIL

Dare to embrace your inner-Carmen Miranda. Drink these, and wear bananas on your head.

1/2 ounce banana liqueur
1/2 ounce Cointreau
1/2 ounce light cream

1. Fill cocktail shaker with ice.
2. Add banana liqueur, Cointreau, and light cream.
3. Shake.
4. Strain into a sour glass half-filled with crushed ice.

542. GORILLA MILK

It takes a brave man to milk a gorilla. Well worth the risk.

1 ounce light rum
1/2 ounce coffee liqueur
1/2 ounce Irish cream liqueur
1/2 ounce crème de banana
1 ounce light cream

1. Fill cocktail shaker with ice.
2. Add rum, liqueurs, crème de banana, and cream.
3. Shake.
4. Strain into a hurricane glass.
5. Garnish with a banana slice.

543. CASABLANCA

Bogie and Bacall. They had it all. Pour it again, Sam.

2 ounces light rum
1 1/2 teaspoon triple sec
1 1/2 teaspoon lime juice
1 1/2 teaspoon cherry liqueur

1. Fill cocktail shaker with ice.
2. Add light rum, triple sec, lime juice, and cherry liqueur.
3. Shake.
4. Strain into a chilled cocktail glass.

544. PINEAPPLE DREAM COCKTAIL

Serve these up while roasting the whole hog at the next family luau.

1/2 ounce pineapple juice
Juice of 1/2 lime
1 ounce rum

1. Fill cocktail shaker with ice.
2. Add pineapple juice, lime juice, and rum.
3. Shake.
4. Strain into a cocktail glass.

545. CALYPSO

Day-o. Day-ay-ay-o. Daylight come but me no wanna go home.

3/4 ounce Tia Maria
3/4 ounce Jamaican rum
Hot coffee

1. Pour Tia Maria and rum into a coffee mug.
2. Fill with hot coffee.
3. Top with whipped cream, if desired.

546. PINEAPPLE FIZZ

Beware: Too much of this concoction will leave you with dancing pineapple hallucinations.

1 ounce pineapple juice
1/2 teaspoon powdered sugar
2 ounces rum
Club soda

1. Fill cocktail shaker with ice.
2. Add pineapple juice, powdered sugar, and rum.
3. Shake.
4. Strain into a highball glass.
5. Fill with club soda.

547. BRASS MONKEY

That funky monkey…you can be a brass monkey junkie. Try one and see.

1/2 ounce vodka
1/2 ounce light rum
5 ounces orange juice

1. Fill highball glass with ice.
2. Add vodka, rum, and orange juice.
3. Stir.

548. SHANGHAI COCKTAIL

A (Shanghai) surprise in every drop.

Juice of 1/4 lemon
1 teaspoon anisette
1 ounce Jamaican rum
1/2 teaspoon grenadine

1. Fill cocktail shaker with ice.
2. Add lemon juice, anisette, rum, and grenadine.
3. Shake.
4. Strain into a cocktail glass.

549. BEE STUNG LIPS

Think Angelina Jolie and Mick Jagger. Pout accordingly.

2 ounces light rum
1 teaspoon honey
1 teaspoon heavy cream

1. Fill cocktail shaker with ice.
2. Add rum, honey, and cream.
3. Shake.
4. Strain into a chilled cocktail glass.

550. ASTRONAUT

After a few of these, Major Nelson calls Genie "master."
Master of the bottle, that is.

1 1/2 ounces Jamaican rum
1 1/2 ounces vodka
1 1/2 teaspoon lemon juice
1 1/2 teaspoon passion fruit juice

1. Fill cocktail shaker with ice.
2. Add rum, vodka, and juices.
3. Shake.
4. Strain into a collins glass with ice.

551. FROZEN MARGARITA

Buffett. Wastin' Away. You get the picture.

1 1/2 ounces tequila
1/2 ounce triple sec
1 ounce sour mix
Dash Rose's lime juice
4 ounces ice

1. Pour ingredients into a blender.
2. Blend for 15 seconds until smooth.
3. Pour into large wine glass or margarita goblet.
4. Garnish with a lime slice.

552. BANANA MAMA

Say a toast. Nani Wahine: To a beautiful woman.

1 1/2 ounces light rum
1/2 ounce dark rum
1 ounce banana liqueur
1 ounce cream of coconut
1 ounce fresh strawberries
2 ounces pineapple juice
3 ounces crushed ice

1. Pour all ingredients into a blender.
2. Blend until smooth.
3. Pour into a goblet.

553. BANANA BOAT

Gilligan made one of these to leave the island. Mr. Howell gulped it down and fell asleep in a hammock. Foiled again!

1 1/2 ounces tequila
1/2 ounce banana liqueur
1 ounce lime juice
2 ounces crushed ice

1. Pour all ingredients into a blender.
2. Blend until smooth.
3. Pour into a sour glass.

554. RUM JULEP

The sassy Caribbean cousin to the famous Mint Julep.

1 1/2 ounces light rum
1 teaspoon sugar
1 ounce water
8 mint sprigs

1. Muddle four mint sprigs, sugar, and water in a collins glass.
2. Fill glass with crushed ice.
3. Stir until glass frosts.
4. Add four mint springs to glass.
5. Add rum.

555. PSYCHO TSUNAMI

Also called The Ex-girlfriend.

1/2 ounce blue curacao
1/2 ounce fresh lime juice
1/2 ounce tequila
2 dashes Tabasco sauce

1. Layer curacao, lime juice, tequila, and Tabasco sauce in shot class.
2. Allow Tabasco to settle before drinking.

556. SHARK BITE

Not as deadly as the Great White. Consider this the Jab-berjaw of rum drinks.

1 1/2 ounces dark rum
3 ounces orange juice
1/2 ounce sour mix
3/4 ounce grenadine
3 ounces ice

1. Pour all ingredients into a blender.
2. Blend until smooth.
3. Pour into a goblet.

557. COBBLER'S COOLER

Geppetto, the cobbler, and Pinocchio, the real boy, drank these on tropical holidays in the later years.

2 1/2 ounces white rum
1 ounce vodka
Dash Grand Marnier
1 banana
Dash Angostura bitters
Dash nutmeg
3 ounces cracked ice
Orange juice

1. Pour rum, vodka, Grand Marnier, and banana into a blender with ice.
2. Blend until smooth.
3. Add bitters and nutmeg.
4. Top with orange juice.
5. Pour into a zombie glass.
6. Garnish with an orange slice and an edible flower.
7. Serve with a straw.

558. SHARK'S TOOTH

The surfer's reward for cresting the killer wave and surviving.

1 1/2 ounces dark rum
1 1/2 ounces lime juice
1 1/2 ounces lemon juice
1/4 ounce grenadine
Club soda

1. Fill cocktail shaker with ice.
2. Add rum, juices, and grenadine.
3. Shake.
4. Strain into a highball glass with ice.
5. Fill with club soda.

559. COCOTINI

A fave of Malibu Barbies. Perfect for relaxing poolside at the Dream House.

3 ounces coconut flavored rum
1 ounce triple sec
Coconut shavings

1. Fill cocktail shaker with ice.
2. Add rum and triple sec.
3. Shake.
4. Strain into a chilled martini glass rimmed with coconut shavings.
5. Garnish with a lime wheel.

560. TROPICAL ITCH

Drink up! This one is worth the Calamine lotion.

1 ounce vodka
1 ounce light rum
1/2 ounce orange curacao
4 ounces passion fruit juice

1. Fill cocktail shaker with ice.
2. Add vodka, light rum, orange curacao, and passion fruit juice.
3. Shake.
4. Strain into a double old-fashioned with ice.

561. LAVA FLOW

This lava flow will send people stampeding...toward the bar.

1 ounce light rum
1 ounce coconut-flavored rum
2 ounces strawberries
1 ripe banana
2 ounces unsweetened pineapple juice
2 ounces coconut cream

1. Pour strawberries and rums into a blender.
2. Blend until a smooth paste.
3. Pour paste into a hurricane glass.
4. Rinse blender.
5. Add banana, pineapple juice, and coconut cream into the blender.
6. Blend until smooth.
7. Slowly pour blender mix into the hurricane glass.

562. BLUE DIABLO

What Satan looks like when hell freezes over.

1 1/4 ounces tequila
4 ounces lemon-lime soda
Splash blue curacao
Salt

1. Pour tequila and lemon-lime soda into a salt-rimmed old-fashioned glass filled with ice.
2. Add splash of curacao.

563. SEX ON THE BEACH

Confession time...Have you had it?

1 1/2 ounces vodka
1/2 ounce peach schnapps
1 1/2 ounces cranberry juice
1 1/2 ounces orange juice

1. Build vodka, peach schnapps, and juices into a highball with ice.

564. BEACHCOMBER

Ah, a fitting end to a hard day of shell seeking.

1 1/2 ounces light rum
1/2 ounce triple sec
1/2 ounce grenadine
1 ounce sour mix
Sugar

1. Fill cocktail shaker with ice.
2. Add rum, triple sec, grenadine, and sour mix.
3. Shake.
4. Strain into a sugar-rimmed cocktail glass.
5. Garnish with a lime wedge.

565. RUMBAS

Drink two and get out on the dance floor. Clap, clap.

1/4 cup fresh papaya cubes (or chunks)
1/4 cup fresh cantaloupe cubes (or chunks)
3/4 cup pineapple juice
3/4 cup orange juice
6 ounces light rum
1 tablespoon grenadine

1. Pour all ingredients into a blender.
2. Fill blender with ice.
2. Blend until slushy.
3. Pour into highball glasses.
4. Garnish with orange slices and cherries.
(Serves 4)

566. TROPICAL PINEAPPLE PARADISE

The Shangri-la of tropical drinks. Tastes best when consumed in the presence of palm trees, sand, and plenty of bikinis.

2 ounces pineapple liqueur
1 ounce coconut rum
Cranberry juice

1. Pour pineapple liqueur and rum into a tall glass.
2. Fill with cranberry juice.
3. Garnish with a pineapple wedge.

567. REEF RUNNER

The ideal drink for a three-hour tour.

1 ounce dark rum
1/2 ounce blackberry brandy
1/2 ounce apricot brandy

1. Fill cocktail shaker with ice.
2. Add rum and brandies.
3. Shake.
4. Strain into a highball glace filled with ice.
5. Fill with a favorite tropical juice. Bartender's choice.

568. TEQUILA SUNRISE

Drink this while the sun is coming up...

2 ounces tequila
4 ounces orange juice
1 ounce grenadine

1. Pour tequila into a highball glass with ice.
2. Top with orange juice.
3. Stir.
4. Add grenadine by tilting the glass and pouring down the side.
5. Garnish with an orange slice and a cherry.

569. TEQUILA SUNSET

...and drink this while the sun is going down.

1 ounce tequila
Orange juice
1/2 ounce blackberry brandy
1 cherry

1. Pour tequila into a collins glass filled with ice.
2. Fill with orange juice.
3. Stir.
3. Top with blackberry brandy.
4. Stir lightly.
5. Add cherry on top.

570. POLYNESIAN PARADISE

A sure-fire gateway drink to nirvana.

1 1/2 ounces golden rum
1 teaspoon brown sugar
3/4 ounce lime juice
1/2 ounce sweet vermouth
1/4 ounce triple sec
1/3 cup crushed ice

1. Pour all ingredients into a blender.
2. Blend for 15 seconds on low speed.
3. Pour into a chilled deep-saucer champagne glass.

571. FLAMINGO COCKTAIL

After three, it's guaranteed: You'll be standing on one leg. Turning pink optional.

1/2 ounce lime juice
1 ounce gin
1/2 ounce apricot brandy
1/4 ounce grenadine

1. Fill cocktail shaker with ice.
2. Add lime juice, gin, brandy, and grenadine.
3. Shake.
4. Strain into a cocktail glass.

572. ROSEATE SPOONBILL

Fun fact: This pink Caribbean bird has a wing-span of over five feet and a bill shaped like a spoon. Guard that drink!

1/2 ounce rum
1/2 ounce spiced rum
1/2 ounce Licor 43
1 ounce grapefruit juice
1 ounce guava nectar
2 dashes grenadine
3 ounces ice

1. Pour rums, Licor 43, grapefruit juice, and guava nectar into a blender.
2. Place a dash of grenadine in a chilled margarita glass.
2. Blend until smooth.
3. Pour into the glass.
4. Add second dash of grenadine.
5. Swirl with swizzle stick or piece of sugar cane.

573. JAMAICA GLOW

Are you part firefly, baby? Cause Jamaican me glow.

1 1/2 ounces gin
1/2 ounce dry red wine
1/2 ounce orange juice
1 teaspoon dark Jamaican rum
Sugar

1. Fill cocktail shaker with ice.
2. Add gin, wine, orange juice, and rum.
3. Shake.
4. Strain into a chilled sugar-rimmed cocktail glass.
5. Garnish with a lime slice.

574. PINK CREOLE

King Creole's little sister.

1 1/2 ounces golden rum
1/2 ounce lime juice
1 teaspoon cream
1 teaspoon grenadine
1 rum-soaked black cherry

1. Fill cocktail shaker with ice.
2. Add rum, lime juice, cream, and grenadine.
3. Shake.
4. Strain into a chilled cocktail glass.
5. Add black cherry.

575. RUM AND PINEAPPLE COOLER

Be nice to the cabana boy, and he'll put in an extra shot of rum for you.

2 1/2 ounces light rum
2 ounces pineapple juice
1/2 ounce lemon juice
1 teaspoon 151-proof rum
1 teaspoon sugar
Dash Angostura bitters
Iced club soda

1. Fill cocktail shaker with ice.
2. Add rums, juices, sugar, and bitters.
3. Shake.
4. Strain into a collins glass.
5. Add splash of club soda and ice to fill glass.
6. Garnish with a spear of pineapple and papaya chunks.

576. RUM AND COCONUT COOLER

If castaways indulge in this drink, they may never want to leave the island.

2 1/2 ounces light rum
1 ounce cream of coconut
1/2 ounce lemon juice
Iced club soda

1. Fill cocktail shaker with ice.
2. Add rum, cream of coconut, and lemon juice.
3. Shake.
4. Strain into a collins glass half-filled with ice.
5. Add splash of club soda.
6. Garnish with a lemon slice and a cherry.

577. SLEEPY LAGOON

One relaxes. Two sedates. Three, indeed, will make you meditate.

1 ounce brandy
1 ounce dry gin
1/2 ounce orange juice
Dash lemon juice

1. Fill cocktail shaker with ice.
2. Add brandy, gin, orange, and lemon juices.
3. Shake.
4. Strain into a chilled cocktail glass.

578. A LITTLE DINGHY

Have a few of these and your friends just might call you "a little dinghy." Take it as a compliment.

3 ounces of Captain Morgan's Parrot Bay rum
3 ounces of Malibu coconut rum
1 part cranberry juice
1 part pineapple juice
1 part orange juice

1. Pour rums into a highball glass filled with ice.
2. Fill the glass with equal parts cranberry, pineapple, and orange juices.
3. Garnish with a pineapple wedge, an orange slice, and a cocktail umbrella.

579. CARIBBEAN ROMANCE

Popular with match-making cruise ship directors. Sure to spark a kiss or two under the moonlight.

1 1/2 ounces light rum
1 ounce amaretto
1 1/2 ounces orange juice
1 1/2 ounces pineapple juice
Splash of grenadine

1. Fill cocktail shaker with ice.
2. Add rum, amaretto, and juices.
3. Shake.
4. Strain into a highball glass.
5. Float grenadine on top.
6. Garnish with an orange slice.

580. A DAY AT THE BEACH

...never felt so good.

1 ounce coconut flavored rum
1/2 ounce amaretto
4 ounces orange juice
1/2 ounce grenadine

1. Fill cocktail shaker with ice.
2. Add rum, amaretto, orange juice, and grenadine.
3. Shake.
4. Strain into a highball glass with ice.
5. Top with grenadine.
6. Garnish with a pineapple wedge and a strawberry.

581. RUM ROYALE

The king of all tropical drinks.

1 ounce light rum
2 ounces Sauternes
1 1/2 ounces lemon juice
2 ounces pineapple juice
1 teaspoon sugar
Dash Peychaud's bitters

1. Fill cocktail shaker with ice.
2. Add rum, Sauternes, juices, sugar, and bitters.
3. Shake.
4. Strain into a chilled collins glass.
5. Add ice to fill glass.
6. Garnish with a pineapple cube and a cherry.

582. PINEAPPLE PLANTER'S PICKUP

If you had to pick pineapples all day, wouldn't you need a pick-me-up?

2 ounces gin
2 ounces pineapple juice

1. Fill cocktail shaker with ice.
2. Add gin and pineapple juice.
3. Shake.
4. Strain into a chilled cocktail glass.

583. POKER COCKTAIL

Deal these and you're guaranteed a full house.

1 1/2 ounces sweet vermouth
1 1/2 ounces light rum

1. Fill cocktail shaker with ice.
2. Add vermouth and rum.
3. Stir.
4. Strain into a cocktail glass.

584. MANHATTAN HAWAII

For the vacationing city slicker who can't bear to leave the metropolis behind.

1 1/2 ounces whiskey
3/4 ounce sweet vermouth
Dash Angostura bitters

1. Fill cocktail shaker with ice.
2. Add whiskey, vermouth, and bitters.
3. Stir.
4. Strain into a chilled cocktail glass.

585. PINEAPPLE BOOMERANG

The drink that returns with a knockout punch.

1 1/2 ounces gin
1/2 ounce vermouth
1/2 ounce pineapple juice

1. Fill cocktail shaker with ice.
2. Add gin, vermouth, and pineapple juice.
3. Shake.
4. Strain into a chilled cocktail glass.

586. TAHITI MILKMAID

Her name is Lola, and she mixes the most wicked cocktails on the isle of Tahiti. This creation will leave you wanting more.

2 ounces gin
1 ounce grenadine
1 teaspoon cream

1. Fill cocktail shaker with ice.
2. Add gin, grenadine, and cream.
3. Shake.
4. Strain into a chilled cocktail glass.

587. SWEET LEILANI

One look at Sweet Leilani and Dave knew he wasn't in Kansas anymore.

2 ounces gin
1/2 ounce grenadine
1/2 ounce lemon juice
2 dashes Angostura bitters
Club soda

1. Fill cocktail shaker with ice.
2. Add gin, grenadine, lemon juice, and bitters.
3. Shake.
4. Strain into a highball cocktail glass with ice.
5. Top with club soda.
6. Garnish with a lemon peel.

588. PREACHER'S PANIC PUNCH

A preacher's worst nightmare. This punch at a church social? Heavens to Betsy!

2 ounces rum
1/2 ounce lime juice
1 ounce pineapple juice
1/2 ounce guava juice
1/2 ounce grenadine
Club soda

1. Pour rum, juices, and grenadine into a zombie glass filled with shaved ice.
2. Stir.
3. Fill with chilled club soda.

589. MISSIONARY'S MISTAKE

Legend has it a missionary traveled deep into the African jungle, made a wrong turn, and threw caution to the wind. St. Peter was not amused.

2 ounces gin
1 1/2 ounces apricot brandy
1 ounce lemon juice
3 mint stalks

1. Fill cocktail shaker with ice.
2. Add gin, apricot brandy, and lemon juice.
3. Shake until mint stalks are crushed.
4. Strain into a chilled cocktail glass.

590. AUSSIE BEACH BLOND

As author Anita Loos once remarked, "Gentlemen always seem to remember blondes." Indeed, this cocktail is one to remember.

2 1/4 ounces white rum
2 ounces Cointreau
1 1/2 teaspoon sugar
3/4 ounce lime juice
1 1/4 ounces orange juice
Juice of 1 passion fruit
1/4 cup crushed ice

1. Pour rum, Cointreau, juices, and sugar in a blender with ice.
2. Blend until slushy.
3. Pour into a hurricane glass.
4. Garnish with lemon, lime, and orange slices.

7

SHOTS AND SLAMMERS FOR THE PERPETUAL 21-YEAR-OLD—

Sorority and Fraternity Fantasia

Admit it. You'd order a shot called a Blow Job in college and snicker about it for days. Even brag about it. You know you would. But would you order that drink when you were thirty-five? Only if you were in the midst of a midlife crisis, craving a college-aged cutie, and a red sports car. We can't promise you the car or the girl, but, no question, these shots and slammers will send you down memory lane. Some of them flame. Literally. Some even wiggle, thanks to Jell-O. Down a couple—or four—with lethal names like Kamikaze and Alien Secretion, and you'll rocket to Mars faster than anything NASA could invent. Remember to buckle up!

591. AFTER FIVE

Another sweet reason to finish your TPS reports on time.

1/3 ounce coffee liqueur
1/3 ounce peppermint schnapps
1/3 ounce Irish cream liqueur

1. Layer coffee liqueur, peppermint schnapps, and Irish cream liqueur in a shot glass.

592. AFTER EIGHT

Clarification: Drink's name is not an invitation to demonstrate what great tricks you can do after eight servings.

1/3 ounce coffee liqueur
1/3 ounce Irish cream liqueur
1/3 ounce white crème de menthe

1. Layer coffee liqueur, Irish cream liqueur, and crème de menthe in a shot glass.

593. ALABAMA SLAMMER

Drink four, say name three times fast, win a prize.

1 1/2 ounces sloe gin
1 1/2 ounces amaretto
1 1/2 ounces Southern Comfort
1 1/2 ounces orange juice

1. Fill cocktail shaker with ice.
2. Add sloe gin, amaretto, Southern Comfort, and orange juice.
3. Shake.
4. Strain into four shot glasses.

(Serves 4)

594. ANTIFREEZE

Proper system maintenance is critical to maximizing your engine's performance.

1/2 ounce green crème de menthe
1/2 ounce vodka

1. Fill cocktail shaker with ice.
2. Add crème de menthe and vodka.
3. Shake.
4. Strain into a shot glass.

595. B-53

Now with even more flavor than the B-52!

1/2 ounce coffee liqueur
1/2 ounce Irish cream liqueur
1/2 ounce Grand Marnier
1/2 ounce vodka

1. Layer coffee liqueur, Irish cream liqueur, Grand Marnier, and vodka into a shot glass.

596. PURPLE HOOTER SHOOTER

Note: In the event hooters remain purple for more than four hours, seek immediate medical attention.

3 ounces vodka
1 ounce Rose's lime juice
Dash of Chambord

1. Fill a cocktail shaker with ice.
2. Add vodka, Rose's lime juice, and Chambord.
3. Stir.
4. Strain into a shot glass.

597. JOLLY RANCHER

Like a trip to the candy store. A candy store where you get carded.

3/4 ounces vodka
1/4 ounce melon liqueur
1/4 ounce peach schnapps
Splash of cranberry juice

1. Fill a cocktail shaker with ice.
2. Add vodka, melon liqueur, peach schnapps, and cranberry juice.
3. Shake.
4. Strain into a shot glass.

598. BABY RUTH

In the 1927 World Series, Babe Ruth called his shot and homered. Time for you to call yours.

1/2 ounce Frangelico
1/2 ounce vodka
Three peanuts

1. Layer Frangelico and vodka in a shot glass.
2. Add peanuts.

599. BUTTERY NIPPLE

"The lady will have the linguine with white clam sauce and a Buttery Nipple." Who says chivalry can't be fun?

1/2 ounce butterscotch schnapps
1/2 ounce Irish cream liqueur

1. Layer butterscotch schnapps and Irish cream liqueur.

600. MELTDOWN

Designed to thaw even the iciest of hearts. Recommended for standoffish blind dates.

1 ounce chilled vodka
1/2 ounce peach schnapps

1. Pour chilled vodka into a shot glass.
2. Top with peach schnapps.

601. PURPLE HAZE

Actin' funny, and you don't know why? S'cuse me while I…

1/2 ounce sambuca
1/2 ounce Chambord

1. Pour sambuca into shot glass.
2. Slowly add Chambord.

602. HAWAIIAN PUNCH

Please resist the urge to smack the guy who requests this drink. It just means you're old enough to remember the commercial.

1/4 ounce crème de almond
1/4 ounce Southern Comfort
1/4 ounce vodka
1/4 ounce pineapple juice

1. Fill a cocktail shaker with ice.
2. Add crème de almond, Southern Comfort, vodka, and pineapple juice.
3. Stir.
4. Strain into a shot glass.

603. BEAM ME UP SCOTTY

Don't be a Klingon—passing this one up is simply not logical.

1/3 ounce coffee liqueur
1/3 ounce Irish cream liqueur
1/3 ounce banana liqueur

1. Layer coffee liqueur, Irish cream liqueur, and banana liqueur.

604. KAMIKAZE

Tora! Tora! Tora!

2 ounces vodka
1/2 ounce triple sec
1/4 ounce Rose's lime juice

1. Fill a cocktail shaker with ice.
2. Add vodka, triple sec, and Rose's lime juice.
3. Shake.
4. Strain into two shot glasses.
(*Serves 2*)

605. BLOW JOB

Makes Monday morning's break room recounting of Friday night a lot more interesting.

1/2 ounce vodka
1/2 ounce coffee-flavored brandy
1/2 ounce coffee liqueur

1. Fill a cocktail shaker with ice.
2. Add vodka, coffee-flavored brandy, and coffee liqueur.
3. Shake.
4. Strain into a shot glass.
5. Top with whipped cream.

606. MISSION ACCOMPLISHED

Banner not included.

2 ounces vodka
1/2 ounce triple sec
1/4 ounce Rose's lime juice
Dash of grenadine

1. Fill a cocktail shaker with ice.
2. Add vodka, triple sec, Rose's lime juice, and grenadine.
3. Shake.
4. Strain into a shot glass.

607. E.T.

Serve with side order of Reese's Pieces.

3/4 ounce melon liqueur
3/4 ounce vodka
3/4 ounce Irish cream liqueur

1. Layer melon liqueur, vodka, and Irish cream liqueur.

608. PEANUT BUTTER AND JELLY

Mmm...just like Mom used to make when you weren't looking.

3/4 ounce Frangelico
3/4 ounce Chambord

1. Fill a cocktail shaker with ice.
2. Add Frangelico and Chambord.
3. Shake.
4. Strain into a shot glass.

609. LEMON DROP

Giggly coeds frequently lose their grip on this one.

1/2 ounce chilled tequila
1/2 ounce chilled vodka
Lemon slice
Sugar

1. Moisten inside of a shot glass with lemon slice.
2. Coat inside of shot glass with sugar.
2. Add tequila and vodka.

610. CANDY BAR

The bouncer at the Candy Bar? A surly, aging Willy Wonka.

1/2 ounce Frangelico
1/2 ounce vodka

1. Fill a cocktail shaker with ice.
2. Add Frangelico and vodka.
3. Strain into a shot glass.

611. MEXICAN FLAG

Order one for the Mexican head of state, win additional NAFTA concessions. Never underestimate the power of drunken diplomacy.

1/2 ounce sloe gin
1/2 ounce vodka
1/2 ounce melon liqueur

1. Pour sloe gin into a shot glass.
2. Float vodka on top of sloe gin.
3. Float melon liqueur on top of vodka.

612. PANCHO VILLA

Pancho Villa was a tough, hardcore Mexican revolutionary. No better way to salute this brave man than with a fruity cocktail.

1 ounce light rum
1 ounce gin
1/2 ounce apricot brandy
1 teaspoon cherry brandy
1 teaspoon pineapple juice

1. Fill a cocktail shaker with ice.
2. Add light rum, gin, brandies, and pineapple juice.
3. Shake.
4. Strain into a rocks glass filled with ice.

613. TO THE MOON

"One of these days, Alice, one of these days...POW!" Pour a little out for Jackie Gleason, RIP.

1/2 ounce coffee liqueur
1/2 ounce amaretto
1/2 ounce Irish cream liqueur
1/2 ounce 151-proof rum

1. Fill a cocktail shaker with ice.
2. Add coffee liqueur, amaretto, Irish cream liqueur, and 151-proof rum.
3. Stir.
4. Strain into a shot glass.

614. BLOODY CAESAR

"Et tu? Okay, you got the first round, I'll pick up this one. Who wants peanuts?"

1 littleneck clam
2 drops Worcestershire sauce
2 drops Tabasco sauce
Dash of horseradish
1 ounce vodka
1 1/2 ounces tomato juice

1. Place littleneck clam in bottom of shot glass.
2. Add Worcestershire sauce, Tabasco sauce, and horseradish.
3. Add vodka and tomato juice.
4. Sprinkle celery salt on top.
5. Garnish with lime juice.

615. PIGSKIN SHOT

Soon to be the official stadium smuggled drink for Arkansas Razorback fans everywhere. Woo Pig Sooiee!

1 ounce vodka
1 ounce melon liqueur
1/2 ounce sour mix

1. Fill a cocktail shaker with ice.
2. Add vodka, melon liqueur, and sour mix.
3. Shake.
4. Strain into a shot glass.

616. SNOW CAP

Like a favorite hat, this one will keep your head nice and warm.

1/2 ounce tequila
1/2 ounce Irish cream liqueur

1. Layer tequila and Irish cream liqueur into a shot glass.

617. WOO WOO

Hard to order this one with a straight face, but give it a try. Well worth the bartender's raised eyebrow.

1/2 ounce vodka
1/2 ounce peach schnapps
1/2 ounce cranberry juice

1. Fill a cocktail shaker with ice.
2. Add vodka, peach schnapps, and cranberry juice.
3. Stir.
4. Strain into a shot glass.

618. ROCK LOBSTER

A shout out to one of the best dance songs ever.

1/3 ounce Irish cream liqueur
1/3 ounce amaretto
1/3 ounce white crème de cacao

1. Layer Irish cream liqueur, amaretto, and crème de cacao in a shot glass.

619. TEQUILA POPPER

This one has scarred many a bachelor party table.

1 ounce tequila
1/2 ounce 7-up

1. Pour tequila into a shot glass.
2. Add 7-Up.
3. Place napkin over top of glass.
4. Bang glass on table.
5. Drink immediately.

620. NUTTY PROFESSOR

Consumed by wildhaired academics around the globe.

1/2 ounce Grand Marnier
1/2 ounce Frangelico
1/2 ounce Irish cream liqueur

1. Fill a cocktail shaker with ice.
2. Add Grand Marnier, Frangelico, and Irish cream liqueur.
3. Stir.
4. Strain into a shot glass.

621. SILVER SPIDER

Like the übercool Italian car, this one handles like a champ.

1/2 ounce vodka
1/2 ounce rum
1/2 ounce triple sec
1/2 ounce white crème de menthe

1. Fill a cocktail shaker with ice.
2. Add vodka, rum, triple sec, and crème de menthe.
3. Stir.
4. Strain into a shot glass.

622. WOMBAT

Fun Fact: The wombat is the world's largest burrowing mammal—and now a delicious beverage.

2 ounces dark rum
1/2 ounce strawberry liqueur
2 ounces orange juice
3 ounces pineapple juice
6 ounces fresh watermelon juice

1. Fill a cocktail shaker with dark rum, strawberry liqueur, orange juice, pineapple juice, and watermelon juice.
3. Shake.
4. Pour into shot glasses.
(Serves 4)

623. RUSSIAN QUAALUDE

How do you say "duuuude...look at my hand..." in Russian?

1/3 ounces Frangelico
1/3 ounces Irish cream liqueur
1/3 ounces vodka

1. Layer Frangelico, Irish cream liqueur, and vodka in a shot glass.

624. TIDY BOWL

Drink the Tidy Bowl now and hug the bowl later. Perfect!

1 1/2 ounces vodka
1 to 2 drops blue curacao
2 raisins

1. Fill a cocktail mixer with ice.
2. Add vodka and blue curacao.
3. Stir.
4. Strain into a shot glass.
5. Plop in raisins.

625. SILK PANTIES

Get these down as fast as possible.

3/4 ounce peach schnapps
3/4 ounce sambuca

1. Fill a cocktail mixer with ice.
2. Add peach schnapps and sambuca.
3. Stir.
4. Strain into a shot glass.

626. GREEN DEMON

Seen this guy on your shoulder once or twice? Fun guy, terrible adviser.

1/2 ounce vodka
1/2 ounce rum
1/2 ounce melon liqueur
1/2 ounce lemonade

1. Fill a cocktail mixer with ice.
2. Add vodka, rum, melon liqueur, and lemonade.
3. Shake.
4. Strain into a shot glass.

627. SNACK BITE

Word around the campfire is that former Girl Scouts like these. Enjoy with a box of cookies.

2 ounces Canadian whiskey
1 ounce Rose's lime juice

1. Pour Canadian whiskey and Rose's lime juice in a shot glass.
2. Garnish with a lime wedge.

628. TEDDY BEAR

At last: The real reason Paddington got lost.

1/2 ounce root beer schnapps
1/2 ounce vodka

1. Layer root beer schnapps and vodka in a shot
   glass.

629. SNOW SHOE

*Surely, Santa has downed a few of these on his annual
journey.*

1 1/2 ounce Wild Turkey
1/2 ounces peppermint schnapps

1. Fill a rocks glass with ice.
2. Add Wild Turkey and peppermint schnapps.
3. Stir.
4. Strain into a shot glass.

630. MONKEY SHINE

Why Curious George hangs around that man in the yellow hat.

1/2 ounce Southern Comfort
1/2 ounce crème de banana
1/2 ounce Irish cream liqueur

1. Fill a cocktail mixer with ice.
2. Add Southern Comfort, crème de banana, and Irish cream liqueur.
3. Shake.
4. Strain into a cordial glass.

631. MELON BALL

Rumored around frat houses to be the real last name of John Cougar.

1 ounce melon liqueur
1 ounce vodka
1 ounce pineapple juice

1. Fill a cocktail mixer with ice.
2. Add melon liqueur, vodka, and pineapple juice.
3. Shake.
4. Strain into a shot glass.

632. GALACTIC ALE

Set phasers to "stun"...a drink for terrestrials and extra-terrestrials alike.

1 1/4 ounces vodka
1 1/4 ounces blue curacao
1 ounce lime juice
1/2 ounce Chambord

1. Fill a cocktail mixer with ice.
2. Add vodka, blue curacao, lime juice, and Chambord.
3. Shake.
4. Strain into two shot glasses.
(*Serves 2*)

633. ORGASM

You know what they say: Even when it's bad, it's still pretty good.

1/2 ounce Irish cream liqueur
1/2 ounce amaretto
1/2 ounce coffee liqueur

1. Fill a cocktail mixer with ice.
2. Add Irish cream liqueur, amaretto, and coffee liqueur.
3. Shake.
4. Strain into a shot glass.

634. SCREAMING ORGASM

This is why the neighbors in the next apartment giggle when they see you. The walls have ears.

1/2 ounce vodka
1/2 ounce Irish cream liqueur
1/2 ounce amaretto
1/2 ounce coffee liqueur

1. Fill a cocktail mixer with ice.
2. Add vodka, Irish cream liqueur, amaretto, and coffee liqueur.
3. Shake.
4. Strain into a rocks glass.

635. IRISH FROST

Begorrah! With this drink handy, who needs to find the end of the rainbow?

1 1/2 ounces Irish cream liqueur
Splash cream of coconut
Splash half and half

1. Fill a cocktail mixer with ice.
2. Add Irish cream liqueur, cream of coconut, and half and half.
3. Shake.
4. Strain into cordial glass.
5. Garnish with cinnamon.

636. OATMEAL COOKIE

Just like Grandma used to make. After you went to bed.

1/2 ounce Irish cream liqueur
1/2 ounce Goldschlager
1/2 ounce butterscotch schnapps

1. Fill a cocktail mixer with ice.
2. Add Irish cream liqueur, Goldschlager, and butterscotch schnapps.
3. Shake.
4. Strain into rocks glass.

637. ORIENTAL RUG

The man who drinks too many of these ends up flat on the floor.

1/2 ounce Irish cream liqueur
1/2 ounce Frangelico
1/2 ounce Jagermeister
1/2 ounce coffee liqueur
Dash of cola

1. Fill a cocktail mixer with ice.
2. Add Irish cream liqueur, Frangelico, Jagermeister, coffee liqueur, and cola.
3. Shake.
4. Strain into a rocks glass.

638. INTERNATIONAL INCIDENT

Some drinks are not worth causing trouble over. Here's an exception. Thank heavens for diplomatic immunity.

1/4 ounce vodka
1/4 ounce coffee liqueur
1/4 ounce amaretto
1/4 ounce Frangelico
1/2 ounce Irish cream liqueur

1. Fill a cocktail mixer with ice.
2. Add vodka, coffee liqueur, amaretto, Frangelico, and Irish cream liqueur.
3. Shake.
4. Strain into a shot glass.

639. OH MY GOSH!

"Oh My Gosh": A popular sorority often linked with the frat boys from I Tappa Kegg.

1 ounce amaretto
1 ounce peach schnapps

1. Fill a cocktail mixer with ice.
2. Add amaretto and peach schnapps.
3. Stir.
4. Strain into a shot glass.

640. MIND ERASER

There's something to be said for truth in advertising. Kudos to this drink for telling it like it is.

3/4 ounce coffee liqueur
1 1/4 ounces vodka
1 ounce tonic water

1. Fill a rocks glass with ice.
2. Add coffee liqueur and vodka.
3. Top with tonic water.
4. Stir gently.
5. Drink through a straw in one shot.

641. JELLY BEAN

Some would say this should be the after-dinner drink of the Reagan Presidential Library.

1 ounce anisette
1 ounce blackberry brandy

1. Pour anisette and blackberry brandy into cordial glass.
2. Stir.
3. Add ice, if desired.

642. WINDEX

Whether drinking it or using it to clean windows, one firm rule: no streaking.

3/4 ounce vodka
3/4 ounce triple sec
3/4 ounce blue curacao
3/4 ounce Rose's lime juice

1. Fill a cocktail mixer with ice.
2. Add vodka, triple sec, blue curacao, and Rose's lime juice.
3. Shake.
4. Strain into a rocks glass.

643. SCOOBY SNACKS

"That's not a real bartender! It's....Mr. Johnson!!??" Drink up, meddling kids.

3/4 ounce vodka
3/4 ounce melon liqueur
3/4 ounce coconut rum liqueur
1 ounce pineapple juice
1/2 ounce of cream

1. Fill a cocktail mixer with ice.
2. Add vodka, melon liqueur, coconut rum liqueur, pineapple juice, and cream.
3. Shake.
4. Strain into a rocks glass.

644. SLIPPERY NIPPLE

A real mouthful for gutter boys.

2 ounces sambuca
1 1/2 ounces Irish cream liqueur
Drop grenadine

1. Pour sambuca into a cocktail glass.
2. Float Irish cream liqueur on top of sambuca.
3. Pour a drop of grenadine in the middle.

645. MEXICAN ROSE

Watch out for the golden thorn.

3/4 ounce Chambord
1/4 ounce gold tequila
Sugar

1. Fill a cocktail mixer with ice.
2. Add Chambord and gold tequila.
3. Shake.
4. Strain into a sugar-frosted chilled cordial glass.

646. HONOLULU SHOOTER

Don't you know Don Ho-wannabees are all about drinking these with the ladies? Add ukulele music at bartender's discretion.

1 ounce gin
1 teaspoon pineapple juice
1 teaspoon orange juice
1 teaspoon lemon juice
1 teaspoon pineapple syrup
Dash Angostura bitters

1. Fill a cocktail mixer with ice.
2. Add gin, juices, pineapple syrup, and bitters.
3. Shake.
4. Strain into a rocks glass.

647. KALASHNIKOV SHOT

Liquor, fire, and a famed Russian weapon? Count me in!

3/4 ounce vodka
1/4 ounce absinthe
1 slice Lemon
Pinch of cinnamon
Pinch of sugar

1. Fill a shot glass with vodka.
2. Place a lemon slice halfway across the top of the glass.
3. Fill the rest of the shot glass with absinthe, pouring so that it passes through the lemon.
4. Add cinnamon and sugar to the lemon.
5. Ignite the lemon.
6. When it extinguishes itself, down the shot and eat the lemon.

648. BARBIE SHOT

Note: 1 ounce + 1 ounce + 1 ounce + 1 ounce...math is hard!

1 ounce coconut rum liqueur
1 ounce vodka
1 ounce cranberry juice
1 ounce orange juice

1. Fill a cocktail mixer with ice.
2. Add coconut rum liqueur, vodka, and juices.
3. Shake.
4. Strain into two rocks glass.
(Serves 2)

649. FUZZY SCREW SHOT

Sounds like some sort of porno script direction. Drink up before the director (or bartender) yells, "Cut!"

1 ounce vodka
1/2 ounce peach schnapps
1/2 ounce triple sec

1. Pour a double shot glass half full of vodka.
2. Pour the peach schnapps into the next quarter.
3. Pour the triple sec in the remaining quarter.
4. Stir and shoot.

650. THE FIG

Ever heard that expression, "I don't give a fig"? Taste this—it's so good, you'd surely keep it, too.

1 1/2 ounces coconut rum liqueur
1 ounce pineapple juice
1 ounce cranberry juice

1. Fill a cocktail mixer with ice.
2. Add coconut rum liqueur and juices.
3. Shake.
4. Pour into a rocks glass.

651. BABY ASPIRIN

You can't drink this without wanting to stay home from school and watch game shows.

1/2 ounce orange juice
1/2 ounce sour mix
1/2 ounce triple sec
1/2 ounce raspberry schnapps

1. Pour equal parts into cocktail mixer, mix and pour into shot glass.

652. BLACK LEATHER WHIP

Crraack! Get me another, bartender.

1/4 ounce sour mix
1/4 ounce triple sec
1/4 ounce Grand Marnier
1/4 ounce gold tequila
1 splash orange juice

1. Fill a cocktail mixer with ice.
2. Add sour mix, triple sec, Grand Marnier, tequila, and orange juice.
3. Shake.
4. Pour into a rocks glass.

653. BLUE POLAR BEAR

What the Great White One drinks when the Coca-Cola people aren't looking. Mmmmm....

1 1/2 ounces vodka
1 1/2 ounces chilled peppermint schnapps
1 ounce crushed ice

1. Fill a cocktail mixer with ice.
2. Add vodka and peppermint schnapps.
3. Shake until well-mixed.
4. Add ice.
5. Shake lightly.
6. Strain.
7. Pour into two shot glasses.
(Serves 2)

654. COCAINE SHOOTER

Consumed by good girls who want to be bad girls. For tonight, anyway.

1/2 ounce amaretto
1/2 ounce Irish cream liqueur
1/2 ounce dark crème de cacao
1/2 ounce coffee liqueur
1/4 ounce cream
1 splash cola

1. Fill a cocktail mixer with ice.
2. Add amaretto, Irish cream liqueur, dark crème de cacao, coffee liqueur, cream, and cola.
3. Shake.
4. Strain into a chilled rocks glass.

655. FRUITY PEBBLE

Yabba Dabba Doo—dibs on the prize!

1 1/2 ounces vodka
1/2 ounce blue curacao
Dash grenadine
1 ounce milk

1. Fill a cocktail mixer with ice.
2. Add vodka, curacao, grenadine, and milk.
3. Shake.
4. Strain into a rocks glass.

656. GEISHA RECIPE

Here's a good reason to emigrate.

1 part Canadian whiskey
2 parts melon liqueur
Pineapple juice

1. Fill a cocktail mixer with ice.
2. Add Canadian whiskey and melon liqueur.
3. Shake.
4. Fill with pineapple juice.

657. GOLDEN EYE

007 might quaff this tasty shot, careful to dodge the peanut. Beware!

1 ounce Goldschlager
1 peanut
1 ounce Irish cream liqueur

1. Pour Goldschlager into a cordial glass.
2. Add a peanut.
3. Top with Irish cream liqueur.

658. GREEN VOODOO

Come do...the voodoo...that you do...so well.

1 ounce melon liqueur
1 ounce coconut rum liqueur
Splash triple sec
Splash sour mix
1 ounce lemon-lime soda

1. Fill a cocktail mixer with ice.
2. Add melon liqueur, coconut rum liqueur, triple sec, sour mix, and lemon-lime soda.
3. Shake.
4. Strain into a two shot glasses.
(Serves 2)

659. HAWAIIAN VOLCANO

Oh great God of Liquor! Shower us with your blessings! Make it a double!

2 ounces vodka
2 ounces Southern Comfort
2 ounces sloe gin
2 ounces Grand Marnier
Splash or two of orange juice

1. Fill a cocktail mixer with ice.
2. Add vodka, Southern Comfort, sloe gin, Grand Marnier, and orange juice.
3. Shake.
4. Strain into a four shot glasses.
(Serves 4)

660. HONEYDEWME

More wives should add this to their hubbies' chore lists.

1/2 ounce Barenjager liqueur
1/4 ounce melon liqueur
1 ounce orange juice

1. Fill a cocktail mixer with ice.
2. Add Barenjager liqueur, melon liqueur, and orange juice.
3. Shake.
4. Strain into a shot glass.

661. KINKY

Handcuffs and leather pants optional.

1/3 ounce cranberry vodka
1/3 ounce raspberry vodka
1/3 ounce peach schnapps

1. Layer vodkas and peach schnapps into a shot glass.

662. MAD HATTER

If Lewis Carroll was drinking this while writing, it explains everything.

1 ounce vodka
1 ounce peach schnapps
1 ounce lemonade
1 ounce cola

1. Fill a cocktail mixer with ice.
2. Add vodka, peach schnapps, lemonade, and cola.
3. Shake.
4. Strain into a shot glass.

663. MAD SCIENTIST

It's alive, it's alive! A great one to whip up in the laboratory for that special...specimen.

3/4 ounce blueberry schnapps
3/4 ounce raspberry schnapps
Grenadine
Irish cream liqueur

1. Add blueberry and raspberry schnapps to a shot glass.
2. Slowly top with grenadine.
3. Dribble a small amount of Irish cream liqueur on top.

664. MEXICAN STANDOFF

Fun party game: Make one shot, quickdraw for it with your nemesis.

1/3 ounce vodka
2/3 ounce gold tequila
1/3 ounce Passoa

1. Layer into a shot glass in order.

665. MORANGUITO

Be enamored of any drink that combines the twin evils, er, "joys," of absinthe and tequila.

2/3 ounce absinthe
2/3 ounce tequila
1/3 ounce grenadine

1. Layer the ingredients in a shot glass.

666. RATTLESNAKE RECIPE

Truth be told, it's more scared of you than you are of it.

1/2 ounce Irish cream liqueur
1/2 ounce coffee liqueur
1/2 ounce crème de cacao

1. Carefully layer into a shot glass or test tube.

667. SANGRITA

New England and Mexico...two great tastes that taste great together.

1 ounce gold tequila
1 ounce Clamato juice
Tabasco sauce
Dash of Worcestershire sauce

1. Fill one shot glass with tequila.
2. Fill second shot glass with Clamato juice
3. Add two drops Tabasco and Worcestershire sauce.
4. Shoot the tequila.
5. Chase it with the second shot.

668. SMARTY

Sweet as a mother's love.

1 ounce amaretto
1 ounce Southern Comfort
1 ounce blackberry brandy
1/2 ounce sour mix

1. Fill a cocktail mixer with ice.
2. Add amaretto, Southern Comfort, blackberry brandy, and sour mix.
3. Shake.
4. Strain into a shot glass.

669. SOLARIS

Spicy and sweet, like a pirate with a heart of gold.

3/4 ounce spiced rum
3/4 ounce grenadine
1 teaspoon sugar

1. Measure the parts so the shot glass is 2/3 full.
2. Skim sugar on top.
3. Stir slightly.

670. SOUTHERN BONDAGE

This one will have you tied up in knots. But in a good way.

1/4 ounce Southern Comfort
1/4 ounce amaretto
1/4 ounce peach schnapps
1/4 ounce triple sec
1 splash cranberry juice
1 splash sour mix

1. Fill a cocktail mixer with ice.
2. Add Southern Comfort, amaretto, peach schnapps, triple sec, cranberry juice, and sour mix.
3. Shake.
4. Strain into a rocks glass.

671. SPRINGBOK

A creamy moon beam dream.

3/4 ounce white crème de menthe
1/4 ounce Amarula cream liqueur
Dash cream

1. Pour crème de menthe into a cordial glass.
2. Gently layer Amarula cream liqueur.
3. Add a thin layer of cream.

672. STARDUST

Surely created by a hippie mixologist inside the lime green VW van, named in honor of his soul mate.

1/2 ounce citrus vodka
1/2 ounce peach schnapps
1/2 ounce blue curacao
1 ounce sour mix
1 ounce pineapple juice
1 splash grenadine

1. Fill a cocktail mixer with ice.
2. Add vodka, peach schnapps, curacao, sour mix, pineapple juice, and grenadine.
3. Shake.
4. Strain into two rocks glasses.
(Serves 2)

673. THE LADY IN RED

Best ordered by a dashing, tuxedoclad gentleman, for his smoldering chanteuse.

1/2 ounce peppermint schnapps
1/2 ounce peach schnapps
1/2 ounce vodka
1/2 ounce grenadine

1. Pour the schnapps, vodka, and grenadine into rocks glass.
2. Let stand for 30 seconds.

674. THE LIQUEURICE DREAM

An unusual concoction that shoots back but leaves a sweet aftertaste.

1/4 ounce Irish cream liqueur
1/4 ounce scotch whiskey
1/4 ounce tequila
1/4 ounce Galliano

1. Pour Irish cream liqueur, scotch whiskey, tequila, and Galliano into a shot glass.
2. Stir.

675. THE PERNOD DEMON

France and Switzerland banned Pernod (and true absinthe) for part of the early twentieth century, fearing its hallucinogenic effects. Bottoms up, you madmen.

1 lemon wedge
Sugar
6 dashes Tabasco sauce
1 1/2 ounces Pernod

1. Coat the lemon wedge with sugar.
2. Add dashes of Tabasco sauce to lemon.
3. Suck the lemon.
4. Shoot the Pernod.

676. TROPICAL PASSION

One might think that "passion" and "shots" are polar opposites. Think again, pal. Nothing says romance like a fruity shooter.

1/2 ounce peach schnapps
1/2 ounce rum
1/2 ounce sloe gin
1/2 ounce triple sec
Splash of orange juice

1. Fill a cocktail mixer with ice.
2. Add peach schnapps, rum, sloe gin, triple sec, and orange juice.
3. Shake.
4. Strain into a shot glass.

677. YELLOW CAKE

Not the uranium, silly. The drink!

1/3 ounce vanilla vodka
1/3 ounce triple sec
1/3 ounce pineapple juice

1. Fill a cocktail mixer with ice.
2. Add vanilla vodka, triple sec, and pineapple juice.
3. Shake.
4. Strain into a shot glass.

678. INDULGENCE

Doesn't get much better than this. One delicious mistress.

1/3 ounce dark crème de cacao
1/3 ounce amaretto
1/3 ounce Amarula cream liqueur

1. Layer in above order in a shot glass.

679. VANILLA CREAM SHOOTER

Even white boys got to shout!

1/3 ounce amaretto
1/3 ounce Amarula cream liqueur
1/3 ounce vanilla vodka

1. Layer in above order in a shot glass.

680. BANANA SPLIT

Even better than that crazy 70s kids TV show.

1/3 ounce amaretto
1/3 ounce white crème de cacao
1/3 ounce crème de banana

1. Layer in above order in a shot glass.

681. LITTLE RED TEDDY

Whether in a shot glass or a lingerie store, everyone's happy to see this little number. Rowr.

4 ounces vodka
1 ounce Chambord
1 ounce white crème de cacao

1. Fill a cocktail mixer with ice.
2. Add vodka, Chambord, white crème de cacao.
3. Shake.
4. Strain into four shot glasses.
(Serves 4)

682. ORANGE CRUSH

Better than the soft drink, naturally, since it has a certain kick courtesy of Russia.

1/2 ounce vodka
1/2 ounce triple sec
1/2 ounce orange juice

1. Fill a cocktail mixer with ice.
2. Add vodka, triple sec, and orange juice.
3. Shake.
4. Strain into a shot glass.

683. ZAMBODIAN

If Zambo were a country, this would be its national drink.

1/2 ounce vodka
1/2 ounce blackberry brandy
1/2 ounce pineapple juice

1. Fill a cocktail mixer with ice.
2. Add vodka, blackberry brandy, and pineapple juice.
3. Shake.
4. Strain into a shot glass.

684. SOUTHERN BEACH

The perfect accompaniment for a day of shell seeking and romping in the sand.

1 ounce Southern Comfort
1/2 ounce peach schnapps
1/4 ounce crème de noyaux
1 ounce orange juice

1. Fill a cocktail mixer with ice.
2. Add Southern Comfort, peach schnapps, crème de noyaux, and orange juice.
3. Shake.
4. Strain into a shot glass.

685. AQUA TIDAL WAVE

Hang ten, Spicoli. This one's for you.

1/3 ounce blue curacao
1/3 ounce vodka
1/3 ounce melon liqueur
Dash pineapple juice
Dash cranberry juice

1. Fill a cocktail mixer with ice.
2. Add curacao, vodka, melon liqueur, and juices.
3. Shake.
4. Strain into a shot glass.

686. MEMPHIS BELLE

As reliable as the World War II B17 for which this drink is named, and much more tolerable than the film version.

3/4 ounce Southern Comfort
3/4 ounce Irish cream liqueur

1. Fill a cocktail mixer with ice.
2. Add Southern Comfort and Irish cream liqueur.
3. Shake.
4. Strain into a shot glass.

687. TIE ME TO THE BEDPOST

If your date orders this without blushing, things are going very well indeed.

1/2 ounce melon liqueur
1/2 ounce citrus vodka
1/2 ounce coconut flavored rum
Splash of sour mix

1. Fill a cocktail mixer with ice.
2. Add melon liqueur, citrus vodka, coconut flavored rum, and sour mix.
3. Shake.
4. Strain into a shot glass.

688. SKIP AND GO NAKED

While weary students have been operating under this philosophy for years, your version is much less drafty.

1 ounce gin
Dash grenadine
Splash sour mix
Splash draft beer

1. Fill a cocktail mixer with ice.
2. Add gin, grenadine, sour mix, and beer.
3. Shake.
4. Strain into a shot glass.

689. ESKIMO KISS

Be warned: Rubbing noses over this sweet delight may melt even the sturdiest igloo.

1/2 ounce Swiss chocolate liqueur
1/2 ounce cherry brandy
1/2 ounce amaretto

1. Fill a cocktail mixer with ice.
2. Add Swiss chocolate liqueur, cherry brandy, and amaretto.
3. Shake.
4. Strain into a shot glass.

690. FUNKY MONKEY

Official drink of Koko the Gorilla.

1/2 ounce peach schnapps
1/2 ounce coffee liqueur
1/2 ounce Irish cream liqueur

1. Fill a cocktail mixer with ice.
2. Add peach schnapps, coffee liqueur, and Irish cream liqueur.
3. Shake.
4. Strain into a shot glass.

691. ALIEN SECRETION

Trekkies: Set phasers to yum and call the mother ship.

1/2 ounce vodka
1/2 ounce melon liqueur
1/2 ounce coconut rum
1/2 ounce pineapple juice

1. Fill a cocktail mixer with ice.
2. Add vodka, melon liqueur, rum, and pineapple juice.
3. Shake.
4. Strain into a shot glass.

VINTAGE COCKTAILS—
Gone but Not Forgotten

For every generation, there's a drink that raises some eyebrows. In the 1980s, it was Sex on the Beach. In the 1930s, it was Symphony of Moist Joy. Sometimes, a drink lives on through the decades and becomes a classic. Other times, a simply fantastic drink fades away only to be found in the yellowed pages of an antique cookbook collecting dust on your grandmother's shelf. Many cocktails were named after Hollywood starlets and notorious rogues who drank at popular Los Angeles haunts in the heyday of silver screen glamour. Many cocktails created before the Prohibition were certainly not for the faint of heart and included absinthe, the legendary liqueur which was later made illegal in the United States. Don't fear—absinthe substitutes remain, but heed this warning: One common theme runs through the drinks of the first half of the twentieth century—heavy on the alcohol, easy on the mixer.

692. ABSINTHE COCKTAIL

Indulge, relax, and witness the magic of wicked little green fairies dancing in your glass.

1 1/2 ounces absinthe
3/4 ounce water
1/4 ounce anisette
Dash orange bitters

1. Fill cocktail shaker with ice.
2. Add absinthe, water, anisette, and bitters.
3. Shake.
4. Strain into a cocktail glass.

693. AMARETTO ALEXANDER

A nutty nightcap for a willing pleasure victim.

1 1/2 ounces amaretto
1 1/2 ounces crème de cacao
1 1/2 ounces cream

1. Fill cocktail shaker with ice.
2. Add amaretto, crème de cacao, and cream.
3. Shake.
4. Strain into a brandy snifter.
5. Garnish with sprinkled nutmeg.

694. BLANCHE

A vintage potable for tragically flawed Southern belles.

3/4 ounce anisette
1/2 ounce Cointreau
1/2 ounce triple sec

1. Fill cocktail shaker with ice.
2. Add anisette, Cointreau, and triple sec.
3. Stir.
4. Strain into a cocktail glass.

695. BANFF

Fun Fact: With snow-capped mountains and sparkling glaciers, Banff National Park is Canada's oldest and most famous national park.

2 ounces Canadian whiskey
1 ounce Grand Marnier
1 ounce Kirsch
Dash Angostura bitters

1. Fill cocktail shaker with ice.
2. Add whiskey, Grand Marnier, Kirsch, and bitters.
3. Stir.
4. Strain into a cocktail glass.
5. Garnish with a lemon twist.

696. WIDOW'S KISS

As mysterious and alluring as its name.

1 ounce apple brandy
3/4 ounce yellow Chartreuse
3/4 ounce Benedictine
Dash Angostura bitters

1. Fill cocktail shaker with ice.
2. Add apple brandy, yellow Chartreuse, Benedictine, and bitters.
3. Shake.
4. Strain into a cocktail glass.
5. Garnish with a strawberry.

697. THE LILY

A drink for those who prefer purity.

3/4 ounce dry gin
3/4 ounce crème de noyaux
3/4 ounce Lillet Blonde
Dash lemon juice

1. Fill cocktail shaker with ice.
2. Add gin, crème de noyaux, and Lillet.
3. Stir.
4. Strain into a cocktail glass.

698. FALLEN ANGEL

(FROM THE VENDOME CLUB IN HOLLYWOOD 1930)

Drink of choice for the good girl gone bad who tossed her shiny halo in a ditch and never looked back.

2 1/2 ounces gin
1/2 ounce white crème de menthe
1/4 ounce lemon juice
2 dashes Angostura bitters

1. Fill a cocktail mixer with ice.
2. Add gin, white crème de menthe, lemon juice, and bitters.
3. Shake.
4. Strain into a chilled martini glass.

699. VIOLET FIZZ

Purple: a color that symbolizes Lent. Good luck giving this one up for forty days.

1 ounce lemon juice
1/2 teaspoon sugar
1 1/2 ounces gin
1/2 ounce crème de violette
Club soda

1. Fill cocktail shaker with ice.
2. Add lemon juice, sugar, gin, and crème de violette.
3. Shake.
4. Strain into a highball glass with ice.
5. Fill with club soda.

700. SOPHIA LOREN

Two of these and your inner Italian starlet shines.

1 teaspoon vermouth
1 ounce orange juice
2 ounces gin
1/2 ounce Campari
2 teaspoons Cointreau

1. Pour vermouth in a tall glass.
2. Swirl to coat inside of glass.
3. Toss out extra vermouth.
4. Fill cocktail shaker with ice.
5. Add orange juice, gin, Campari, and Cointreau.
6. Shake.
7. Strain into the glass filled with ice.

701. NAKED LADY

Odd to begin the night with one of these rather than end it that way.

1 ounce light rum
1 ounce sweet vermouth
4 dashes apricot brandy
2 dashes grenadine
4 dashes lemon juice

1. Fill cocktail shaker with ice.
2. Add rum, vermouth, apricot brandy, grenadine, and lemon juice.
3. Shake.
4. Strain into a cocktail glass.

702. THE PEGU

Signature drink of Burma's Pegu Club. The club fell victim to World War II, but the drink lives on.

1 1/2 ounces gin
1/2 ounce Cointreau
3/4 ounce lime juice
2 dashes Angostura bitters

1. Fill cocktail shaker with ice.
2. Add gin, Cointreau, lime juice, and bitters.
3. Shake.
4. Strain into a chilled cocktail glass.

703. MAIDEN'S PRAYER COCKTAIL

Maidens always pray for a nice boy. With a nice car. And a flask handy.

1/4 teaspoon orange juice
1/4 teaspoon lemon juice
1/4 teaspoon triple sec
2 ounces dry gin

1. Fill cocktail shaker with ice.
2. Add juices, triple sec, and gin.
3. Shake.
4. Strain into a cocktail glass.

704. JACK ROSE

Named for a mysterious chap who created an intoxicating elixir. Kudos to Jack Rose.

1 1/2 ounces apple jack or calvados
1 ounce sugar syrup
3/4 ounce lemon juice
2 dashes grenadine

1. Fill cocktail shaker with ice.
2. Add apple jack (or calvados), sugar syrup, lemon juice, and grenadine.
3. Shake.
4. Strain into a cocktail glass.

705. AVIATION

Enjoy while sitting on the dunes of Kitty Hawk.

1 1/2 ounces gin
1/4 ounce apricot brandy
1/4 ounce maraschino liqueur
1/2 ounce lemon juice

1. Fill cocktail shaker with ice.
2. Add gin, apricot brandy, maraschino liqueur, and lemon juice.
3. Stir.
4. Strain into a cocktail glass.

706. FRISCO SOUR

The official drink of any earthquake party.

2 ounces bourbon
1/2 ounce grenadine
Juice of 1/2 lime
Juice of 1/4 lemon
Club soda

1. Fill cocktail shaker with ice.
2. Add bourbon, grenadine, and juices.
3. Shake.
4. Strain into a sour glass.
5. Fill with club soda.

707. CONTINENTAL

When you dance, you're charming, and you're gentle. While you're up, get me another Continental.

1 1/2 ounces light rum
1/2 ounce lime juice
1/4 ounce green crème de menthe
1/4 teaspoon sugar

1. Fill cocktail shaker with ice.
2. Add rum, lime juice, crème de menthe, and sugar.
3. Shake.
4. Strain into a cocktail glass.

708. SCOFFLAW

True scofflaws drink wherever they want. Whenever they want.

1 ounce Canadian whiskey
1 ounce dry vermouth
Dash orange bitters
Dash grenadine
1/4 ounce lemon juice

1. Fill cocktail shaker with ice.
2. Add whiskey, vermouth, bitters, grenadine, and lemon juice.
3. Stir.
4. Strain into a chilled cocktail glass.

709. ASTORIA

Stately and classic like the hotel that bears its name.

1 1/2 ounces gin
3/4 ounce dry vermouth
Dash orange bitters

1. Fill cocktail shaker with ice.
2. Add gin, vermouth, and bitters.
3. Stir.
4. Strain into a cocktail glass.
5. Garnish with an olive.

710. HI HO COCKTAIL

Starlets and leading men lollygagged and indulged in these at Hollywood's Hi Ho Club. Recapture the moment.

2 ounces gin
1 ounce white port
4 dashes orange bitters

1. Fill a cocktail mixer with ice.
2. Add gin, port, and bitters.
3. Shake.
4. Strain into a chilled cocktail glass.
5. Garnish with a lemon peel.

711. HONEYMOON COCKTAIL

(FROM THE BROWN DERBY, HOLLYWOOD CIRCA 1930)

Created in Hollywood, the town that practically invented "happily ever after."

2 ounces apple jack
1/2 ounce Benedictine
1/2 ounce orange curacao
1/2 ounce fresh lemon juice

1. Fill a cocktail mixer with ice.
2. Add apple jack, Benedictine, curacao, and lemon juice.
3. Shake.
4. Strain into a chilled cocktail glass.
5. Garnish with a lemon peel.

712. DOUGLAS FAIRBANKS

Guaranteed to play a leading role in your night's activities.

1 1/2 ounces gin
1 ounce apricot brandy
1/2 ounce lime juice
3/4 ounce egg white

1. Fill cocktail shaker with ice.
2. Add gin, brandy, lime juice, and egg white.
3. Shake very well.
4. Strain into a chilled cocktail glass.

713. PARK AVENUE COCKTAIL

First choice of the poodle crowd.

1 1/2 ounces gin
1/2 ounce pineapple juice
1/4 ounce sweet vermouth
1/4 ounce orange curacao

1. Fill cocktail shaker with ice.
2. Add gin, pineapple juice, vermouth, and curacao.
3. Shake.
4. Strain into a cocktail glass.

714. BEE'S KISS

This drink's slight sting is quickly masked by its sticky-sweet finish.

1 1/2 ounces light rum
1/2 ounce honey
1/2 ounce cream

1. Fill cocktail shaker with ice.
2. Add rum, honey, and cream.
3. Shake.
4. Strain into a cocktail glass.

715. FLORIDITA

A favorite of Papa Hemingway and other old men by the sea.

1 ounce lime juice
2 ounces light rum
1/4 ounce grapefruit juice
1/4 ounce maraschino liqueur
1/2 teaspoon sugar

1. Fill cocktail shaker with ice.
2. Add lime juice, rum, grapefruit juice, maraschino liqueur, and sugar.
3. Shake.
4. Strain into a cocktail glass.

716. EL DIABLO

The Mexican devil that will cha-cha on your head.

1 1/2 ounces tequila
1/2 ounce crème de cassis
1/2 ounce lime juice
Ginger ale

1. Fill cocktail shaker with ice.
2. Add tequila, crème de cassis, and lime juice.
3. Shake.
4. Strain into a highball glass with ice.
5. Fill with ginger ale.
6. Garnish with lime wedge.

717. BROWN DERBY COCKTAIL

In the 1945 cinema classic Mildred Pierce, *Joan Crawford said of this Hollywood hot spot, "People have to drink somewhere. Why not here?"*

1/2 ounce whiskey
1/4 ounce grapefruit juice
1/4 ounce honey

1. Fill cocktail glass with ice.
2. Add whiskey, grapefruit juice, and honey.
3. Shake.
4. Strain into a cocktail glass.

718. WHEEL OF FORTUNE

Raise a glass to Lady Luck and hope she bestows a free spin on the golden wheel.

1 1/2 ounces sambuca
1 ounce brandy

1. Fill cocktail shaker with ice.
2. Add sambuca and brandy.
3. Stir.
4. Strain into a cocktail glass.
5. Garnish with a lemon twist.

719. WHISKEY DAISY

Oopsy Daisy! I'm drunk!

2 ounces blended whiskey
1/2 teaspoon powdered sugar
1 teaspoon grenadine
Juice 1/2 lemon

1. Fill cocktail shaker with ice.
2. Add whiskey, powdered sugar, grenadine, and lemon juice.
3. Shake.
4. Strain into a beer mug with one ice cube.
5. Garnish with a cherry and an orange slice.

720. MARLENE DIETRICH COCKTAIL

"No girly drinks for this starlet. I am, at heart," said Ms. Dietrich, "a gentleman."

3/4 wineglass of rye or Canadian whiskey
2 dashes Angostura bitters
2 dashes curacao

1. Fill cocktail shaker with ice.
2. Add whiskey, bitters, and curacao.
3. Shake.
4. Strain into a cocktail glass.
5. Squeeze orange and lemon peel on top.

721. DEVIL'S TORCH

Go toward the flame...burns a little, but it's well worth the pain.

1 1/2 ounces vodka
1 1/2 ounces dry vermouth
3 dashes grenadine

1. Fill cocktail shaker with ice.
2. Add vodka, vermouth, and grenadine.
3. Shake.
4. Strain into a chilled cocktail glass.
5. Garnish with a lemon peel.

722. DIXIE WHISKEY

Old times here are not forgotten. At least not until the fourth glass.

1 1/2 ounces bourbon
1/2 ounce orange curacao
1/4 ounce white crème de menthe
2 dashes Angostura bitters
3/4 ounce lemon juice

1. Fill cocktail shaker with ice.
2. Add bourbon, orange curacao, white crème de menthe, bitters, and lemon juice.
3. Shake.
4. Strain into a martini glass.

723. EMBASSY COCKTAIL

The drink that launched a thousand treaties.

3/4 ounce brandy
3/4 ounce Cointreau
3/4 ounce Jamaican rum
1/2 ounce lime juice
Dash Angostura bitters

1. Fill cocktail shaker with ice.
2. Add bourbon, Cointreau, rum, lime juice, and bitters.
3. Shake.
4. Strain into a chilled martini glass.
5. Garnish with a lime wedge.

724. WHIZ BANG

Drink this, and you get a very pleasant whiz-bang feeling bouncing around in your head. Do not be alarmed.

2 ounces scotch
1/2 ounce dry vermouth
2 dashes grenadine
2 dashes Pernod
2 dashes orange bitters

1. Fill cocktail shaker with ice.
2. Add scotch, vermouth, grenadine, Pernod, and bitters.
3. Shake.
4. Strain into a chilled martini glass.

725. SAVANNAH COCKTAIL

Drink these at midnight in the garden of good and evil.

Juice of 1 orange
1 1/2 ounces dry gin
1 egg white
Dash crème de cacao

1. Fill cocktail shaker with ice.
2. Add orange, gin, egg white, and crème de cacao.
3. Shake.
4. Strain into a claret glass.

726. VENDOME

The Vendome was a Los Angeles nightclub to remember. One suspects that this cocktail selection has made more than one person forget.

1 ounce red Dubonnet
1 ounce gin
1 ounce dry vermouth

1. Fill cocktail shaker with ice.
2. Add Dubonnet, gin, and vermouth.
3. Stir.
4. Strain into a chilled cocktail glass.
5. Garnish with a lemon peel.

727. STORK CLUB COCKTAIL

Opened in 1929 as an NYC speakeasy, this swanky night spot was the site of many cagey shenanigans and illicit romances. Toast it!

1 1/2 ounces gin
1/2 ounce triple sec
1/4 ounce lime juice
1 ounce orange juice
Dash Angostura bitters

1. Fill cocktail shaker with ice.
2. Add gin, triple sec, juices, and bitters.
3. Shake.
4. Strain into a martini glass.
5. Garnish with an orange peel.

728. SOUTH COAST COCKTAIL

A drink for any coastal tourist or those luckless enough to be landlocked.

2 1/2 ounces scotch
1/2 ounce curacao
1/2 ounce lemon juice
1/4 ounce sugar syrup
2 1/2 ounces club soda

1. Fill cocktail shaker with ice.
2. Add scotch, curacao, lemon juice, sugar syrup, and club soda.
3. Stir.
4. Strain into two chilled martini glasses.
5. Garnish with a flame orange peel.

(Serves 2)

729. SATAN'S WHISKERS

He keeps 'em neatly trimmed, but they still manage to tickle a bit. Especially the morning after.

1 ounce gin
1/2 ounce sweet vermouth
1/2 ounce dry vermouth
1/2 ounce Grand Marnier
1 ounce orange juice
Dash Angostura bitters

1. Fill cocktail shaker with ice.
2. Add gin, vermouths, Grand Marnier, orange juice, and bitters.
3. Shake.
4. Strain into a chilled martini glass.
5. Garnish with an orange peel.

730. LOS ANGELES COCKTAIL

One sip, and you'll see why L.A. is known as the City of Angels.

1 1/2 ounces bourbon
1/4 ounce sweet vermouth
1 ounce sugar syrup
1 small egg
1/2 ounce lemon juice

1. Fill cocktail shaker with ice.
2. Add bourbon, sweet vermouth, sugar syrup, egg, and lemon juice.
3. Shake extra well.
4. Strain into a chilled port glass.
5. Dust with nutmeg.

731. HONOLULU COCKTAIL

Okole Maluna! (Bottoms Up!)

2 ounces gin
1/2 ounce pineapple juice
1/2 ounce orange juice
1/4 ounce lemon juice
1/4 ounce sugar syrup
Dash Angostura bitters

1. Fill cocktail shaker with ice.
2. Add gin, juices, sugar syrup, and bitters.
3. Shake.
4. Strain into a sugar-rimmed chilled martini glass.
5. Garnish with a lemon peel.

732. CHARLIE CHAPLIN

This little tramp will make your mustache wiggle.

1 1/2 ounces lime juice
1 1/2 ounces sloe gin
1 1/2 ounces apricot brandy

1. Fill cocktail shaker with ice.
2. Add lime juice, sloe gin, and brandy.
3. Shake.
4. Strain into a cocktail glass.

733. CREOLE

Spicy and feisty...a drink that fights back.

1 1/2 ounces light rum
Dash Tabasco sauce
1 teaspoon lemon juice
1 1/2 ounces beef bouillon
Salt and pepper to taste

1. Fill cocktail shaker with ice.
2. Add rum, Tabasco sauce, lemon juice, beef bouillon, salt, and pepper.
3. Shake.
4. Strain into an old-fashioned glass with ice.

734. CORONATION '37

Created to commemorate the crowning of King George VI, who became King of England after the unexpected abdication of his brother, King Edward VIII. Lucky devil.

1 1/8 ounces gin
1 1/8 ounces orange curacao
1 1/8 ounces rum
1 1/8 ounces lemon juice

1. Fill cocktail shaker with ice.
2. Add gin, curacao, rum, and lemon juice.
3. Shake.
4. Strain into a cocktail glass.

735. FLORIDA

Believe it or not, this drink has no oranges. Crazy, but good.

1 1/2 ounces grapefruit juice
3/4 ounce Galliano
1 ounce gin
1/4 ounce Campari

1. Fill cocktail shaker with ice.
2. Add grapefruit juice, Galliano, gin, and Campari.
3. Shake.
4. Strain into cocktail glass.
5. Garnish with an orange slice.

736. HARVARD

Drink this one and start talking like a Hah-vahd grad.

1 1/2 ounces brandy
3/4 ounce sweet vermouth
Dash Angostura bitters
1 teaspoon grenadine
2 teaspoons lemon juice

1. Fill cocktail shaker with ice.
2. Add brandy, vermouth, bitters, grenadine, and lemon juice.
3. Stir.
4. Strain into a cocktail glass.

737. MARCONI WIRELESS

Fun fact: Guglielmo Marconi first offered his radio signal invention to the Italians. They turned him down. So he moved to England where in 1898, he flashed the results of the Kingstown Regatta to a Dublin newspaper.

1 1/2 ounces apple brandy
1/2 ounce sweet vermouth
2 dashes orange bitters

1. Fill cocktail shaker with ice.
2. Add apple brandy, vermouth, and bitters.
3. Shake.
4. Strain into a chilled cocktail glass.

738. METROPOLITAN

Sipped in the dark confines of sophisticated urban watering holes everywhere.

1 1/4 ounce brandy
1 1/4 ounce sweet vermouth
1/2 teaspoon sugar syrup
Dash of Angostura bitters

1. Fill cocktail shaker with ice.
2. Add brandy, vermouth, sugar syrup, and bitters.
3. Stir.
4. Strain into a cocktail glass.

739. 1915

With World War I gearing up and Prohibition on its way, tavern-dwellers had precious little time to enjoy this cocktail—but they gave it their best.

1 1/2 ounces curacao
1 1/2 ounces cream
1 1/2 ounces gin

1. Fill cocktail shaker with ice.
2. Add curacao, cream, and gin.
3. Shake.
4. Strain into a cocktail glass.

740. RAINBOW POUSSE CAFÉ

This rainbow comes complete with a pot o' gold.

1/4 ounce grenadine
1/4 ounce maraschino liqueur
1/4 ounce green crème de menthe
1/4 ounce yellow Chartreuse
1/4 ounce curacao
1/4 ounce brandy

1. Layer carefully in the above order in a pousse café glass.

741. BABY TITTY

Order and proceed to giggle.

2/3 ounce anisette
2/3 ounce crème de yvette
2/3 ounce whipped cream
Cherry

1. Layer the ingredients in the above order in a sherry glass.
2. Add a cherry.

742. CHRYSANTHEMUM COCKTAIL

Fun fact: In Japanese culture, the chrysanthemum is a symbol of perfection.

1 ounce Benedictine
1 ounce dry vermouth
1 teaspoon absinthe

1. Fill cocktail shaker with ice.
2. Add Benedictine, vermouth, and absinthe.
3. Shake.
4. Strain into a cocktail glass.

743. GILROY

Not to be confused with Kilroy.

Juice of 1/4 lemon
1/2 ounce dry vermouth
3/4 ounce cherry brandy
3/4 ounce dry gin
Dash of orange bitters

1. Fill cocktail shaker with ice.
2. Add lemon, vermouth, brandy, gin, and bitters.
3. Stir.
4. Strain into a cocktail glass.

744. GIN & IT

It, presumably, being vermouth.

2 ounces dry gin
1 ounce sweet vermouth

1. Pour gin and vermouth in a cocktail shaker.
2. Stir with no ice.
3. Pour into cocktail glass.

745. GOLDEN GATE COCKTAIL

Cool as an October night on the bay.

1 1/2 ounces dry gin
1 scoop orange sherbet

1. Fill cocktail shaker with ice.
2. Add gin and sherbet.
3. Shake.
4. Strain into a cocktail glass.

746. MOON RAKER

Share this with her, and you just might fly to the moon. Careful not to burn up on re-entry.

3/4 ounce brandy
3/4 ounce red Dubonnet
3/4 ounce peach brandy
1/4 ounce pastis

1. Fill cocktail shaker with ice.
2. Add brandy, Dubonnet, brandy, and pastis.
3. Shake.
4. Strain into a cocktail glass.

747. MONKEY GLAND

Fun fact: Believe it or not, this drink is named for a late-nineteenth-century practice of transplanting simian testicles into impotent men. No word on whether it worked, but a Russian doctor became very rich.

3 ounces dry gin
1 1/2 ounces orange juice
2 dashes absinthe
2 dashes grenadine

1. Fill cocktail shaker with ice.
2. Add gin, orange juice, absinthe, and grenadine.
3. Shake.
4. Strain into a cocktail glass.

748. RED DEVIL

"The devil is most devilish when respectable." —Elizabeth Barrett Browning

2 ounces Irish whiskey
Dash Worcestershire sauce
1 1/2 ounces clam juice
1 1/2 ounces tomato juice
1/4 ounce lime juice

1. Fill cocktail shaker with ice.
2. Add whiskey, Worcestershire sauce, and all juices.
3. Shake.
4. Strain into a highball glass with ice.
5. Sprinkle with pinch of pepper.

749. SYMPHONY OF MOIST JOY

One really cool aspect of being a composer: getting an entire orchestra to perform in harmonious rhythm, about any subject you choose.

1/4 ounce grenadine
1/4 ounce green crème de menthe
1/4 ounce yellow Chartreuse
1/4 ounce cognac

1. Build grenadine, crème de menthe, Chartreuse, and cognac in a cordial glass.

750. LOVING CUP

Winner takes all!

6 ounces shaved ice
1 1/2 ounces passion fruit
2 ounces dry vermouth
4 ounces white rum
4 ounces champagne

1. Fill cocktail shaker with 6 ounces ice.
2. Add passion fruit, vermouth, and rum.
3. Shake.
4. Fill a loving cup with ice.
5. Add passion fruit mixture into the loving cup.
6. Decorate with a half peach, red and green cherries, and 4 colored straws.
7. Add 4 ounces champagne.

751. SIX FEET UNDER

You'd have to be six feet under to refuse another glass of this.

1 1/2 ounces Bacardi rum
1 1/2 ounces Swedish punch
1 1/2 ounces calvados

1. Fill cocktail shaker with ice.
2. Add rum, Swedish punch, and calavdos.
3. Shake.
4. Strain into a cocktail glass.
5. Squeeze orange peel on top.

752. HOT TODDY

Classic cure for the flu.

1 teaspoon sugar
3 whole cloves
1 cinnamon stick
1 thin lemon slice
1 ounce bourbon
4 ounces boiling water

1. Put sugar, cloves, cinnamon stick, and lemon slice in a heat-resistant mug.
2. Add 1 ounce boiling water.
3. Stir.
4. Let stand for 5 minutes.
5. Add bourbon and 3 ounces boiling water.
6. Stir.
7. Dust with nutmeg.

753. ZAZA

Made famous by the Astoria Hotel, this drink was a popular Depression-era cocktail.

1 3/4 ounces gin
3/4 ounce red Dubonnet

1. Fill cocktail shaker with ice.
2. Add gin and Dubonnet.
3. Stir.
4. Strain into a cocktail glass.

754. PRINCESS MARY

A drink for ladies who fancy the lush life.

1 1/2 ounces crème de cacao
1 1/2 ounces cream
1 1/2 ounces dry gin

1. Fill cocktail shaker with ice.
2. Add crème de cacao, cream, and gin.
3. Stir.
4. Strain into a cocktail glass.

755. ROYAL SMILE

"Grin, wave to the subjects...turn...grin, wave to the subjects..."

1 ounce apple jack
1/2 ounce gin
1/2 ounce lemon juice
1/2 ounce grenadine

1. Fill cocktail shaker with ice.
2. Add apple jack, gin, lemon juice, and grenadine.
3. Shake.
4. Strain into a cocktail glass.

756. WEDDING BELLE

A true southern belle serves this at each of her weddings.

3/4 ounce gin
3/4 ounce red Dubonnet
1/2 ounce orange juice
1/2 ounce cherry brandy

1. Fill cocktail shaker with ice.
2. Add gin, Dubonnet, orange juice, and cherry brandy.
3. Shake.
4. Strain into a cocktail glass.

757. GIGOLO COCKTAIL

The go-to drink for gigolos of all eras.

1 teaspoon honey
1 ounce cream
1 ounce parfait amour

1. Pour honey and cream into a cocktail glass.
2. Stir.
2. Add parfait amour.
3. Stir.
4. Dust with freshly grated nutmeg.

758. COCONUT GROVE

(FROM 1940S HOLLYWOOD NIGHTCLUB, THE
COCONUT GROVE)

*Indulge in these in a private cabana. No one will know
you're being naughty.*

1 1/2 ounces sweet vermouth
1 1/2 ounces dry vermouth
1 1/2 ounces dry gin

1. Fill cocktail shaker with ice.
2. Add vermouths and gin.
3. Shake.
4. Strain into a cocktail glass.
5. Garnish with a pineapple slice.

759. SARDI'S DELIGHT

Located near Broadway, this landmark NYC restaurant features walls covered with sketches of stars. The perfect drink for a well-planned Oscar party.

1 1/2 ounces gin
1/4 ounce passion fruit juice
1/4 ounce lemon juice
1/4 ounce grenadine
1/4 ounce pastis
Dash Angostura bitters

1. Fill cocktail shaker with ice.
2. Add gin, juices, grenadine, pastis, and bitters.
3. Shake.
4. Strain into a cocktail glass.

760. MAX BAER COCKTAIL

Named for a heavyweight boxing champion with an equally famous son, Max Baer, Jr. —Jethro on The Beverly Hillbillies.

1 ounce gin
1 ounce apple brandy
1/4 ounce grenadine
1/4 ounce pastis

1. Fill cocktail shaker with ice.
2. Add gin, apple brandy, grenadine, and pastis.
3. Stir.
4. Strain into a cocktail glass.

761. MONTMARTRE SPECIAL COCKTAIL

A fitting tribute to the highest hill in Paris.

3 ounces Bacardi rum
1 1/2 ounces cream
Dash grenadine

1. Fill cocktail shaker with ice.
2. Add rum, cream, and grenadine.
3. Shake.
4. Strain into a cocktail glass.

762. CABLEGRAM

Order up. STOP. Drink. STOP. Order another. DON'T STOP.

2 ounces blended whiskey
Juice of 1/2 lemon
1/2 teaspoon sugar
4 ounces ginger ale

1. Fill cocktail shaker with ice.
2. Add whiskey, lemon juice, and sugar.
3. Shake.
4. Strain into a highball glass with crushed ice.
5. Fill with ginger ale.
6. Garnish with a lemon twist.

763. CORONATION

King me!

8 ounces sherry
8 ounces vermouth
Dash maraschino liqueur
2 dashes orange bitters

1. Fill cocktail shaker with ice.
2. Add sherry, vermouth, maraschino liqueur, and bitters.
3. Shake.
4. Strain into a pint glass.

764. HUNTRESS COCKTAIL

For all modern-day Dianas, mistresses of the hunt.

3/4 ounce bourbon
3/4 ounce cherry liqueur
1 teaspoon triple sec
1 ounce cream

1. Fill cocktail shaker with ice.
2. Add bourbon, cherry liqueur, triple sec, and cream.
3. Shake.
4. Strain into a chilled cocktail glass.

765. ETHEL DUFFY

For brazen women everywhere who won't take no for an answer.

1 ounce apricot brandy
3/4 ounce white crème de menthe
3/4 ounce curacao

1. Fill cocktail shaker with ice.
2. Add brandy, crème de menthe, and curacao.
3. Shake.
4. Strain into a cocktail glass.

766. PEGGY COCKTAIL

The early twentieth century song says, "Peg o' my heart, I love you, We'll never part for I love you, dear little girl, sweet little girl, sweeter than the Rose of Erin." This drink will have you echoing those sentiments.

1 1/2 ounces gin
3/4 ounce dry vermouth
1/4 ounce pastis
1/4 ounce red Dubonnet

1. Fill cocktail shaker with ice.
2. Add gin, vermouth, pastis, and Dubonnet.
3. Stir.
4. Strain into a cocktail glass.

767. PRESIDENT ROOSEVELT COCKTAIL

Both President Roosevelts enjoyed a cocktail. This one calls for a fireside chat about world affairs.

1 1/2 ounces light rum
1 ounce orange juice
Dash grenadine

1. Fill cocktail shaker with ice.
2. Add rum, orange juice, and grenadine.
3. Shake.
4. Strain into a cocktail glass.

768. ROSCOE TURNER COCKTAIL

Named for the greatest air racing pilot of the Golden Age. On your mark, get set...Jet!

1 1/2 ounces lemon juice
3 ounces gin
2 dashes of maraschino liqueur

1. Fill cocktail shaker with ice.
2. Add lemon juice, gin, and maraschino liqueur.
3. Shake.
4. Strain into a cocktail glass.
5. Garnish with a cherry.

769. GINGER ROGERS

Dances gracefully across your palate.

1 1/2 ounces dry vermouth
1 1/2 ounces dry gin
1 1/2 ounces apricot brandy
4 dashes of lemon juice

1. Fill cocktail shaker with ice.
2. Add vermouth, gin, apricot brandy, and lemon juice.
3. Shake.
4. Strain into a cocktail glass.
5. Garnish with a cherry.

770. HESITATION COCKTAIL

This will buy you a few more seconds to decide which direction to go—down the aisle or out the door.

Dash of lemon juice
1 ounce whiskey
3 ounces Swedish punch

1. Fill cocktail shaker with ice.
2. Add lemon juice, whiskey, and Swedish punch.
3. Shake.
4. Strain into a cocktail glass.

771. JOHNNY WEISMULLER

Me Tarzan. You Jane. Want drink?

1 1/2 ounces gin
1 1/2 ounces Bacardi rum
1 1/2 ounces lemon juice
Dash of grenadine
1/2 teaspoon powdered sugar

1. Fill cocktail shaker with ice.
2. Add gin, rum, lemon juice, grenadine, and powdered sugar.
3. Shake.
4. Strain into a cocktail glass.

772. JEAN HARLOW COCKTAIL

Spencer Tracy said of her, "A square shooter if there ever was one." Raise your glass to this silent film diva.

2 ounces Bacardi rum
2 ounces sweet vermouth

1. Fill cocktail shaker with ice.
2. Add rum and vermouth.
3. Shake.
4. Strain into a cocktail glass.
5. Garnish with a lemon peel.

773. SAUCY SUE COCKTAIL

We like 'em like this. The saucier, the better.

1/2 teaspoon apricot brandy
1/2 teaspoon absinthe
2 ounces apple jack

1. Fill cocktail shaker with ice.
2. Add apricot brandy, absinthe, and apple jack.
3. Stir.
4. Strain into a cocktail glass.

774. FIFTH AVENUE

Finish this one up and head to Saks.

1/3 ounce crème de cacao
1/3 ounce apricot nectar
1/3 ounce cream

1. Carefully layer in a cordial glass.

775. HAVANA

Made especially for enjoying on snow white Cuban beaches.

1 1/4 ounces pineapple juice
3/4 ounce rum
1/2 teaspoon lemon juice

1. Fill cocktail shaker with ice.
2. Add rum and juices.
3. Shake.
4. Strain into a cocktail glass.

776. BRANDY MILK PUNCH

Who knew you could visit the bar and build healthy teeth and bones at the same time? Does a body good!

1 teaspoon powdered sugar
2 ounces brandy
1/2 pint milk

1. Fill cocktail shaker with ice.
2. Add powdered sugar, brandy, and milk.
3. Shake.
4. Strain into a collins glass.
5. Dust with nutmeg.

777. FRANKENJACK COCKTAIL

Not nearly as frightening as the name might suggest. Just don't turn your back on it.

1 ounce dry gin
3/4 ounce dry vermouth
1/2 ounce apricot brandy
1 teaspoon triple sec

1. Fill cocktail shaker with ice.
2. Add gin, vermouth, apricot brandy, and triple sec.
3. Stir.
4. Strain into a cocktail glass.
5. Garnish with triple sec.

778. HOT BUTTERED RUM

A winter classic best sipped by the fire with family and friends.

2 ounces rum
Square of butter
1 sugar cube
Water, boiling

1. Place sugar cube into heat-resistant mug.
2. Fill two-thirds with boiling water.
3. Add butter and rum.
4. Stir.
5. Dust with nutmeg.

779. MERRY WIDOW COCKTAIL

As *Helen Rowland once said, "A widow is a fascinating being with the flavor of maturity, the spice of experience, the piquancy of novelty, the tang of practiced coquetry, and the halo of one man's approval." We couldn't have said it any better.*

1 1/4 ounces dry gin
1 1/4 ounces dry vermouth
1/2 teaspoon Benedictine
1/2 teaspoon absinthe
Dash of Orange bitters

1. Fill cocktail shaker with ice.
2. Add gin, vermouth, Benedictine, absinthe, and bitters.
3. Stir.
4. Strain into a cocktail glass.
5. Garnish with a lemon peel.

780. MILLION DOLLAR COCKTAIL

If your name is Rockefeller, you get to run a tab.

1 1/2 ounces bourbon
1/2 ounce curacao
1/4 teaspoon grenadine
1 egg white

1. Fill cocktail shaker with ice.
2. Add bourbon, curacao, grenadine, and egg white.
3. Shake.
4. Strain into a cocktail glass.

781. MIKADO COCKTAIL

For intermission at the opera house.

2 ounces brandy
1/2 teaspoon crème de cacao
1/2 teaspoon curacao
2 dashes of Angostura bitters

1. Fill cocktail shaker with ice.
2. Add brandy, crème de cacao, curacao, and bitters.
3. Shake.
4. Strain into a cocktail glass.

782. MORNING GLORY FIZZ

What's the story, Morning Glory?

2 ounces scotch
1/2 teaspoon absinthe
1 egg white
1 teaspoon powdered sugar
Juice of 1/2 lemon
Club soda

1. Fill cocktail shaker with ice.
2. Add scotch, absinthe, egg white, powdered sugar, and lemon.
3. Shake.
4. Strain into a highball glass.
5. Fill with club soda.

783. POLLYANNA COCKTAIL

Go ahead and order it. The glass is half full, and everything will work out just fine.

3 slices pineapple
3 slices orange
2 ounces dry gin
1/2 ounce sweet vermouth
1/2 teaspoon grenadine

1. Muddle pineapple and orange slices.
2. Put mixture into a cocktail glass.
3. Fill cocktail shaker with ice.
4. Add gin, vermouth, and grenadine.
5. Shake.
6. Strain into the cocktail glass.

784. SEVILLA COCKTAIL

A delicious delight from southern Spain.

1 ounce rum
1 ounce port
1 egg
1/2 teaspoon powdered sugar

1. Fill cocktail shaker with ice.
2. Add rum, port, egg, and powdered sugar.
3. Shake.
4. Strain into a cocktail glass.

785. UNION JACK COCKTAIL

Hail, Britannia!

1 1/2 ounces dry gin
3/4 ounce crème de yvette
1/2 teaspoon grenadine

1. Fill cocktail shaker with ice.
2. Add gin, crème de yvette, and grenadine.
3. Shake.
4. Strain into a cocktail glass.

786. CHARLIE ROSE

If we ever get invited onto his talk show, we'll be sure to bring some of these to break the ice.

1 ounce brandy
Lemon slice

1. Pour brandy into a pony glass.
2. Add lemon slice on top.

787. FAIRY BELLE COCKTAIL

A magical, pixie-dusted place where fairy dreams come true. The drinker will float there on gossamer wings.

1 egg white
1 teaspoon grenadine
1 ounce apricot liqueur
3 ounces dry gin

1. Fill cocktail shaker with ice.
2. Add egg white, grenadine, apricot liqueur, and gin.
3. Shake.
4. Strain into a cocktail glass.

788. JUPITER COCKTAIL

This largest of the planets features one big red eye. You may end up with two.

1 teaspoon orange juice
1 teaspoon parfait amour
1/2 ounce dry vermouth
1 1/2 ounces dry gin

1. Fill cocktail shaker with ice.
2. Add orange juice, parfait amour, vermouth, and gin.
3. Shake.
4. Strain into a cocktail glass.

789. SABBATH CALM

Sip liberally on the day of rest.

1 ounce brandy
1 ounce coffee
1 ounce port
1 whole egg
1/2 teaspoon sugar
2 ounces cream

1. Fill cocktail shaker with ice.
2. Add brandy, coffee, port, egg, and sugar.
3. Add cream.
4. Shake.
5. Strain into a goblet.
6. Dash with nutmeg.

790. PANZERWAGEN

A model of German efficiency. Smooth as silk and purrs like a kitten.

1/2 ounce vodka
1/2 ounce gin
1/2 ounce Cointreau

1. Fill cocktail shaker with ice.
2. Add vodka, gin, and Cointreau.
3. Shake.
4. Strain into a cocktail glass.
5. Serve with side of green olives and almonds.

791. LOTUS CLUB COCKTAIL

Fun fact: Lotus flowers, native to Asia, have long symbolized spiritual enlightenment.

1 lump sugar
2 to 3 drops Angostura bitters
Dash Pernod
2 ounces whiskey

1. Muddle a lump of sugar with a few drops of bitters in cocktail shaker.
2. Add a dash of Pernod and whiskey.
3. Stir.
4. Pour over one ice cube in an old-fashioned glass.
5. Garnish with lime peel.

792. TANGO

Named after the tango craze of 1915, certainly meant to make you hit the dance floor. In more ways than one.

1 1/2 ounces gin
1 1/2 ounces sweet vermouth
1 egg white

1. Fill cocktail shaker with ice.
2. Add gin, vermouth, and egg white.
3. Shake.
4. Strain into a cocktail glass.

9

TEMPTING TIPPLES FOR FESTIVE FROLICS—
'Tis the Season

Your friend calls and insists that you throw a Fourth of July party. She suggests you serve more than beer and wine this time. The creative stakes are high but not impossible. Move beyond the traditional drinks for summer celebrations, yuletide gatherings, and even Easter events. Try a funky cocktail called The Betsy Ross for Independence Day or The Black Turncoat for a Cinco de Mayo bash. For the most romantic holiday of the year—Valentine's Day—think outside the champagne and chocolate box. Wow your honey with a glass of Red Hot Passion or a Soul Kiss, sure to make the heart, and senses, melt. Often, traditional holidays like Christmas call for traditional drinks like eggnog and wassail, but you can add an international twist to the family feast by introducing the German "Gluhwein." Bottoms up!

YULETIDE DRINKS

793. POINSETTIA

Unlike its namesake, this cocktail is hardly poisonous to its drinker.

2 ounces lemon-flavored vodka
8 ounces cranberry juice
Splash champagne

1. Fill cocktail shaker with ice.
2. Add vodka and cranberry juice.
3. Shake.
4. Strain into a martini glass.
5. Splash with champagne.
(Serves 2)

794. SHERRY COBBLER

Santa Claus likes for a sherry to greet him in England on Christmas Eve. Not milk.

2 ounces club soda
1 teaspoon sugar
2 1/2 ounces sherry
1/2 ounce orange juice

1. Fill a double old-fashioned glass with crushed ice.
2. Add club soda, sugar, sherry, and orange juice.
3. Garnish with fruit.

795. SNOW BUNNY

Every man hopes to find one of these on his ski weekend getaway.

1 1/2 ounces triple sec
Hot chocolate

1. Pour triple sec into a heavy mug.
2. Fill with hot chocolate.
3. Garnish with a cinnamon stick.

796. PEPPERMINT STICK

If you've been good, maybe you'll find one of these waiting for you before bedtime on Christmas Eve.

1 ounce peppermint schnapps
1 1/2 ounces white crème de menthe
1 ounce light cream

1. Fill cocktail shaker with ice.
2. Add schnapps, crème de menthe, and cream.
3. Shake.
4. Strain into a champagne flute.

797. ICEBALL

Avoid getting hit in the head with one of these in a snow-ball fight, but be sure to mix one up for an evening relaxing by the fire.

1 1/2 ounces gin
3/4 ounce white crème de menthe
3/4 ounce sambuca
2 to 3 teaspoons cream
3 ounces crushed ice

1. Pour gin, crème de menthe, sambuca, cream, and ice in a blender.
2. Blend for 15 seconds at medium speed until smooth.
3. Pour into a goblet.

798. WASSAIL

If some yells "wassail" during the holidays, the proper reply is "be in good health."

2 quarts apple cider
1/2 cup brown sugar
1 1/3 cups lemon juice
6 cinnamon sticks
12 whole cloves
12 whole allspice
1 1/2 teaspoons nutmeg
2 fifths dry sherry

1. Place apple cider, brown sugar, lemon juice, and all spices in a pot.
2. Bring to a boil.
3. Cover and simmer for 20 minutes.
4. Remove spices from mixture.
5. Add sherry.
6. Heat until just below boiling.
7. Fill a punch bowl with boiling water.
8. Let stand for one minute to heat bowl.
9. Pour water out of punch bowl.
10. Pour wassail mixture from stove to punch bowl.
11. Garnish with orange or lemon slices studded with cloves.

(Serves 25)

799. WINTER SPARKLER

A bubbly concoction designed to lighten up any family festivity.

Juice of 1 lemon
Juice of 1 lime
8 ounces Southern Comfort
8 ounces peach schnapps
2 fifths brut champagne
3 peaches
30 whole cloves
Ice block

1. Place ice in punch bowl.
2. Add juices.
3. Add peach schnapps and Southern Comfort.
4. Stir.
5. Stud peach skins with cloves and add to bowl.
6. Add champagne.
7. Stir gently.
(Serves 25)

800. MULLED WINE

Fun Fact: Mull is an old English word for "dust," which explains why the drink is dusted with so many spices.

3/5 red wine
Juice of one orange
1/2 teaspoon nutmeg
1/2 teaspoon cinnamon
1/2 teaspoon powdered cloves
2 tablespoons whole cloves

1. Pour wine, juice of the orange, and all spices into a pot.
2. Heat until warm.
3. Pour into mugs.
4. Add honey or brown sugar to taste.
(*Serves 12–15*)

801. BLIZZARD

Floridian snow birds can enjoy these frosty nips on the patio at Christmas while the rest of the country freezes.

3 ounces bourbon
1 ounce cranberry juice
1 tablespoon lemon juice
2 tablespoons sugar syrup
3 ounces crushed ice

1. Pour bourbon, juices, sugar syrup, and ice into blender.
2. Blend on low speed until smooth.
3. Pour into a large wineglass or a highball glass.

802. CHRISTMAS CHEER

Ready? Okay! Give me an S! A! N! T! A! Go Santa!

1 gallon apple cider
8 cinnamon sticks
1 1/2 cups rum
1 cup applejack
3/4 cup apple schnapps

1. Bring cider and cinnamon to a boil in a pot.
2. Reduce heat and add rum, applejack, and apple schnapps.
3. Stir until heated.
4. Serve in pousse café glasses.
5 .Garnish with cinnamon sticks.
(Serves 50)

803. CHRISTMAS WONDERLAND

It's a beautiful sight, we're drinking tonight…stumbling in a Christmas wonderland.

1 ounce vanilla vodka
1 ounce crème de cacao
1 ounce green crème de menthe

1. Fill cocktail shaker with ice.
2. Add vodka, crème de cacao, and crème de menthe.
3. Shake.
4. Strain into a chilled cocktail glass.

804. SILK STOCKINGS

Mrs. Claus's preferred nightcap after Santa's big sleigh ride.

2 ounces tequila
1 ounce crème de cacao
2 ounces light cream
Dash grenadine

1. Fill cocktail shaker with ice.
2. Add tequila, crème de cacao, cream, and grenadine.
3. Shake.
4. Strain into a chilled cocktail glass.
5. Dust with cinnamon.

805. SNOWBALL

No need to cross your fingers. You do have a chance in hell of tasting one of these.

1 ounce gin
1/4 ounce white crème de cacao
1/4 ounce Pernod
1/4 ounce crème de yvette
1/4 ounce cream

1. Fill cocktail shaker with ice.
2. Add gin, crème de cacao, Pernod, crème de yvette, and cream.
3. Shake.
4. Strain into a chilled deep-saucer champagne glass.

806. GLUHWEIN

A German "glowing wine" to share with your fräulein.

5 ounces claret wine or sweet red wine
1 sugar cube
Dash Angostura bitters
Juice of 1/2 lemon
Dash cinnamon
Dash nutmeg

1. Simmer all ingredients in a pot on the stove until just boiling.
2. Pour into a glass coffee mug.

807. GLOGG

A classic Scandinavian hot spiced wine punch that warms the soul at Christmas.

1 bottle full-bodied red wine
1/3 cup raisins
1/3 cup blanched almonds
5 crushed cardamom
5 whole cloves
1 cinnamon stick
1 peel of a small orange
4 ounces vodka or cognac (bartender's choice)
Sugar to taste

1. Mix wine, raisins, almonds, and spices in a container with a lid. Reserve a few raisins and almonds for garnish.
2. Let the mixture stand in a closed container at room temperature for 24 hours.
3. Before serving, heat the mixture on the stove on medium-high heat until boiling.
4. Add vodka and sugar.
5. Serve hot with a few raisins and blanched almonds in each cup.

(Serves 6)

808. COOL YULE MARTINI

For the hip kids who crave Rat Pack status during the holidays.

3 ounces vodka
1/2 ounce dry vermouth
1 teaspoon peppermint schnapps

1. Fill cocktail shaker with ice.
2. Add vodka, vermouth, and peppermint schnapps.
3. Shake.
4. Strain into a cocktail glass.
5. Garnish with a small candy cane.

809. STAR

I wish I may, I wish I might, have another sip of this tonight.

1 1/2 ounces apple brandy
1 1/2 ounces sweet vermouth
2 dashes orange bitters

1. Fill cocktail shaker with ice.
2. Add apple brandy, vermouth, and bitters.
3. Shake.
4. Strain into a chilled cocktail glass.

810. PEPPERMINT PATTY

Sir, can I pour you another?

1/2 ounce peppermint schnapps
1/2 ounce dark crème de cacao
1 ounce cream

1. Pour peppermint schnapps and crème de cacao into an old-fashioned glass with ice.
2. Add cream.
3. Stir.

811. MISTLETOE MARTINI

Instructions: Hold over your head. Hope for the best.

1 ounce vodka
3/4 ounce melon liqueur
Dash of grenadine syrup

1. Fill cocktail shaker with ice.
2. Add vodka and melon liqueur.
3. Shake.
4. Strain into a chilled martini glass rimmed with red sugar.
5. Float with red grenadine.
6. Garnish with a cherry.

812. EGGNOG FOR TWO

A snuggle bunny drink to share while watching the lights twinkle on the tree.

3 eggs
4 ounces sugar
1/4 teaspoon vanilla extract
1/4 teaspoon ground nutmeg
1/2 ounce brandy
1/2 ounce dark rum
8 ounces heavy cream
8 ounces milk
Note: Keep <u>all</u> ingredients refrigerated in advance of making this drink.

1. Beat the eggs and sugar until thick.
2. Add vanilla and nutmeg.
3. Continue to beat mixture.
4. Add brandy, rum, heavy cream, and milk.
5. Stir.
6. Chill before serving.
7. Dust with nutmeg.

813. EGGNOG CARIBBEAN STYLE

Bring out the nog and the Christmas calypso music and watch Aunt Margo shimmy the night away.

3 eggs
1/2 cup sugar
1/4 teaspoon vanilla extract
1/4 teaspoon ground nutmeg
1 ounce light rum
8 ounces heavy cream
4 ounces milk
4 ounces of coconut milk
Note: Keep **all** ingredients refrigerated in advance of making this drink.

1. Beat the eggs and sugar until thick.
2. Add vanilla and nutmeg.
3. Continue to beat mixture.
4. Add rum, heavy cream, milk, and coconut milk.
5. Stir.
6. Chill before serving in highball glasses.
7. Garnish with coconut flakes.

(Serves 2)

814. CHRISTMAS MARTINI

'Tis the season to act like Dean Martin and the gang. Baby, it's cold outside, but we've got our love to keep us warm.

3 ounces gin
1/2 ounce dry vermouth
1 teaspoon peppermint schnapps

1. Fill cocktail shaker with ice.
2. Add gin, vermouth, and peppermint schnapps.
3. Shake.
4. Strain into a chilled cocktail glass.
5. Garnish with a candy cane.

815. SANTA CLAUS IS COMING TO TOWN

And he'll be expecting this by the fireside. Don't disappoint him.

1 1/2 ounces peppermint schnapps
1 1/2 ounces cinnamon schnapps
1 1/2 ounces melon liqueur

1. Pour schnapps and melon liqueur in a chilled deep-saucer champagne glass.
2. Top with whipped cream.

816. CAROLING WINE

The carols sound quite different at the tenth house than they did at the first when carolers take a thermos of this along.

8 ounces water
8 ounces brown sugar
16 ounces pineapple juice
8 ounces orange juice
6 whole cloves
3 whole allspice berries
2 cinnamon sticks
Rind of 2 oranges
1/2 teaspoon salt
32 ounces red wine

1. Pour water, brown sugar, pineapple juice, and orange juice in a large nonaluminum saucepan.
2. Add cloves, allspice, 2 cinnamon sticks, and salt.
3. Add orange rinds.
4. Bring mixture to a boil.
5. Reduce heat and simmer for 15 minutes.
6. Add wine.
7. Heat to just boiling and remove from heat.
8. Serve hot with a cinnamon stick for garnish.

(Serves 8)

817. HOLIDAY CHEER

Good tidings to you and all of your kin.

1 bottle champagne
1 can frozen cranberry juice concentrate, thawed

1. Pour champagne and cranberry juice concentrate into a punch bowl.
2. Stir.
3. Decorate with lime slices.
(Serves 10)

818. SIBERIAN SLEIGH RIDE

Giddy up, giddy up, let's go.

1 1/4 ounces vodka
3/4 ounce créme de cacao
1/2 ounce white créme de menthe
3 ounces light cream

1. Fill cocktail shaker with ice.
2. Add vodka, crème de cacao, crème de menthe, and light cream.
3. Shake.
4. Strain into a snifter.
5. Sprinkle with chocolate shavings.

819. NEW YEAR MARTINI

It's almost midnight. Hang on to this one with your right hand. Grab someone to kiss with your left.

Blue curacao
Champagne
1 ounce vodka
1 sugar cube

1. Soak the sugar cube in blue curacao in a small bowl.
2. Pour the champagne into a cocktail shaker.
3. Let stand for 5 seconds.
4. Add vodka.
5. Stir.
6. Strain into a chilled martini glass.
7. Drop in the curacao-soaked sugar cube.

820. RESOLUTION MARTINI

This year I promise to behave…Another one please. It's not midnight yet.

3 ounces gin
1 ounce apricot brandy
1/2 ounce lemon juice

1. Fill cocktail shaker with ice.
2. Add gin, apricot brandy, and lemon juice.
3. Shake.
4. Strain into a chilled cocktail glass.

821. BLACK TURNCOAT

Tis the season to toast the treason.

2 ounces chilled tequila
Juice of 1/2 lime
Splash water
Chilled cola
2 ice cubes

1. Pour chilled tequila and lime juice into a rocks glass with ice cubes.
2. Add a splash of water.
3. Stir.
4. Top with chilled cola.
5. Garnish with lime twists.

822. THE COCKROACH

La Cucaracha! Nothing says a party like flaming cockroaches.

1 1/2 ounces tequila
1 ounce coffee liqueur

1. Pour tequila and coffee liqueur into an old-fashioned glass.
2. Flame with a lighter.

823. THE GIRAFFE

Fun fact: Giraffes have 18-inch prehensile tongues. Guard drink accordingly.

1 1/2 ounces tequila
Grapefruit juice

1. Pour tequila into an old-fashioned glass with ice.
2. Swirl.
3. Fill with grapefruit juice.
4. Garnish with a cherry.

824. SWEET TEQUILA

Sip slowly. Have deep thoughts.

2 ounces tequila
1 ounce Pernod

1. Pour tequila and Pernod in a cocktail shaker.
2. Stir.
3. Pour into a brandy snifter.

825. COCKTAIL ATTACK

Take cover! When cocktails attack...Next on the Food Channel.

2 ounces tequila
1 ounce triple sec
1 ounce dry vermouth
1/2 lime
Crushed ice

1. Pour tequila, triple sec, and vermouth into a cocktail glass.
2. Squeeze in the juice from the lime.
3. Add crushed ice.
4. Shake.
5. Strain into a chilled champagne glass.
6. Garnish a lime twist.

826. LA TUNA

Sorry Charlie. This drink is mine.

4 dashes of Angostura bitters
1 1/2 ounces tequila
1 teaspoon lime juice
Club soda
Salt

1. Pour bitters, tequila, and lime juice into an old-fashioned glass with ice.
2. Fill with club soda.
3. Sprinkle salt on top.

827. TEQUILA DRY

Ssssh. Don't tell anyone. Top secret info says super spies love to indulge in these "Mexican martinis" when looking for bad guys south of the border.

1 1/2 ounces tequila
1/2 ounce dry vermouth
1/4 ounce grenadine
2 ice cubes

1. Pour the tequila, vermouth, and grenadine into a cocktail shaker.
2. Stir.
3. Add the two ice cubes.
4. Garnish with lime or orange wheel.

828. TURBO

Grab the handle bars and buckle up. Zero to sixty in five seconds flat.

1 ounce tequila
1 ounce vodka
4 ounces tropical fruit punch

1. Fill cocktail shaker with ice.
2. Add tequila, vodka, and fruit punch.
3. Shake.
4. Strain into a collins glass.

829. TEQUILA FURNACE

Turn up the heat.

5 to 10 drops Tabasco sauce
1 1/2 ounces tequila
Salt
Lime wedge

1. Drip Tabasco into a shot glass.
2. Top with tequila.
3. Consumed in the classic style: lick the salt, shoot the tequila, and suck the lime.

830. NUBE NUEVE

Cloud Nine...Up, up and away.

1 ounce tequila
1 ounce brandy
1 egg beaten
Juice of 2 limes

1. Fill cocktail shaker with ice.
2. Add tequila, brandy, egg, and lime juice.
3. Shake.
4. Strain into a cocktail glass.
5. Garnish with a mint sprig.

831. SENORITA

A staple at Rose's Cantina consumed by many a victim of Felina's enchanting charms.

6 ounces tequila
6 ounces lime juice
4 1/2 ounces curacao
Salt

1. Fill cocktail shaker with ice.
2. Add tequila, lime juice, and curacao.
3. Shake.
4. Strain into salt-rimmed goblets.
(Serves 6)

832. EL PRESIDENTE

Worthy of a head of state.

1 1/2 ounces light rum
1/2 ounce vermouth
2 dashes of grenadine
Juice of 1/2 lime

1. Fill cocktail shaker with ice.
2. Add rum, vermouth, grenadine, and lime juice.
3. Shake.
4. Strain into a cocktail glass.

INCOME TAX DAY—APRIL 15

833. INCOME TAX

Fill out the forms. Write the check. Drink until you forget.

1 ounce gin
1 teaspoon dry vermouth
1 teaspoon sweet vermouth
1/2 ounce orange juice
2 to 3 dashes Angostura bitters

1. Fill cocktail shaker with ice.
2. Add gin, vermouths, orange juice, and bitters
3. Shake.
4. Strain into an old-fashioned glass with ice.

EARTH DAY

834. SAVE THE PLANET

You have the whole world in your glass.

1 ounce vodka
1 ounce melon liqueur
1/2 ounce blue curacao
1 to 2 dashes green Chartreuse

1. Fill cocktail shaker with ice.
2. Add vodka, melon liqueur, blue curacao, and green Chartreuse.
3. Shake.
4. Strain into a chilled cocktail glass.

ST. PATRICK'S DAY

835. BLARNEY STONE COCKTAIL

Fun Fact: Kissing the Blarney Stone gives the kisser the gift of great persuasiveness.

2 ounces Irish whiskey
1/2 teaspoon absinthe
1/2 curacao
1/4 teaspoon maraschino liqueur
Dash Angostura bitters

1. Fill cocktail shaker with ice.
2. Add whiskey, absinthe, curacao, maraschino liqueur, and bitters.
3. Shake.
4. Strain into a cocktail glass.
5. Garnish with an orange peel twist and an olive.

836. ST. PATRICK'S DAY

Raise a toast to St. Patrick. Blessed is he who chases snakes out of a country.

3/4 ounce green crème de menthe
3/4 ounce green Chartreuse
3/4 ounce Irish whiskey
Dash Angostura bitters

1. Fill cocktail shaker with ice.
2. Add crème de menthe, Chartreuse, whiskey, and bitters.
3. Stir.
4. Strain into a cocktail glass.

837. CHILLY IRISHMAN

Begorrah! Get this man a scarf.

3 ounces cold espresso
1 ounce Irish whiskey
1/2 ounce coffee liqueur
1/2 ounce Irish cream liqueur
1 scoop vanilla ice cream
Dash sugar syrup
4 cups crushed ice

1. Combine all ingredients in a blender.
2. Blend until smooth.
3. Pour into a parfait glass.
4. Garnish with a three-leaf clover.

838. IRISH DREAM

An iridescent vision of rainbows and lush green hills where fairies scamper.

1/2 ounce hazelnut liqueur
1/2 ounce Irish cream liqueur
3/4 ounce crème de cacao
4 ounces vanilla ice cream

1. Combine all ingredients in a blender.
2. Blend until smooth.
3. Pour into a frosted pilsner glass.
4. Top with whipped cream and chocolate sprinkles.

839. EVERYBODY'S IRISH COCKTAIL

At least on March 17th they are.

1 teaspoon green crème de menthe
1 teaspoon green Chartreuse
2 ounces Irish whiskey

1. Fill cocktail shaker with ice.
2. Add crème de menthe, Chartreuse, and whiskey.
3. Stir.
4. Strain into a cocktail glass.
5. Garnish with a green olive.

840. CLOVER LEAF COCKTAIL

I'm looking over a four-leaf clover. Oh, maybe it's my glass.

Juice of 1 lime
2 teaspoons grenadine
1 egg white
1 1/2 ounces gin

1. Fill cocktail shaker with ice.
2. Add lime, grenadine, egg white, and gin.
3. Shake.
4. Strain into a cocktail glass.
5. Garnish with a mint leaf.

841. DUBLIN COCKTAIL

If you order two, is it a double Dublin?

2 ounces Irish whiskey
1 teaspoon green Chartreuse
3 dashes green crème de menthe

1. Fill cocktail shaker with ice.
2. Add whiskey, Chartreuse, and crème de menthe.
3. Stir.
4. Strain into a cocktail glass.
5. Garnish with an olive.

842. EMERALD ISLE COCKTAIL

As William Drennan said in 1795, "Nor one feeling of vengeance presume to defile/The cause, or the men, of the Emerald Isle."

2 ounces dry gin
1 teaspoon green crème de menthe
3 dashes Angostura bitters

1. Fill cocktail shaker with ice.
2. Add dry gin, crème de menthe, and bitters.
3. Stir.
4. Strain into a cocktail glass.

843. GREEN FIZZ

Pink hearts, yellow moons, orange stars...green fizz.

2 ounces dry gin
1 teaspoon green crème de menthe
1/2 teaspoon powdered sugar
1 egg white
Juice of 1/2 lemon
Club soda

1. Fill cocktail shaker with ice.
2. Add gin, crème de menthe, powdered sugar, egg white, and lemon.
3. Shake.
4. Strain into a highball glass.
5. Fill with club soda.

844. GREEN ROOM COCKTAIL

Where leprechauns wait before their Tonight Show appearance.

3/4 ounce brandy
1 1/2 ounces dry vermouth
1/2 teaspoon curacao

1. Fill cocktail shaker with ice.
2. Add brandy, dry vermouth, and curacao.
3. Shake.
4. Strain into a cocktail glass.

845. SHAMROCK COCKTAIL

The man who has luck in the morning has luck in the afternoon. And a shamrock never hurts either.

1 1/2 ounces Irish whiskey
1/2 ounce dry vermouth
1 teaspoon green crème de menthe

1. Fill cocktail shaker with ice.
2. Add whiskey, vermouth, and crème de menthe.
3. Stir.
4. Strain into a cocktail glass.
5. Garnish with an olive.

846. GREEN SWIZZLE

Here's to the old lady up on the hill. If she won't drink it, oh, well—I will!

2 ounces dry gin
2 dashes Angostura bitters
1 tablespoon green crème de menthe
1 teaspoon powdered sugar
Juice of 1 lime
Club soda

1. Pour gin, bitters, crème de menthe, powdered sugar, and lime in a collins glass with shaved ice.
2. Stir.
3. Fill with club soda.
4. Stir again.

847. LEPRECHAUN

Magically delicious, so sayeth one lucky pixie.

2 ounces Irish whiskey
Tonic water

1. Pour whiskey in an old-fashioned glass with ice.
2. Fill with tonic water.
3. Stir.
4. Garnish with a lemon twist.

848. LEPRECHAUN LIBATION

A popular favorite in leprechaun haunts all over Erin.

1 ounce green crème de menthe
2 1/2 ounces Irish whiskey
3 1/2 ounces ice

1. Pour crème de menthe, whiskey, and ice into a blender.
2. Blend.
3. Pour into a goblet or large wine glass.

849. PADDY COCKTAIL

As my uncle Paddy once said, "May the enemies of Ireland never meet a friend."

1 1/2 ounces Irish whiskey
3/4 ounce sweet vermouth
3 dashes Angostura bitters

1. Fill cocktail shaker with ice.
2. Add whiskey, vermouth, and bitters.
3. Shake.
4. Strain into a chilled cocktail glass.

850. EMERALD ISLE COOLER

May the leprechauns be near you to spread luck along your way.

3 scoops vanilla ice cream
1 ounce green crème de menthe
1 ounce Irish whiskey
1 ounce club soda

1. Pour vanilla ice cream, green crème de menthe, and Irish whiskey into a blender.
2. Blend until smooth.
3. Pour into a chilled highball glass.
4. Add club soda.
5. Stir gently.

851. TOP OF THE MORNING

A good laugh and a long sleep are the two best cures for all that ails you. Along with this drink.

1 ounce brandy
1/2 ounce apple brandy
1/2 ounce sweet vermouth
Dash of lemon juice

1. Fill cocktail shaker with ice.
2. Add brandies, vermouth, and lemon juice.
3. Stir well from bottom.
4. Strain into a cocktail glass.
5. Serve with one olive.

852. LITTLE GREEN FAIRY

Tinkerbell's tipple of choice.

2 ounces green Chartreuse
2 ounces Benedictine
1/5 bottle white dinner wine
2 ounces blue curacao
2 ounces cherry brandy
2/5 bottle brut champagne

1. Pour Chartreuse, Benedictine, wine, curacao, and brandy in a pitcher.
2. Stir and chill.
3. When ready to serve, pour into a champagne bowl.
4. Add champagne.
(Serves 25)

853. GREEN FIRE

The burning ring of green fire. It's caused many a good Irishman to chase the rainbow.

1 1/2 ounces gin
2 teaspoons green crème de menthe
2 teaspoons kummel

1. Fill cocktail shaker with ice.
2. Add gin, crème de menthe, and kummel.
3. Shake.
4. Strain into a highball glass.
5. Add ice.

FOURTH OF JULY

854. AMERICAN FLAG

When mixed properly, these colors don't run.

1/2 ounce grenadine
1/2 ounce cream
1/2 ounce blue curacao

1. Layer in above order carefully in pousse café glass or a pony.

855. LIBERTY COCKTAIL

Take this cocktail to your tired, poor, huddled masses.

1 1/2 ounces apple brandy
3/4 ounce light rum
1/4 teaspoon sugar syrup

1. Fill cocktail shaker with ice.
2. Add apple brandy, rum, and sugar syrup.
3. Stir.
4. Strain into a chilled cocktail glass.

856. FIREWORKS

Toss one back and prepare to witness mental pyrotechnics. Kaboom!

1/2 ounce vodka
1/2 ounce light rum
1/2 ounce tequila
3 ounces pineapple juice
1 ounce cream of coconut
2 teaspoons milk
1 drop grenadine

1. Fill cocktail shaker with ice.
2. Add vodka, rum, tequila, pineapple juice, cream of coconut, milk, and grenadine.
3. Shake.
4. Strain into a collins glass half filled with ice.
5 Garnish with a cherry.

857. BETSY ROSS

Fun Fact: Betsy Ross was excommunicated by the Quakers. Maybe because she enjoyed too much brandy.

1 1/2 ounces brandy
1 1/2 ounces port
2 dashes Angostura bitters
2 dashes blue curacao

1. Fill cocktail shaker with ice.
2. Add brandy, port, bitters, and blue curacao.
3. Stir.
4. Strain into a brandy snifter.

858. YANKEE DOODLE COCKTAIL

One word: Dandy.

1 3/4 ounces gin
1/4 ounce cream
1/4 ounce lemon juice
1/4 ounce crème de yvette

1. Fill cocktail shaker with ice.
2. Add gin, cream, lemon juice, and crème de Yvette.
3. Shake.
4. Strain into a cocktail glass.

859. AMERICAN GLORY HIGHBALL

Keep your eye on the grand old flag. Hard to do after an afternoon of these.

1 1/2 ounces champagne
1 1/2 ounces orange juice
Club soda

1. Pour champagne and orange juice into a highball glass with ice.
2. Stir.
3. Fill with club soda.

860. STARS AND STRIPES POUSSE CAFE

Every heart beats true for this red, white, and blue.

2/3 ounce grenadine
2/3 ounce white crème de menthe
2/3 ounce crème de yvette

1. Layer carefully in above order in a pousse café glass.

VALENTINE'S DAY

861. THE KISS

Sweet as your first.

1 1/2 ounces vodka
1/2 ounce chocolate liqueur
1/4 ounce cherry liqueur
3/4 ounce heavy cream

1. Fill cocktail shaker with ice.
2. Add vodka, liqueurs, and cream.
3. Shake.
4. Strain into a chilled cocktail glass.

862. HANKY PANKY COCKTAIL

Too little hanky panky can leave your mate very cranky.

1 3/4 ounces gin
3/4 ounce sweet vermouth
1/4 ounce Fernet Branca

1. Fill cocktail shaker with ice.
2. Add gin, vermouth, and Fernet Branca.
3. Stir.
4. Strain into a cocktail glass.
5. Garnish with an orange peel.

863. RED HOT PASSION

A sure-fire recipe for afternoon delight.

1/2 ounce bourbon
1/2 ounce amaretto
1/2 ounce Southern Comfort
1/4 ounce sloe gin
Splash triple sec
Splash orange juice
Splash pineapple juice

1. Pour all ingredients over ice into a hurricane glass.
2. Stir gently.
3. Garnish with an orange slice.

864. KISS IN THE DARK

A nice way to end the day. Or begin the night.

3/4 ounce gin
3/4 ounce cherry brandy
1/4 ounce dry vermouth

1. Fill cocktail shaker with ice.
2. Add gin, cherry brandy, and vermouth.
3. Shake.
4. Strain into a chilled cocktail glass.

865. SWEETIE BABY

Serve with a side of candy hearts and say "I love you."

2 ounces amaretto
5 ounces vanilla ice cream
1/2 ounce milk (optional)

1. Pour amaretto, ice cream, and milk into a blender.
2. Blend at medium speed until smooth.
3. Pour into a goblet.
4. Garnish with crushed almonds.

866. SOUL KISS

The best way to kiss your soul mate.

1 ounce whiskey
1 ounce dry vermouth
1/2 ounce Dubonnet
3/4 ounce orange juice

1. Fill cocktail shaker with ice.
2. Add whiskey, vermouth, Dubonnet, and orange juice.
3. Stir.
4. Strain into an old-fashioned glass with ice.

867. CHOCOLATE COFFEE KISS

The consummate accent to a snowy Valentine's Day spent watching An Affair to Remember.

3/4 ounce coffee liqueur
3/4 ounce Irish cream liqueur
Splash crème de cacao
Splash Grand Marnier
1 1/2 ounces chocolate syrup
Hot coffee

1. Pour liqueurs into an Irish coffee glass.
2. Add chocolate syrup.
3. Fill with coffee.
4. Top with whipped cream.
5. Garnish with shaved chocolate and a cherry.

868. HOT KISS

e.e. Cummings said it best: "Kisses are a better fate than wisdom."

1/2 ounce white crème de menthe
1 ounce Irish whiskey
1/2 ounce white crème de cacao
6 ounces hot coffee

1. Pour liqueurs and whiskey into an Irish coffee glass.
2. Add coffee.
3. Stir.
4. Top with whipped cream.
5. Garnish with a chocolate-covered mint.

869. LOVER'S DELIGHT COCKTAIL

Sky rockets in flight...

1/2 ounce dry gin
1 teaspoon orange sherbet

1. Fill cocktail shaker with ice.
2. Add gin and orange sherbet.
3. Shake.
4. Strain into a cocktail glass.
5. Dust with nutmeg.

870. CUPID'S COCKTAIL

Draw back bow. Aim arrow at lover. Release.

1 1/2 ounces sherry
1 egg
1 teaspoon powdered sugar
Dash of cayenne pepper

1. Fill cocktail shaker with ice.
2. Add sherry, egg, powdered sugar, and pepper.
3. Shake.
4. Strain into a cocktail glass.

871. AMOROUS DUO

Antony and Cleopatra. Romeo and Juliet. Tracy and Hepburn. Are you next?

1 ounce raspberry schnapps
1/4 ounce amaretto
1 scoop vanilla ice cream
2 ounces crushed ice

1. Pour raspberry schnapps, amaretto, vanilla ice
   cream, and ice into a blender.
2. Blend until smooth.
3. Pour into a brandy snifter.

872. GODDESS OF LOVE COCKTAIL

Aphrodite's favorite concoction for lovers in love.

1 3/4 ounces pastis
3/4 ounce anisette

1. Fill cocktail shaker with ice.
2. Add pastis and anisette.
3. Shake.
4. Strain into a cocktail glass.

873. KISS ME QUICK

Before I change my mind.

2 ounces Pernod
2 dashes Angostura bitters
1 teaspoon Cointreau
1 ounce club soda

1. Add Pernod, bitters, and Cointreau to an old-fashioned glass with ice.
2. Stir.
3. Top with club soda.

874. PINK ROSE FIZZ

Drink this rose and think sweet thoughts.

Juice of 1/2 lemon
1 teaspoon powdered sugar
1 egg white
1/2 teaspoon grenadine
2 teaspoons cream
2 ounces dry gin
Club soda

1. Fill cocktail shaker with ice.
2. Add lemon, powdered sugar, egg white, grenadine, cream, and gin.
3. Shake.
4. Strain into a highball glass.
5. Fill with club soda.

875. WILD FLING

Everybody should have at least one in their lifetime.

1 1/2 ounces wilderberry schnapps
4 ounces pineapple juice
Splash cranberry juice

1. Pour schnapps in a highball glass with ice.
2. Fill with pineapple juice.
3. Splash with cranberry juice.
4. Stir.

876. FRANKENSTEIN COCKTAIL

Don't be surprised if the villagers chase you around with torches.

1 ounce dry gin
1 ounce dry vermouth
1/2 ounce apricot liqueur
1/2 ounce Cointreau

1. Fill cocktail shaker with ice.
2. Add gin, vermouth, apricot liqueur, and Cointreau.
3. Shake.
4. Strain into a cocktail glass.

877. RED DEVIL

Keeper of the "spirits" of the dead.

1/2 ounce sloe gin
1/2 ounce vodka
1/2 ounce Southern Comfort
1/2 ounce triple sec
1/2 ounce banana liqueur
2 tablespoon Rose's lime juice
2 ounces orange juice

1. Fill cocktail shaker with ice.
2. Add gin, vodka, Southern Comfort, triple sec, banana liqueur, and juices.
3. Shake.
4. Strain into a collins glass.

878. BLACK MAGIC

Only devil women with evil on their minds partake in this libation.

1 1/2 ounces vodka
3/4 ounce coffee liqueur
1 to 2 dashes lemon juice

1. Pour vodka, coffee liqueur, and lemon juice into an old-fashioned glass with ice.
2. Garnish with a lemon twist.

879. INCANTATIONS

Take a lesson from the witches of Macbeth. Double, double toil and trouble. Fire burn and cauldron bubble. Repeat as needed.

1 ounce vodka
1/2 ounce green curacao
2 ounces lemonade
2 to 3 drops grenadine
3 ounces ice

1. Add vodka, curacao, and lemonade in a blender with ice.
2. Blend until slushy.
3. Pour into extra large martini glass or goblet.
4. Drip grenadine over glass.
5. Garnish with sugar-coated lime wedge.

880. BLACK WITCH

She's no Glenda the Good Witch.

1 1/2 ounces gold rum
1/4 ounce dark rum
1/4 ounce apricot brandy
1/2 ounce pineapple juice

1. Fill cocktail shaker with ice.
2. Add rums, apricot brandy, and pineapple juice.
3. Shake.
4. Strain into a chilled cocktail glass.

881. CAT'S EYE

Fun fact: Legend has it that when you see a one-eyed cat, you should spit on your thumb, stamp it in the palm of your hand, make a wish, and it will come true. What can it hurt?

2 ounces dry vermouth
1/2 ounce yellow Chartreuse
2 dashes orange bitters

1. Fill cocktail shaker with ice.
2. Add vermouth, Chartreuse, and bitters.
3. Shake.
4. Strain into a chilled cocktail glass.

882. HEADLESS HORSEMAN

Throw back a few of these while you still have a noggin.

2 ounces vodka
3 dashes Angostura bitters
Ginger ale

1. Pour vodka and bitters into a collins glass with ice.
2. Fill with ginger ale.
3. Stir.
4. Garnish with an orange slice.

883. VAMPIRE'S DELIGHT

Dracula enjoys these for a change of pace. Love at first bite, indeed.

2 ounces rum
1 banana
2 scoops vanilla ice cream
Grenadine

1. Place banana, rum, and ice cream in blender.
2. Blend on low for about 15 seconds until smooth.
3. Swirl grenadine into two champagne flutes until it coats the inside of the glasses.
4. Add banana mixture.
5. Serve with cherry.

884. BLACK WIDOW

Less deadly than the spider's venom. At least in small doses.

1/2 ounce strawberry liqueur
1/2 ounce sambuca
1/2 ounce cream

1. Layer in above order in a shot glass.

885. WITCH'S BREW

The popular year-around drink in Salem. Bottoms up, Esmeralda.

2 ounces Strega
1/2 ounce crème de menthe
1 ounce lemon juice
1 ounce orange juice
Pernod

1. Fill cocktail shaker with ice.
2. Add Strega, crème de menthe, and juices.
3. Shake.
4. Strain into a collins glass with shaved ice.
5. Float three or four drops Pernod.
6. Decorate with fresh mint.

886. DEMON POSSESSION

This one may make your head spin.

1 ounce citrus vodka
1 ounce light rum
1/4 ounce blue curacao
Lemonade

1. Fill cocktail shaker with ice.
2. Add vodka, rum, and curacao.
3. Shake.
4. Strain into a highball glass with ice.
5. Fill with lemonade.
6. Garnish with a cherry.

887. SKELETON

Drink in place of barium for your next X-ray.

1/2 ounce white rum
1/2 ounce sour apple vodka
Lemon-lime soda

1. Pour rum and vodka into an old-fashioned glass filled with crushed ice.
2. Top off with soda.

888. GREEN GHOST

Yellow and Blue makes Green.

1 ounce blue curacao
1 ounce gin
1/2 ounce peach schnapps
2 ounces lemonade
Squeeze of an orange wedge

1. Fill cocktail shaker with ice.
2. Add curacao, gin, peach schnapps, lemonade, and orange juice.
3. Shake.
4. Strain into a hurricane glass with ice.
5. Garnish with a lime wedge.

ELECTION DAY

889. VICTORY

Drink early and often while you wait for the results to come in.

1 1/2 ounces Pernod
3/4 ounce grenadine
Club soda

1. Fill cocktail shaker with ice.
2. Add Pernod and grenadine.
3. Shake.
4. Strain into a highball glass filled with ice.
5. Fill with club soda.

890. WASHINGTON

Barry Goldwater said it perfectly: "If everybody in this town connected with politics had to leave town because of chasing women and drinking, you would have no government."

1 1/2 ounces dry vermouth
3/4 ounce brandy
2 dashes sugar syrup
2 dashes Angostura bitters

1. Fill cocktail shaker with ice.
2. Add vermouth, brandy, sugar syrup, and bitters.
3. Stir.
4. Strain into a chilled cocktail glass.

THANKSGIVING

891. THANKSGIVING SPECIAL

Your Turkey Day guests will "gobble" these down.

3/4 ounce apricot liqueur
3/4 ounce dry gin
3/4 ounce dry vermouth
1/4 teaspoon lemon juice

1. Fill cocktail shaker with ice.
2. Add apricot liqueur, gin, vermouth, and lemon juice.
3. Shake.
4. Strain into a cocktail glass.
5. Serve with a cherry.

892. NEW ORLEANS FIZZ

Get your krewe together and have your own parade.

2 ounces gin
1/2 ounce cream
Dash of orange flower water
1/4 to 3/4 ounce sugar syrup
1/2 teaspoon powdered sugar
1 egg white
1 ounce lemon juice
Club soda

1. Fill cocktail shaker with ice.
2. Add gin, cream, orange flower water, sugar syrup, powdered sugar, egg white, and lemon juice.
3. Shake.
4. Strain into a collins glass over ice.
5. Top with club soda.

893. NEW ORLEANS NIGHT

Let the good times roulez!

3/4 ounce vodka
1/2 ounce praline liqueur
2 ounces cream of coconut
1 ounce heavy cream
8 ounces crushed ice

1. Pour vodka, praline liqueur, cream of coconut, heavy cream, and ice in a blender.
2. Blend until smooth on low speed.
3. Pour into a wine glass.
4. Garnish with whipped cream.

EASTER

894. EASTER BUNNY

Here comes Peter Cottontail...invite him in for a drink!

1 1/2 ounces dark crème de cacao
1/2 ounce vodka
1 teaspoon chocolate syrup
1 teaspoon cherry brandy

1. Fill cocktail shaker with ice.
2. Add crème de cacao and vodka.
3. Shake.
4. Strain into an old-fashioned glass.
5. Float chocolate syrup and brandy.

895. JACK RABBIT

Fun fact: Both Bugs Bunny and Brer Rabbit are North American jackrabbits.

3/4 ounce dry gin
3/4 ounce dry vermouth
1/4 ounce apricot nectar liqueur
1/4 ounce triple sec

1. Fill cocktail shaker with ice.
2. Add gin, vermouth, apricot nectar liqueur, and triple sec.
3. Shake.
4. Strain into a cocktail glass.

10

VIRGIN JACKS AND JILLS—
For the Sober One in All of Us

Pssst. Hey you. Yeah, I'm talking to you. Who am I? Well, I'm your weary liver. I'm here to win friends and influence...your drinking habits. Sometimes, you just have to slow down on all the crazy concoctions out there, bro. Rest up, and drink some juices and club soda. It's really okay to be over twenty-one and ask for a Shirley Temple. Say it with me, "Shirley Temple." Non-alcoholic drinks aren't half bad. Give them a try. I'll thank you in the morning.

896. BEACH BLANKET BINGO

Annette and Frankie do the watusi. Everybody kick up some sand!

One part cranberry juice
One part grapefruit juice
Splash of soda

1. Pour juices in a collins glass with ice.
2. Top with soda.
3. Garnish with a lime wedge.

897. PINK LASSIE

This one will make even the worst wayward pup come home.

1 scoop of vanilla ice cream
2 ounces cranberry juice
2 ounces pineapple juice
1 ounce sugar syrup
Splash of club soda

1. Blend vanilla ice cream, juices, sugar syrup, and club soda.
2. Pour into a champagne flute.

898. A.S. MACPHERSON

Sweet and tangy. A less-than-potent potable for camp counselors everywhere.

3 ounces orange juice
3 ounces club soda
Splash sour mix
2 dashes Angostura bitters

1. Fill cocktail shaker with ice.
2. Add orange juice, club soda, sour mix, and bitters.
3. Shake.
4. Strain into a collins glass.
5. Garnish with a small American flag.

899. BITTERS HIGHBALL

A long cool drink of fizz.

3/4 ounce Angostura bitters
Club soda or ginger ale

1. Pour bitters into a highball glass.
2. Fill with soda or ginger ale.
3. Garnish with a lime twist.

900. CARDINAL PUNCHLESS

Even Father Flanigan would approve.

6 ounces cranberry juice
6 ounces ginger ale
Splash orange juice
Dash lemon juice
Dash sugar syrup

1. Pour cranberry juice and ginger ale into a collins glass with ice.
2. Splash with orange juice.
3. Add dashes of lemon juice and syrup.

901. DOWN EAST DELIGHT

A juicy cocktail perfect for a tween sleepover. Get out the Hilary Duff videos!

One part cranberry juice
One part pineapple juice
One part orange juice
Dash sugar syrup

1. Pour juices into a collins glass with ice.
2. Add dash sugar syrup.
3. Garnish with a cherry.

902. GRENADINE RICKEY

Rum and Gin Rickey's virgin sister. Really she is.

1 1/2 ounces grenadine
1 1/2 ounces lime juice
Club soda

1. Combine grenadine and lime juice in a highball glass with ice.
2. Add soda.
3. Garnish with a lime wedge.

903. I'LL FAKE MANHATTAN

For those who dare to face big city life sober.

1 1/2 ounces cranberry juice
1 1/2 ounces orange juice
2 dashes orange bitters
Dash grenadine
Dash lemon juice

1. Fill cocktail shaker with ice.
2. Add juices, bitters, grenadine, and lemon juice.
3. Stir.
4. Strain into a chilled cocktail glass.

904. MARGARITA

Serve these up at your next block party. No permit needed.

2 ounces sour mix
Splash lime juice
Splash orange juice
Salt

1. Pour sour mix and juices into a blender with ice.
2. Blend until smooth.
3. Serve in a salt-rimmed margarita glass.
4. Garnish with a lime wedge.

905. MISSIONARY

Drink this while trying to convert the locals.

2 ounces pineapple juice
1 ounce sugar syrup
1 ounce sour mix

1. Fill cocktail shaker with ice.
2. Add pineapple juice, sugar syrup, and sour mix.
3. Stir.
4. Strain into a cocktail glass.
5. Garnish with a pineapple wedge.

906. MONTEGO BAY

Hey, mon, drink as much as you like.

2 ounces orange juice
2 ounces sour mix
Splash grenadine
Splash club soda

1. Fill cocktail shaker with ice.
2. Add orange juice, sour mix, and grenadine.
3. Shake.
4. Strain into an old-fashioned glass.
5. Top with club soda.
6. Garnish with a cherry.

907. ORANGEADE

Time for all good drinks to come to the "ade" of their mixer.

One part orange juice
One part soda
Splash sugar syrup

1. Pour juice and soda into a highball glass with ice.
2. Add splash sugar syrup.
3. Garnish with an orange slice.

908. PAC MAN

The drink of choice for video game addicts who want to keep their edge over Inky, Blinky, and the gang.

Dash bitters
Dash grenadine
Splash lemon juice
Ginger ale

1. Add bitters, grenadine, and lemon juice in a highball glass with ice.
2. Stir.
3. Fill with ginger ale.
4. Garnish with an orange slice.

909. PIÑA COLADA

A great drink for prom night or the grad party.

1 ounce pineapple juice
3 or 4 pineapple chunks
1 ounce cream of coconut
1 teaspoon orange juice
1 tablespoon cream
3 ounces ice

1. Add pineapple juice, pineapple chunks, cream of coconut, orange juice, cream, and ice into a blender.
2. Blend until smooth.
3. Pour into a goblet or large wine glass.
4. Garnish with a pineapple wedge and cherry.

910. PONY'S NECK

The G-rated version of a Horse's Neck.

Dash lime juice
2 dashes Angostura bitters
Ginger ale

1. Pour lime juice and bitters into a collins glass with ice.
2. Fill with ginger ale.
3. Garnish with a spiraled lemon peel and a cherry.

911. ROSY PIPPIN

Looking for complete fulfillment like Pippin? Here it is.

4 ounces apple juice
Splash grenadine
Splash sour mix
Ginger ale

1. Fill cocktail shaker with ice.
2. Add apple juice, grenadine, and sour mix.
3. Shake.
4. Strain into a highball glass with ice.
5. Fill with ginger ale.
6. Garnish with an apple slice.

912. ROY ROGERS

Happy Trails—No Hangovers.

Cola soda
Splash grenadine

1. Fill a highball glass with ice.
2. Add soda.
3. Splash with grenadine.
2. Garnish with a flag.

913. SAGINAW SNOOZE

A sweet warm send-off to never-never land.

3 ounces apple juice
3 ounces cranberry juice
1 teaspoon honey

1. Pour juices into a large heat-resistant mug.
2. Heat for 1 minute in microwave.
3. Stir in honey.
4. Garnish with a lemon slice and a cinnamon stick.

914. SAN FRANCISCO

Take this one with you on the cable cars. No brown paper bag necessary.

One part pineapple juice
One part orange juice
One part grapefruit juice
One part sour mix
2 dashes grenadine
Club soda

1. Fill cocktail shaker with ice.
2. Add juices, sour mix, and grenadine.
3. Shake.
4. Strain into a goblet.
5. Top with soda.

915. SONOMA NOUVEAU

Taste the wine country while you drive up the coast.

5 ounces alcohol-free white wine
Club soda
Cranberry juice

1. Pour wine in a highball glass with ice.
2. Splash soda until glass is almost full.
3. Float cranberry juice.
4. Garnish with a lime twist.

916. STRAWBERRY COLADA

A *sweet twist on the classic for long, sultry summer nights.*

2 ounces fresh or frozen strawberries
1 ounce cream of coconut
2 ounces pineapple juice
2 ounces crushed ice

1. Pour strawberries, cream of coconut, pineapple juice, and ice into a blender.
2. Blend until smooth on medium speed for about 15 seconds.
3. Serve in a hurricane glass.
5. Garnish with strawberries and a pineapple chunk.

917. STRAWBERRY DAIQUIRI

Hemingway would not approve. But your mother would.

3 ounces fresh or frozen strawberries
Splash sour mix
Dash grenadine
2 ounces ice

1. Pour strawberries, sour mix, grenadine, and ice into a blender.
2. Blend until smooth on medium speed for about 15 seconds.
3. Serve in a hurricane glass.
4. Garnish with strawberries.

918. SUNSET COOLER

Make a pitcher in the RV. Pull over and watch the sun fade over the horizon.

4 ounces cranberry juice
2 1/2 ounces orange juice
Splash lemon juice
Splash ginger ale
3 ounces ice

1. Add juices with ice into a blender.
2. Blend until smooth on low speed.
3. Pour into a hurricane glass.
3. Top with ginger ale.
4. Garnish with an orange slice.

919. TOMATO COOLER

Gym rats can't get enough of these thirst quenchers.

7 ounces chilled tomato juice
Splash lemon juice
Tonic water

1. Pour juices into a highball glass with ice.
2. Top with tonic water.
3. Garnish with a lemon wedge and a celery stalk.

920. TRANSFUSION

No needle required, so even the squeamish can enjoy this one.

3 ounces grape juice
6 ounces ginger ale
Splash lime juice

1. Combine grape juice and ginger ale in a collins glass with ice.
2. Splash with lime juice.
3. Garnish with a lime wedge

921. VIRGIN MARY

Ave Maria! This one is tasty.

6 ounces tomato juice
Dash Worcestershire sauce
Dash Tabasco sauce
Dash salt
Dash pepper
Celery salt to taste

1. Pour juice into a tall glass or beer mug with ice.
2. Add Worcestershire sauce, Tabasco sauce, salt, pepper, and celery salt.
3. Stir.
4. Garnish with a celery stalk and lime wedge.

922. HAWAIIAN PIÑA

Quench your thirst but keep your balance while hanging ten.

2 1/2 ounces pineapple juice
1 teaspoon coconut cream
1 scoop vanilla ice cream
10 drops blue curacao

1. Pour juice, coconut cream, vanilla ice cream, and curacao into a cocktail shaker.
2. Mix.
3. Pour into a hurricane glass.
4. Garnish with a pineapple slice.

923. UN-FUNKY MONKEY

A birthday party treat for your little monkey and his chimp-a-riffic friends.

1/2 ounce strawberry crush soda
2 1/2 ounces orange juice
1 sliced banana
1 teaspoon honey

1. Pour strawberry soda, orange juice, banana, and honey into a blender.
2. Blend on low until thick and a smooth pink color.
3. Pour into a hurricane glass.
4. Garnish with a banana slice.

924. FIVE ALIVE

Hey Sleepyhead, awaken your five senses!

1 ounce chilled ginger ale
Orange juice
Club soda
Chilled lemon-lime soda
5 to 6 drops grenadine

1. Pour ginger ale into a pilsner glass.
2. Add one ice cube.
3. Pour orange juice until glass is half full.
4. Add equal amounts of club and lemon-lime soda.
5. Add grenadine syrup.
6. Garnish with a lime slice.

925. PEACHY SUNSET

As keen as they come.

1 ounce chilled peach crush
Juice from three lime wedges
Lemonade
3–5 drops grenadine syrup

1. Pour the peach crush into an old-fashioned glass.
2. Add one ice cube and lime juice.
3. Fill with lemonade.
4. Add grenadine.
5. Garnish with a cherry.

926. LOVE POTION #13

A teenage witch favorite for good witches only.

1/2 ounce khus syrup
1 ounce chilled, shaken pineapple juice
Club soda
Lime wedge

1. Pour the khus syrup into an old-fashioned glass.
2. Add one ice cube.
3. Pour in pineapple juice.
4. Add club soda slowly.
5. Drop lime wedge.
6. Decorate with a pineapple slice.

927. ICY BLUSH

The perfect gift for rosy-cheeked lasses on their sweet sixteenth.

1 ounce strawberry crush
Lemon-lime soda
1 ice cube
Juice from 1/2 lime

1. Pour strawberry crush in an old-fashioned glass.
2. Top with lemon-lime soda
3. Add lime juice.
4. Garnish with lime slice.

928. BAMBINO BELLINI

For toasting the arrival of newborns. Mix one up for the mom-to-be at her baby shower.

2 ounces peach nectar
1 ounce lemon juice
Chilled sparkling cider

1. Pour the peach nectar and lemon juice into a chilled champagne flute.
2. Stir.
3. Fill with cider.
4. Stir gently.

929. STARRY STARRY NIGHT

A jug of this, a telescope, and you.

4 ounces papaya juice
2 ounces pineapple juice
4 ounces ginger ale
Sugar

1. Pour juices and ginger ale into a sugar-rimmed tall glass with ice.
2. Stir.
3. Garnish with star fruit.

930. METROPOLIS

The Daily Planet's *deadline drink. Even Clark Kent gets thirsty sometimes.*

2 ounces raspberry syrup
2 cups lemonade

1. Fill 24-ounce cocktail shaker with ice.
2. Add raspberry syrup and lemonade.
3. Shake.
4. Strain into martini glasses.
5. Garnish with lemon twists.
(Serves 6)

931. MAI TAI MOCKTAIL

Mmmm. Mai Tai have another?

1 ounce vanilla syrup
1/2 ounce almond syrup
3 ounces orange juice
2 ounces cranberry juice

1. Pour syrups and juices into a highball glass with ice.
2. Stir.
3. Garnish with an orange slice and a cherry.

932. VIRGIN LEMON DROP

Give the sourpusses a taste of their own medicine.

1 1/4 ounces lemon syrup
2 1/2 ounces club soda
1/4 ounce lemon juice
Sugar

1. Fill cocktail shaker with ice.
2. Add lemon syrup, club soda, and lemon juice.
3. Shake.
4. Strain into a sugar-rimmed martini glass.
5. Garnish with a lemon twist.

933. MOONLIGHT COCKTAIL

Bring these along for a night of stargazing.

6 ounces grapefruit juice
Dash grenadine

1. Fill cocktail shaker with ice.
2. Add grapefruit juice and grenadine.
3. Shake.
4. Pour into an old-fashioned glass.

934. BLACKBERRY LEMON FUSION

Dr. Oppenheimer would be proud.

1 ounce blackberry syrup
Juice of 1 lemon
Cold club soda

1. Combine blackberry syrup and lemon in a tall glass.
2. Add ice.
3. Fill with club soda.

935. RASPBERRY LEMON FUSION

An explosion of flavor with none of the fallout.

1 ounce raspberry syrup
Juice of 1 lemon
Cold club soda

1. Combine raspberry syrup and lemon in a tall glass.
2. Add ice.
3. Fill with club soda.

936. SANGREETA

Greet your guests with a goblet of this little number.

1 1/2 tablespoons grenadine
2 tablespoons lime juice
12 ounces orange juice
Tabasco sauce to taste

1. Fill cocktail shaker with ice.
2. Add grenadine, lime juice, orange juice, and Tabasco sauce.
3. Shake.
4. Strain into a goblet.
5. Garnish with lime wedges.

937. AFTERGLOW

A peaceful, easy feeling.

1 ounce grenadine
4 ounces orange juice
4 ounces pineapple juice

1. Pour grenadine and juices into a cocktail shaker.
2. Mix.
3. Pour into a highball glass with ice.
4. Garnish with a pineapple chunk.

938. BATMAN

Holy Mocktails, Batman! Make mine a double!

6 ounces orange juice
1/2 teaspoon grenadine

1. Pour the juice and grenadine into a tall glass almost filled with ice cubes.
2. Stir well.
3. Garnish with an orange slice.

939. LEMON FIN

Just when you thought it was safe to go back in the water…it is!

Club soda
2 to 3 teaspoons powdered sugar
1 ounce lemon juice

1. Fill a highball glass halfway with ice.
2. Pour club soda stopping an inch from the top.
3. Add powdered sugar and lemon juice.
4. Stir well.
5. Garnish with lemon slice.

940. TEMPERANCE TANTRUM

Serve these at the next meeting of the Anti-Saloon League.

3 ounces cranberry juice
2 ounces orange juice
Squeeze lemon
Ginger ale
2 ounces ice

1. Pour juices in a blender with ice.
2. Blend until smooth.
3. Top with the ginger ale.
4. Garnish with a red chili pepper.

941. BIG PANTS

Having a pity party because your date laughed at your oversized bloomers? This one will drive you to the edge of reason.

One part orange juice
One part mango juice
Ginger ale
Dash grenadine

1. Pour equal parts orange and mango juices into a highball glass with crushed ice.
2. Top with ginger ale.
3. Add grenadine.
4. Garnish with a slice of lime or a cherry.

942. MISTER DARCY

Best consumed while wearing a hideous holiday jumper.

4 ounces orange juice
1 peach or nectarine
Dash grenadine
3 ounces ice

1. Pour juice, fruit, and grenadine in a blender with ice.
2. Blend until smooth.

943. STARFRUIT SPRITZER

Mix these up and win the approval of your teetotaling future mother-in-law.

3 ounces mango juice
3 ounces peach juice
Club soda

1. Fill a cocktail glass with crushed ice.
2. Add juices.
3. Top with club soda.
4. Stir.
5. Garnish with a star fruit.

944. DIXIE'S RAINBOW COOLER

The first choice for Southern belles who must be on their best behavior.

2 ounces orange juice
2 ounces pineapple juice
2 ounces passion fruit juice
1/4 ounce lemon juice
1 teaspoon grenadine

1. Fill cocktail shaker with ice.
2. Add juices and grenadine.
3. Shake.
4. Strain into highball glass filled with ice.
5. Garnish with fresh kiwi.

945. ENGLISH AFTERNOON

Ideal take away for your journey down the Thames.

4 ounces iced tea
4 ounces raspberry juice

1. Fill a tall glass with ice.
2. Add iced tea and raspberry juice.
3. Stir.
4. Garnish with fresh lemon and raspberries.

946. CHERRY ALE

Like a night at the drive-in, but no need to strap on the roller skates.

2 ounces cherry juice
1 ounce lime juice
Ginger ale

1. Fill a juice glass with ice.
2. Add cherry and lime juices.
3. Top with ginger ale.
4. Garnish with a lime wheel or cherries.

947. VIENNA COLD NIGHT SOOTHER

Like a pleasant stroll along the Danube. Freud would be envious.

4 ounces cold strong coffee
2 ounces cream
1/4 ounce chocolate syrup
1/2 teaspoon cinnamon

1. Fill cocktail shaker with ice.
2. Add coffee, cream, chocolate syrup, and cinnamon.
3. Shake.
4. Strain into a tumbler.
5. Top with whipped cream and shaved chocolate.

948. SUPPER SIPPER

Give this to Dad while he's slaving over the grill. He may raise your allowance.

3 ounces grape juice
3 ounces lemonade
Sparkling water

1. Pour grape juice and lemonade into a goblet with ice.
2. Top with sparkling water.
3. Garnish with a lemon wheel.

949. BERRY HAPPY

A berry frothy treat for those who have been berry good to you.

2 scoops vanilla ice cream
2 ounces fresh blueberries
2 ounces fresh raspberries
2 ounces strawberries
1/2 cup milk

1. Put vanilla ice cream, blueberries, raspberries, strawberries, and milk in a blender.
2. Blend thoroughly.
3. Pour into a tumbler or a large cocktail glass.
4. Top with fresh berries.

950. CAESAR JR.

A drink for all up-and-coming conquerors.

1/2 teaspoon Worcestershire sauce
1/4 teaspoon Tabasco to taste
Juice of 1/4 lime
1/2 teaspoon grated horseradish
Clamato juice

1. Fill a celery-salted rimmed double old-fashioned glass with ice.
2. Add Worcestershire sauce, Tabasco, lime juice, and horseradish.
3. Top with Clamato juice.
4. Stir.
5. Garnish with a celery stalk and a cherry tomato.

951. SOFT BUCKET OF BUNNIES

Don't you just want to dive in?

1/2 ounce grenadine
3 ounces milk

1. Fill cocktail shaker with ice.
2. Add grenadine and milk.
3. Shake.
4. Strain into cocktail glass.
5. Top with whipped cream.

952. PUSSY FOOT

Guaranteed to make you land on your feet.

1/3 ounce grenadine
1 1/3 ounces pineapple juice
1 1/3 ounces orange juice
1 1/3 ounces grapefruit juice

1. Fill cocktail shaker with ice.
2. Add grenadine and juices.
3. Shake.
4. Strain into cocktail glass.

953. ORANGE JULIA

Orange juice: It's not just for breakfast anyone.

2 cups milk
1 can unsweetened orange juice concentrate
1 teaspoon vanilla
10 crushed ice cubes

1. Pour all ingredients into a blender.
2. Blend on medium speed for 30 seconds.
3. Pour into champagne tulips.
(Serves 5)

954. CITRUS COLLINS

Tom, John, Vodka, Rum, and Mint's baby cousin.

2 ounces orange juice
1 ounce lemon juice
1 ounce sugar syrup
Club soda

1. Pour juices and sugar syrup in a highball glass with ice.
2. Fill with club soda.
3. Garnish with an orange slice or a cherry.

955. PERSIAN POEM

A sweet, fruity ode to temperance.

1/2 cup frozen or fresh raspberries
1/2 cup frozen or fresh sliced peaches
2 tablespoons honey
2 teaspoons lemon juice
2 teaspoons grenadine
6 1/2 ounces chilled Perrier water

1. Put fruit, honey, lemon juice, grenadine, and 2 ounces of Perrier water into a blender.
2. Blend until smooth.
3. Pour into goblets.
4. Add remaining Perrier.
5. Garnish with a few raspberries.
(Serves 2)

956. MOON WALKER

Put on your zippered jacket, grab a glass of this, and walk backwards. Come on, you can do it.

5 teaspoons vanilla essence
1/2 cup milk
1 banana
1 teaspoon honey
1 tablespoon yogurt

1. Pour vanilla, milk, banana, honey, and yogurt into a blender.
2. Blend until smooth.
3. Pour into a highball glass.

957. CINDERELLA

Here's a secret: this was in the punch bowl at the Princess' Royal Ball.

One part pineapple juice
One part orange juice
One part lemon juice
Splash club soda
Splash grenadine

1. Fill cocktail shaker with ice.
2. Add juices.
3. Shake.
4. Strain into a highball glass with ice.
5. Top with club soda.
6. Splash with grenadine.
7. Garnish with orange and lemon slices, and a cherry.

958. COCONUT PAW PAW

A popular drink way down yonder in the paw paw patch.

1/2 small paw paw
4 ounces chilled coconut milk
1/2 ounce lime juice
1 teaspoon honey or raw sugar

1. Peel and chop the paw paw.
2. Pour coconut milk, lime juice, and honey in a blender.
3. Add the paw paw.
4. Blend until smooth on medium speed.
5. Pour into a cocktail glass.
6. Garnish with paw paw, strawberries, and mint.

959. BANSHEE DELIGHT

This one will certainly make you wail with glee.

1/2 ounce chocolate syrup
2 inch slice of banana
2 ounces cream
3 ounces ice

1. Pour chocolate syrup, banana, cream, and ice into the blender.
2. Blend for 15 seconds on medium speed.
3. Pour into a parfait glass.
4. Dust with nutmeg.

960. CARIBBEAN FLING

You, that special someone, and seven days with no phones or faxes.

2 ounces unsweetened orange juice
1/2 medium banana
2 ounces unsweetened pineapple juice
2 ounces ice

1. Put the banana, orange juice, pineapple juice, and ice into a blender.
2. Blend for 5–10 seconds or until smooth.
3. Pour into a highball glass.
4. Garnish with banana and orange slices and coconut flakes.

961. MEXICAN SUNRISE

It's 6 a.m. in Guadalajara and the whole day awaits you.

6 ounces chilled orange juice
1/2 ounce grenadine

1. Pour orange juice into a highball glass with ice.
2. Top with grenadine.

962. GINGER HONEY DRINK

Sticky and sweet. Indulge in this gooey treat.

1 tablespoon ginger extract
1 tablespoon honey
1 tablespoon sugar syrup
1 teaspoon lemon juice
Pinch of salt
8 ounces club soda

1. Pour all ingredients into a cocktail shaker.
2. Beat with an electric beater until frothy.
3. Pour into a highball glass.

963. CENTER COURT

Serve with love on a grass court.

1/2 pound fresh strawberries, stems removed
1/2 pint sweet cream
2 teaspoons powdered sugar
1/2 teaspoon powdered ginger
Club soda

1. Combine strawberries, sweet cream, sugar, and ginger in a blender.
2. Blend well.
3. Pour into a pitcher.
4. Add club soda and ice cubes.
5. Stir.

964. DRY GRAPE VINE

For when you are getting no gossip at all.

2 ounces grape juice
1 ounce lemon juice
Dash grenadine

1. Fill a cocktail shaker with ice.
2. Add juices and grenadine.
3. Shake.
4. Strain into a chilled cocktail glass.

965. NO-GIN FIZZ

Ebullient effervescent elixir.

4 ounces lemon juice
1 ounce lime juice
1 tablespoon powdered sugar
Club soda

1. Pour juices and sugar into a collins glass with ice.
2. Stir until sugar is dissolved.
3. Fill with club soda.
4. Garnish with a lime wedge.

966. ORANGE FIZZ

A citrus circus in every sip.

5 ounces orange juice
1 ounce sour mix
Club soda

1. Pour orange juice and sour mix into a collins glass with ice.
2. Top with club soda.

967. ORANGE AND BITTERS

Simple and delicious. Sometimes life doesn't have to be complicated.

Orange juice
2 to 3 dashes Angostura bitters

1. Pour orange juice and bitters into a highball glass with ice.
2. Stir.

968. SHIRLEY TEMPLE

For those voyages on the good ship lollipop.

Dash grenadine
Ginger ale

1. Fill a collins glass with ice.
2. Add grenadine.
3. Fill with ginger ale.
4. Garnish with a cherry and an orange slice.

969. SAFE SEX ON THE BEACH

Condom maven Joycelyn Elders would be proud.

1 ounce peach nectar
3 ounces pineapple juice (or grapefruit juice)
3 ounces orange juice

1. Pour peach nectar, pineapple juice (or grapefruit juice), and orange juice into a highball glass with ice.
2. Stir.

970. SOBER THOUGHTS

The on-top-of-your-game drink of choice for debate teams and chess clubs everywhere.

3 ounces orange juice
3 ounces fresh lime juice
1 tablespoon grenadine
Tonic water

1. Pour juices and grenadine into a highball glass with ice.
2. Stir.
3. Fill with tonic water.

971. MUTED TEQUILA SUNSET

Picture perfect every day at six.

2 ounces orange juice
1 tablespoon grenadine

1. Pour orange juice into a rocks glass with ice.
2. Slowly add grenadine by pouring over the back of a spoon.
3. Let grenadine rise from the bottom of the glass.

972. EGG CREAM

Which came first? The chicken or the egg cream?

1 1/2 ounces chocolate syrup
Cold milk
Seltzer

1. Pour chocolate syrup into a highball glass.
2. Fill 2/3 with milk.
3. Top with seltzer.
4. Stir.

973. BUBBLETART

Relax in a steamy tub with this refresher. The more bubbles the merrier.

3 ounces cranberry juice
1 ounce lime juice
3 ounces mineral water

1. Fill cocktail shaker with ice.
2. Add juices and mineral water.
3. Shake.
4. Strain into a highball glass with ice.
5. Fill with mineral water.
6. Garnish with a lime wheel.

974. CROW'S NEST

Ahoy! Tasty drink now being served off the port bow.

4 ounces orange juice
1 ounce cranberry juice
1/2 teaspoon grenadine

1. Fill cocktail shaker with ice.
2. Add juices and grenadine.
3. Shake.
4. Strain into an old-fashioned glass almost filled with ice.
5. Garnish with a lime slice.

975. CREAMSICLE

Yummy. You'll want to gobble this one up whole, but beware of the brain freeze.

8 ounces orange juice
2 scoops vanilla ice cream

1. Put orange juice and vanilla ice cream in blender.
2. Blend at low speed.
3. Pour into highball glass.
4. Garnish with orange slice.

976. INNOCENT PASSION

Abstinence never tasted so good.

4 ounces passion fruit juice
Dash cranberry juice
Dash lemon juice
Club soda

1. Pour juices into a highball glass filled with ice.
2. Top with club soda.
3. Add a cherry and a long straw.

977. LAVA FLOW

The word "volcano" derives from Vulcan, the Roman god of fire. This is what he drank on his more mellow days.

4 ounces light cream
1/2 ounce coconut cream
3 ounces pineapple juice
1/2 banana
1/2 cup frozen strawberries, thawed

1. Pour light cream, coconut cream, pineapple juice, and banana into a blender with ice.
2. Blend until smooth.
3. Put strawberries in the bottom of a parfait glass.
4. Quickly pour in fruit and cream mixture for a starburst effect.

978. PEACH MELBA

A classic British dessert—in a glass.

8 ounces peach nectar
2 scoop vanilla ice cream
1/2 peach, sliced
3 ounces ripe raspberries

1. Put ingredients in a blender.
2. Blend at low speed until smooth.
3. Pour in a highball glass.
4. Garnish with raspberries.

979. BLACKBERRY SOFT DRINK

Teach the kiddies to make this one by themselves.

4 ounces ripe blackberries
1 ounce sugar
1 tablespoon lemon juice
Club soda

1. Mix blackberries, sugar, and lemon juice in a cocktail shaker.
2. Strain into a highball glass.
3. Fill with club soda.
4. Garnish with a blackberry.

980. CARLOTA

A glassful of garden fresh goodness.

1 1/2 ounces celery juice
1 1/2 ounces carrot juice
1 1/2 ounces apple juice
Dash lemon juice

1. Pour juices into a highball glass with ice.
2. Stir.
3. Top with chopped parsley.

981. FLORIDA

A more exotic recommendation for getting your Vitamin C.

2 ounces grapefruit juice
1 ounce orange juice
1 ounce lemon juice
2 dashes sugar syrup
Club soda

1. Fill cocktail shaker with ice.
2. Add juices and sugar syrup.
3. Shake.
4. Strain into a highball glass.
5. Top with club soda.

982. TEXAS BBQ

Hang on, cowboy. This bold beverage is liable to provide a much-needed spicy kick.

Lime juice
Cajun spices
Dash of Worcestershire sauce
6 ounces tomato juice
2 teaspoons barbecue sauce
Lime wedge

1. With lime juice, rim a highball glass with cajun spices.
2. Fill halfway with ice.
3. Add Worcestershire sauce, tomato juice, barbecue sauce, and lime wedge.
4. Stir.
5. Garnish with a lime wedge.

983. SUE ELLEN'S NIGHTMARE

Much to Mrs. Ewing's dismay, she'll have to face this one sober.

One part passion fruit juice
One part grapefruit juice
One part guava banana juice

1. Fill cocktail shaker with ice.
2. Add juices.
3. Shake.
4. Strain into an old-fashioned glass.
5. Garnish with lime wedges.

984. VIRGIN HURRICANE

Rank: Category 1. No need to take cover with this storm.

4 ounces orange juice
4 ounces sour mix
3/4 ounce passion fruit syrup
Dash grenadine

1. Build orange juice, sour mix, passion fruit syrup, and grenadine into a highball glass with ice.
2. Stir.
3. Garnish with a lime slice.

985. VIRGIN SEABREEZE

A gentle lilting lift of fresh air.

3 ounces cranberry juice
3 ounces grapefruit juice

1. Fill cocktail shaker with ice.
2. Add juices.
3. Shake.
4. Strain into a highball glass packed with ice.

986. LITTLE PINKIE

Whip him up one of these and he'll be wrapped around your little finger.

3 ounces orange juice
3 ounces sour mix
3/4 ounce peach syrup
Dash grenadine

1. Build ingredients in a highball glass with ice.
2. Garnish with an orange slice and a cherry.

987. CHAPALA

Spicy and spirited for those who like a smidgen of spice.

4 ounces orange juice
2 teaspoons grenadine
Dash salt
Dash cayenne pepper

1. Fill cocktail shaker with ice.
2. Add orange juice, grenadine, salt, and cayenne pepper.
3. Shake.
4. Strain into a highball glass over ice.

988. ORANGE SMILE

Even when breakfast comes too early, this one will make you grin.

1 egg
1 tablespoon grenadine
2 ounces orange juice

1. Fill cocktail shaker with three ice cubes.
2. Add egg, grenadine, and orange juice.
3. Shake.
4. Strain into a cocktail glass.

989. KON-TIKI

In the book of the same name, a biologist traveled thousands of miles across the Pacific Ocean on a wooden raft dubbed Kon-Tiki. Lucky for you, this Kon-Tiki crossing is only as far as the kitchen.

4 ounces milk
3/4 ounce pineapple juice
1 scoop orange ice cream
1/4 teaspoon vanilla
Cola

1. Fill cocktail shaker with ice.
2. Add milk, pineapple juice, orange ice cream, and vanilla.
3. Shake.
4. Strain into a highball glass.
5. Top with cola.
6. Garnish with a chunk of pineapple.

990. GRAPEFRUIT BLAST

We have lift off!

2 ounces grapefruit juice
2 ounces orange juice
2 ounces sour mix

1. Fill cocktail shaker with ice.
2. Add juices and sour mix.
3. Shake.
4. Pour into a highball glass.
5. Garnish with an orange slice.

991. CAFÉ MOCHA

Mochalicious. A caffeine chocolate jolt for any Swiss miss.

4 ounces strong hot black coffee
4 ounces hot chocolate

1. Pour coffee and hot chocolate into a large mug.
2. Top with whipped cream.
3. Dust with cinnamon and nutmeg.

992. JOHNNY APPLESEED

Drink one. Plant a tree. Repeat often.

2 ounces apple juice
2 scoops vanilla ice cream
Splash of orange juice
Splash of club soda

1. Blend juices, vanilla ice cream, and club soda in a blender until smooth.
2. Pour into a champagne flute.

993. TOOTS

One taste of this and you'll want to down the rest tout de suite.

1 scoop orange sherbet
1 scoop chocolate ice cream
2 ounces orange soda

1. Blend sherbet, chocolate ice cream, and orange soda until smooth.
2. Pour into a tumbler.
3. Top with whipped cream.
4. Garnish with an orange wedge.

994. STRAWBERRY WONDERLAND

Strawberry fields forever and ever and ever.

1 ounce coconut cream
2 ounces frozen strawberries
3 ounces pineapple juice
1 ounce sour mix
2 ounces ice

1. Add coconut cream, strawberries, pineapple, sour mix, and ice.
2. Blend until smooth.
3. Pour into a large brandy snifter.
4. Top with whipped cream.
5. Garnish with a strawberry.

995. SANTA'S LITTLE HELPER

The favorite break-time refreshment for elves.

3 ounces lemonade
2 tablespoons lime juice
1 scoop raspberry sorbet
1 scoop vanilla ice cream
1 cup ice
Splash cola
Splash lemon-lime soda
Splash grenadine

1. Pour lemonade, lime juice, raspberry sorbet, vanilla ice cream, soda, grenadine, and ice into a blender.
2. Blend all ingredients until smooth and thick.
3. Pour into a pint glass.
4. Top with whipped cream.
5. Splash cream with additional grenadine.
6. Garnish with a cherry.

11

CURES WITHOUT CUSSING—
The Morning After

L ore has it that next door to the *Economist* offices in London is a famed and very old-fashioned chemist—D. R. Harris. The shop has a most marvelous hangover cure, which those in need can buy in a bottle or tincture, or better yet, freshly mixed right there by the chemist for a pound note. Every morning, a procession of old gents in pin-striped suits hustle up to the counter for relief. The bufferest of all old buffers. Those of us, not privy to such European remedies can make our own. All that's needed: The ability to stand and mix.

996. NATIONAL ANTHEM

British in its origin, the National Anthem cure "soon gets you on your feet," so sayeth the Avengers' John Steed, consummate Brit, consummate drinker, sure to know how to shake off last night's indulgence and quickly return to saving the world.

1 egg
3 or 4 dashes Worcestershire sauce
Dash salt

1. Mix well.
2. Down quickly.

997. PRAIRIE OYSTER

It's the catsup in this one that makes those pesky morning-after demons vanish.

1 teaspoon Worcestershire sauce
2 dashes vinegar
Dash pepper
1 teaspoon tomato catsup
1 egg yolk

1. Fill cocktail shaker with ice.
2. Add Worcestershire sauce, vinegar, pepper, and tomato catsup.
3. Shake.
4. Strain into an old-fashioned glass.
5. Drop in egg yolk without breaking yolk.

998. ABSINTHE SUISSESSE

Absinthe soothes the sinful soul. And the foggy brain. And the queasy stomach.

1 1/2 ounces Pernod
1/2 ounce orgeat
1 egg white
1/2 ounce cream
4 ounces ice

1. Pour Pernod, orgeat, egg white, cream, and ice into a blender.
2. Blend.
3. Pour into a chilled old-fashioned glass.

999. AUSSIE EYE-OPENER FOR TWO

Even burly Australian beefcakes swig this citrus soother.

1 grapefruit
1/2 ripe pineapple
1 lemon

1. Peel and chop fruit.
2. Use a juice extractor to process the grapefruit, pineapple, and lemon.
3. Pour juices into a cocktail shaker.
4. Mix.
5. Pour into tumblers. (Serve over ice if preferred.)

1000. BANANARAMA

Better than breakfast cereal and you can drink it with your eyes closed.

10 ounces whole milk
1 tablespoon honey
1 tablespoon heavy cream
1 banana
3 ounces ice

1. Pour whole milk, honey, heavy cream, banana, and ice into a blender.
2. Blend until smooth.
3. Pour into a large glass.

INDEX OF LIQUORS

I

L

M

INDEX OF RECIPE NAMES

S

T

ABOUT THE AUTHOR

Photo © Dixie Knight

Suzi Parker is a bartending school graduate as well as an award-winning journalist, focusing extensively on politics, Southern culture, and sexual mores in the Deep South. She is the author of the non-fiction book, *Sex in the South: Unbuckling the Bible Belt* (Justin Charles & Co., 2003).